Praise for "What the Heck Are You

"[Kevin Mattson] lays out the events of th[...] big, rolling banquet . . . The historical ingredients are fascinating and first-rate." **—New York Times**

"A cautionary tale and a great read . . . Those of us who were around back in the day will be ruefully reminded of those bygone times. And those who weren't will be scratching their heads in disbelief at this fascinating and frequently improbable history." **—Wall Street Journal**

"Mattson makes Carter's maligned speech a touchstone for a rich retrospective and backhanded appreciation of the soul-searching '70s." **—Publishers Weekly**

"In *'What the Heck Are You Up To, Mr. President?'* Kevin Mattson revisits Jimmy Carter's speech delivered to a national audience on July 15, 1979. That address came to be known as the 'malaise' speech, though Carter never used the word. The president did mention 'paralysis and stagnation and drift,' but he also spoke of 'strength' and 'a rebirth of the American spirit.' Mattson offers a deep reading of the speech, placing it in the cultural and political contexts of the late 1970s. The result is an eye-opening inquiry into the power of words at a pivotal moment in history." **—Louis P. Masur, author of The Soiling of Old Glory**

"Despite a brief bump in the president's approval ratings, the address became forever disparaged as the 'malaise' speech, and it doomed Carter's reelection chances . . . Ohio University historian Kevin Mattson challenges that conclusion in his feisty new book . . . Chronicling the mood inside the White House and across the nation in the months surrounding the speech—months when gas lines and Three

Mile Island monopolized the news while *Apocalypse Now* and 'disco sucks!' dominated the zeitgeist—Mattson offers a radically different reading." **—Washington Post**

"Mattson's book describes how Carter came to deliver this sermon to an agitated population and how the speech became the turning point, or perhaps the crumbling point, of Carter's presidency . . . Mattson has crafted an interesting story . . . a window into an unforgettably embarrassing time in the national history." **—Roll Call**

"Mattson fully renders the motley array of Carter's 'Georgia Mafia,' along with countless details of this turbulent era in American history. A galloping history full of interesting characters and significant moments." **—Kirkus Reviews**

"Boldly and with great style, Kevin Mattson captures the political, social, and cultural events that shaped Jimmy Carter's 'malaise' speech of July 15, 1979. He reveals how events abroad and at home—in the White House, at gas stations, on TV, and in learned books—shaped an opportunity to confront the energy problem, which the nation avoided at its own peril."
—Daniel Horowitz, professor of American studies at Smith College and author of *The Anxieties of Affluence*

"WHAT THE HECK ARE YOU UP TO, MR. PRESIDENT?"

"WHAT THE HECK ARE YOU UP TO, MR. PRESIDENT?"

Jimmy Carter, America's "Malaise,"
and the Speech That Should Have
Changed the Country

KEVIN MATTSON

BLOOMSBURY

New York   Berlin   London

Published by Bloomsbury USA, New York

All papers used by Bloomsbury USA are natural, recyclable products made
from wood grown in well-managed forests. The manufacturing processes
conform to the environmental regulations of the country of origin.

LIBRARY OF CONGRESS CATALOGING-IN-PUBLICATION DATA

Mattson, Kevin, 1966–
"What the heck are you up to, Mr. President?": Jimmy Carter, America's
"malaise," and the speech that should have changed the country / Kevin
Mattson.—1st U.S. ed.
p. cm.
Includes bibliographical references.
ISBN-13: 978-1-59691-521-3 (hardcover)
ISBN-10: 1-59691-521-8 (hardcover)
1. Carter, Jimmy, 1924– —Oratory. 2. Carter, Jimmy, 1924– —Political and
social views. 3. Rhetoric—Political aspects—United States—History—20th
century. 4. United States—Politics and government—1977–1981. 5. Energy
policy—United States—History—20th century. 6. Petroleum industry
and trade—Political aspects—United States. 7. National characteristics,
American. I. Title.

E873.2.M386 2009
973.926092—dc22
2008054505

First published by Bloomsbury USA in 2009
This paperback edition published in 2010

Paperback ISBN: 978-1-60819-206-9

1 3 5 7 9 10 8 6 4 2

Typeset by Westchester Book Group
Printed in the United States of America by Worldcolor Fairfield

CONTENTS

We have learned that "more" is not necessarily "better," that even our great nation has its recognized limits, and that we can neither answer all questions nor solve all problems. We cannot afford to do everything, nor can we afford to lack boldness as we meet the future. So together, in a spirit of individual sacrifice for the common good, we must simply do our best.

—JIMMY CARTER, INAUGURAL ADDRESS, 1977

FOREWORD TO THE
PAPERBACK EDITION

For those who weren't yet born on July 15, 1979, or were too little to stay up and watch TV that night, the "malaise" address was President Carter's most famous, most notorious, most ambitious, and (in my opinion) most interesting foray into big-time speechifying, a field in which he was only intermittently successful (although, to be fair, he did manage to talk his way into the presidency).

In this rigorous yet accessible history, Kevin Mattson does a fine job of situating the drama of the speech in the context of both the craziness and (such as it was) the intellectual ferment of the time. And he's good on the operatic desperation, infighting, and vertigo that engulfed the White House during that gasoline-parched summer thirty years ago. I learned some things from the book—for example, I hadn't known that Walter Mondale's dismay about it all was so profound that he seriously considered resigning the vice presidency. And I was there.

The "malaise" episode (a) involves the fall of a regime and (b) has elements of sheer, over-the-moon lunacy. In an essay I wrote in 1995, I explain my take on what we, the guilty, prefer to call the "Crisis of Confidence Address."

On one occasion, Carter, seeking to go beyond technocratic approaches, tried to cast the energy problem in sweeping moral terms. This was the so-called "malaise" episode, widely recognized as one of the most memorable moments of the Carter administration and almost as widely scorned as one of the most contemptible. The received version of what happened is simple. It goes like this: in the summer of 1979, President Carter was overwhelmed by energy and economic crises. In desperation, he made a disastrous speech blaming the American people and a national "malaise" for his own manifest failures of policy and leadership. The American people, horrified, turned him out of office at the first opportunity.

Variations on this version were used effectively by both Edward Kennedy and Ronald Reagan in the 1980 election campaign. The "malaise" had proved to have a long shelf life. At the 1988 Republican convention and again in 1992, speaker after speaker trooped to the podium to denounce "Jimmy Carter and the days of malaise." Attacks on Carter and "malaise" have served the Republicans in the eighties and nineties almost as sturdily as attacks on Hoover and "prosperity is just around the corner" served the Democrats in the forties and fifties.

It goes almost without saying that the historical reality and the political caricature do not comport with one another. For example, here are four details of the episode that are at variance with how most people seem to remember it: (1) Carter himself never mentioned the word *malaise*. (2) The speech itself was an enormous popular success. It generated a record amount of positive mail to the White House, and Carter's approval rating in the polls zoomed up by eleven points literally overnight. (3) The sudden political damage came not from the speech but from the cabinet firings a few days later. (4) Although Carter has been flayed for blaming others, the first third of the speech is devoted to the most excoriating self-criticism ever heard from any American president. As these details suggest, the "malaise" episode has become encrusted in myth.

The episode came at a moment of great political and human vulnerability for Carter. He and his staff, myself included, had been preoccupied with two difficult overseas trips—one to Vienna to complete and sign the SALT II treaty with the Soviet Union, the other to Japan and Korea. He and his staff were completely exhausted. Meanwhile, back at home, the country was in an uproar because of gasoline lines triggered by the fall of the shah in Iran. Carter had hoped to stop over in Honolulu for a couple of days and get some rest, but that was politically impossible given the gas lines at home. Almost as soon as we got back to Washington, it was announced that Carter would address the nation on July 5. Actually, Carter had not agreed to deliver a speech, only to look at a draft and then decide. But the premature announcement put him in a corner.

Even so, when Carter got his speech draft he decided that he didn't want to do it. He said he had made the same points about energy policy over and over again, and the people weren't responding, and, as he pungently put it in the conference call in which he told his staff he was canceling the speech, he didn't want to "bullshit the American people." He remained at Camp David and began an extraordinary series of meetings with leaders from all walks of American life. For a long time, Patrick Caddell, Carter's brilliant young pollster, had been saying with increasing urgency that Americans were losing faith in their institutions. The things Carter heard from his visitors at Camp David seemed to confirm Caddell's analysis.

I was the designated writer for the speech that emerged from this curious process. In truth I was more stenographer-typist than author, smoothing and coordinating bits of draft from various people, including Caddell, Stuart Eizenstat, and Carter himself. The speech had three parts. In the first part of it, wholly conceived and written by Carter, the president criticized himself through the words of those he had spoken to over the previous ten days: "Mr. President, you're not leading this nation—you're just managing the government," and so on. The second part described the erosion of public faith in institutions, in the future, and in the economy—an erosion begun by the shocks of Vietnam, the Kennedy and King assassinations, and Watergate; worsened by inflation and energy shortages; and manifested in declining rates of savings and voter participation. The third and final part outlined a series of proposals for tackling the energy problem and, in the process, beginning to pull ourselves out of the crisis of confidence.

The speech engendered a mixed reaction among the elites, although it did get mostly favorable editorial comment in its immediate aftermath. But three days later, Carter asked for the resignations of the whole of his cabinet and senior staff, telling them he would decide which ones to accept. He hoped that this would be the beginning of a regeneration of his administration—an infusion of new blood and new ideas, and a signal that even those whom he would decide to keep on would be starting anew. Instead, the mass resignations created an unanticipated and unwelcome global sensation; many foreign newspapers and governments, whose grasp of the intricacies of the American political system was imperfect, actually believed that the elites decided that Carter was finished. Within a few weeks this view had trickled down to the public, and Carter's popularity ratings dropped back to the abysmal level where they had been prior to the speech.

The episode was consistent with the religious cast of Carter's leadership. It had elements of sin, confession, and redemption, via a process of "witnessing," prayer, and rededication. It was part of a pattern of symbolic death and resurrection that had marked Carter's personal and political life. He had been politically reborn before—after his first, unsuccessful runs for state senator and then governor, and then, as an obscure southern ex-governor, to the presidency itself.

And of course he had been "born again" as a Christian. The "malaise" episode was his most spectacular effort to be born again—and, this time, to bring the country with him.

The episode was an exercise in national pastorship—in national psychotherapy, to use secular terms. Acknowledging the trauma (the "crisis of confidence" brought on by Vietnam, Watergate, and the sense of national vulnerability triggered by energy shortages) was to be the key to healing it. The therapy's failure, of course, opened the way to a period of hedonism and boastfulness.

The episode may also be seen as mythmaking, in the sense popularized by Joseph Campbell. It was an attempt to create one myth (the notion of a crisis of confidence that could be overcome by tackling the energy problem) that inadvertently created another (the notion of Carter as the personification and cause of national weakness and vulnerability). A side effect was the discrediting of candor about unpleasant truths and the enshrinement of "optimism." Carter's diagnosis of the country's spiritual ills was accurate, and was recognized as such by millions of people, but when he proved unequal to the task of curing those ills (or even palliating them, as Reagan did), he was reviled with special bitterness.

In the cabinet and staff shakeup that followed the speech, Carter got rid of a number of officials who, it is fair to say, were disloyal but competent. If he had first gotten rid of a few who were loyal but incompetent, the episode might have turned out quite differently. That, apparently, he could not bring himself to do. The rebirth was stillborn. The speech was a truthful and prescient diagnosis of what was wrong with the country and what in many ways continues to be wrong with the country. But a president who sets out to diagnose a problem had better be able to offer a plausible solution to it. The Carter of the "malaise" episode was a prophet. But he was not a savior.

If you've stuck with me this far, and you're up for an even deeper delve into the Sensational Seventies, you might as well grab your disco purse and/or put on your pale blue jacket with the six-inch lapels and go whole hog: Read the damn speech. Better still, watch it.

Carter was in unusually good form that evening. In fact, he never delivered a television speech better than he did this one. Much of the credit for that must go to Gordon Stewart, who had been a theater director in a previous life. (He was the director of the original off-Broadway production of *The Elephant Man* until felled by a collapsed lung.) Gordon showed chutzpah beyond the call of duty. First, he insinuated himself into the makeshift studio at Camp David where Carter was practicing the speech. That was pretty ballsy right there. But then, having crashed the president's rehearsal, he proceeded to direct the man.

Others had tried to coach Carter before, usually by telling him not to do things (don't grin so much, knock off the singsong, etc.) or by using technical tricks, such as double- or triple-underlining words to be stressed. What Gordon did, as I understand it (I wasn't in the room), was to get his leading man to focus on *what* he was saying, not how. Gordon worked on motivation. He got Carter to imagine that he was telling a story and that he was telling it for the first time. He got him to picture in his mind what he was saying as he was saying it. It certainly helped that Carter cared deeply about what he was saying, that he was committed to it, as he seldom was to the content of a speech. Whatever the reason, the fact is Carter never delivered a television speech better than he delivered this one.

This book describes a meeting during the run-up to the speech that I should have mentioned in my 1995 piece, by way of strengthening my point about the "religious cast" of Carter's leadership. From Carter's point of view, I would guess, and certainly from mine, the most useful of the many confessional-cum-advisory off-the-record skull sessions of which the hastily organized pre-speech "domestic summit" consisted was a meeting with religious leaders and thinkers, including Cardinal Terence Cooke, Rabbi Marc Tanenbaum, Robert Bellah, and a half dozen others. I'm normally not the world's biggest booster of religion—I'm an atheist, especially when it comes to the notion of a "personal" god, which I find bafflingly childish—but it was refreshing, even inspiriting, to listen to these people talk. It wasn't that they said anything especially original or startling. It was enough that they didn't have any legislative axes to grind and that they were interested in spiritual matters, or, as we secular humanists might put it, people's inner lives, not just their identities and their economic interests. The session encouraged Carter to follow his natural inclination to use the speech he would end up giving to say critical things about mindless consumerism, rampant selfishness, and the like.

One of the people at the session was a big shot in the Southern Baptist Convention, but this was back in the days when that organization was still primarily a religious group, not the combination of vice squad (in both senses!) and Fox News auxiliary it has since become. Carter hasn't been a Southern Baptist for nearly a decade now, but he is emphatically still a Christian. I know he's a busy man, and he hasn't got another eighty-five years to spare, but I can't help wishing he would do a speaking tour of evangelical Christian colleges and megachurches. He knows how to speak their language, and he might be able to persuade their students and parishioners, and maybe even their pastors, of something many of them may already be beginning to suspect: Christianity need not be defined by sexual querulousness, morbid Armageddon-mongering, and an obsession with embryos as opposed to all other manifestations of human life and human potential.

Was the "malaise" episode Jimmy Carter's finest hour? Heavens, no. I'd vote for the (politically costly) trifecta of securing passage of the Panama Canal "giveaway," forging the cold peace between Israel and Egypt, and holding back the dogs of war during the Iran hostage crisis. But the remarkable address that Carter delivered when he descended from the wooded hills of Camp David in the middle of July 1979—his sermon from the mount—opened an unprecedented window on the character of a president and the spiritual condition of a nation. Thanks to Kevin Mattson, the story of that address has now been properly told.

—Hendrik Hertzberg
March 2010

"WHAT THE HECK ARE YOU UP TO, MR. PRESIDENT?"

INTRODUCTION

"WHAT THE HECK ARE YOU UP TO, MR. PRESIDENT?"

July 4, Independence Day, 1979: Sheets of rain fell on Washington, D.C., and suspense mounted. Would the nation's biggest fireworks show proceed or be drowned? National Park Service officials huddled in rickety wood structures roped with plastic and decided around three P.M. to make an announcement: *Please be patient.* Then at five P.M., they announced an official delay. Four hours later, they canceled the show altogether.[1]

Close by, a different celebration got under way: the annual smoke-in of the Youth International Party (Yippies), an organization founded twelve years earlier by counterculture celebrities Abbie Hoffman and Jerry Rubin. There was no Vietnam War to protest in 1979, of course, but the right to get high seemed as urgent as stopping a war. In Lafayette Park, across from the White House, scraggly young adults toked joints, swigged beer and Jack Daniel's, and set off firecrackers. The rain turned the tangy smell of pot slightly mellower, but when the high wore off, the crowd went berserk. The mob scrambled over a large black fence onto the White House lawn. Cops pursued, dodging beer bottles flung at them. Nine arrests followed, one just a few feet away from the White House.[2]

Perhaps it was fortunate fewer people were on the Mall to be disappointed by canceled fireworks or freaked out by police-hippie melees. Most gas stations in D.C. were shut down, not for the Fourth of July holiday but as a result of the decision by the Organization of the Petroleum Exporting Countries (OPEC) to cut exports to the United States. This was becoming a summer when people coasted or pushed their cars to stations often to find no gas. Stations with gas reported mile-long lines and three-hour waits. Most D.C. residents simply stayed home on July 4. Those who did search for gas raged. "The greatest country in the world," one person on a gas line told an inquiring journalist, "is stifled by a few sheiks."[3]

An editorial in the *Los Angeles Times* on July 4 stated the obvious: "This Independence Day, the holiday's very name seems to mock us." The grand old document known as the Declaration of Independence trumpeted citizens' rights to "alter" or "abolish" governments in face of a hostile world. Now *this*. Americans couldn't even get the third world to cough up enough gas to roll their cars out of driveways for traditional summer vacations. Stoned teenagers took over the White House lawn. Freedom seemed a cruel joke or an excuse for chaos. The conservative tabloid the *New York Post* intoned that on "Independence Day, 1979 the American paradox is bleakly apparent. As a nation, we appear to have become steadily more dependent on forces seemingly beyond our control, losing confidence in our ability to master events, uncertain of our direction." And then the editors slipped in this zinger: "The United States is now a victim of a loss of nerve and will, wracked by indecision and groping for a glimpse of inspirational and innovative leadership."[4]

It didn't take much to figure out that the *New York Post*'s editors intended those words for Jimmy Carter, the thirty-ninth president of the United States. Carter wasn't in the White House the day Yippies jumped the fence. He was at Camp David in the Catoctin Mountains of rural Maryland, the place where just a year before he had initiated the grandest accomplishment of his presidency, a peace agreement between Egypt and Israel, after long, tiresome meetings and brutal negotiations. Since then, Camp David provided good memories and a refuge from the strains of an increasingly stressful presidency, a place to fish, read, and relax. But on July 4, Carter felt the bad mood setting in on the nation and himself.

Before he had boarded a helicopter to Camp David on July 3, key members of his staff—Gerald (Jerry) Rafshoon, whose advertising background helped his work to improve the president's image; Hamilton "Ham" Jordan, the president's loyal right-hand man and soon-to-be chief of staff; Jody Powell, the press secretary; and Stuart E. Eizenstat, a policy wonk and chief domestic adviser at the White House—hounded Carter to make a speech about the energy crisis, about those long gas station lines exploding with anger. This group, most often called the "Georgia mafia" because they had followed Carter from the governor's mansion of Georgia to the White House, applied pressure.

The member of the mafia that Carter trusted most, Ham Jordan, had been watching over the White House while Carter had bounced around the world on a recent series of diplomatic trips. During the president's June sojourns in Austria, Japan, and Korea, Jordan (pronounced jer-din) would sometimes kick back and watch television news. He saw repeated images of gas lines tinged with violence and heard interviews with angry citizens: "What in the hell is Carter doing in Japan and Korea when all the problems are here at home?" Don't wait, Jordan counseled the president, to calm these people's nerves. Citizens "*want to hear from their President.*" So Jordan applied pressure the best way he knew how: He summoned Jerry Rafshoon to get Hendrik Hertzberg and Gordon Stewart, chief speechwriters at the time, to work up a speech. "With a very heavy heart," they sent a draft to Camp David. They knew it was bland, dry, and not up to the crisis Americans faced.[5]

Pressure, such as it was, never made Carter nervous. Just the opposite. He had a phenomenal ability to grow *calmer* while others went
bonkers. Rafshoon would pace and pull on his curly locks, Jordan
would boil, Eizenstat would blurt out criticisms, and Powell would
smoke cigarette after cigarette. Carter just flashed a steely grin. The political commentator and historian Garry Wills once described Carter's
"ferocious tenderness, the detached intimacy, the cooing which
nonetheless suggests a proximity of lions." But one thing always wound
up driving the president crazy: his need to rely on others to perform
tasks that produced mixed results.[6]

The drafted speech he stared at was a case in point. He could barely
make it past page four. For sure, it had its moments, talking of patriotism and American independence and the need to extol the key virtue
of war—sacrifice for the common good—while battling dependency
on OPEC oil. Those were ideas Carter could get behind. The speech
also mentioned an incident in which a pregnant woman was violently
attacked while on a Los Angeles gas line. That frightening story might
send shivers up the spine of the public's conscience. But the rest of the
speech read like a laundry list of vague energy plans. After falling
asleep reading it, Carter went to bed. Later that night, First Lady Rosalynn Carter stumbled across it on a coffee table. Suffering jet-lag-
related insomnia (she had accompanied Jimmy overseas), Rosalynn
read the speech and then told her husband the next morning that it
was awful. She had a much better ear than the president for the way a
speech like this might play politically, and her judgment mattered im-
mensely to Jimmy. That was it, Carter thought, there was to be no
speech, at least not this one.[7]

So while National Park Service officials and fireworks operators
worried about rain and the citizens of the nation's capital waited in gas
lines or stayed home, Carter placed a call from Camp David to the
White House. Vice President Walter Mondale joined Jordan, Powell,
and Rafshoon on phones. *Cancel it*, the president's words hissed over

telephone wires. Rafshoon flew into a panic. This had never happened before, *never*, not in the course of American history had a president canceled a speech with no explanation. Rafshoon complained that he had already called the television networks and asked them to block out the time. Calling them back wouldn't be easy. This is *not* the image we want to project, Rafshoon argued.

Carter rebuffed his image man. "There's more to it than energy," Carter explained. And then to underscore his point, as if the exhaustion and curtness in his voice weren't enough, he blurted out, "I just don't want to bullshit the American people." The advisers grew shocked at these words but continued to protest. So Carter hung up on them. Jody Powell looked at the others in the room with grief. He knew he'd have to make a statement the next day. The best he could come up with was short and perfunctory: There would be no speech, he announced, and then followed that with a "no further comment."[8]

And then the president seemed to disappear . . .

He remained holed up at Camp David for the rest of Independence Day. The next day, things took a turn for the worse. The dollar fell in international markets. Stock prices ratcheted down. And Jerry Rafshoon's worst nightmares began: Rumors spread. The president had an inexplicable "health problem." No, he was crazy, some politicians and journalists argued, or maybe he had left the country. It didn't help that one White House staffer told reporters that people had asked if the president installed "rubber wallpaper in the offices." Jody Powell—who had a knack for combining openness and distance with the press—tried to tamp down the suspicion. But if the president was in hiding, there must be something wrong, or so most journalists assumed. The bold headline on the cover of the *New York Post* the next day said it all: "What the Heck Are You Up To, Mr. President?"[9]

On July 5, all the president's men—Mondale, Jordan, Powell, Eizenstat, and Rafshoon—piled into a helicopter. They were joined by the president's young pollster, Patrick Caddell. He worked next door to the White House analyzing depressing poll numbers, his salary paid by the Democratic National Committee (DNC). When Caddell joined the others for their flight, they all seemed a little punch-drunk, laughing nervously and making jokes as the copter took off. They even wondered: What if we arrive and the president isn't there?[10]

They landed around three P.M., and cars whisked them to the Laurel Lodge where Jimmy and Rosalynn waited. Immediately, the conversation turned raucous; the participants seemed to mirror the anger heard on the gas lines. Mondale and Eizenstat realized that the president had become hopped up with ideas presented by Pat Caddell three months before in a long memo full of numbers and ponderous thoughts about a psychic crisis setting into America. To talk to the American people about such a crisis was "too negative," Mondale explained. "You can't castigate the American people or they will turn you off once and for all," the vice president pleaded, his voice shaking. Mondale looked on the cusp of a nervous breakdown, so Carter invited him on a walk around Camp David while the others took a break. But when they reassembled, fights broke out again. Eizenstat called Caddell's ideas "bullshit." Rafshoon worried about sounding apocalyptic. Through it all, Carter remained iron-willed, arguing that he wanted to confront the "crisis of confidence" plaguing America. His young pollster had won the argument after a meeting that went almost to midnight.[11]

Carter stayed at Camp David for ten days. He invited a string of visitors from different walks of life. Details were mysterious; the press was locked out for seven days during which reporters speculated about who was invited. The president had vanished to search his soul—and the nation's soul—on his mountaintop retreat. Then he came out of hiding on July 15, a Sunday, and went in front of the television cameras.

People talked about Moses coming down from the mountain, ready to impart God's word. They tuned in for a jeremiad.

Carter sat at his desk, leaned toward the cameras, pounded his fist, grinned his grin, and let big words and ideas fly. He condemned the American way of life. We as a people, Carter explained, "worship self-indulgence and consumption" and are mired in "fragmentation and self-interest." "Our people are losing" faith in "the ability as citizens to serve as the ultimate rulers and shapers of our democracy." He didn't have to say it but he did anyway: "This is not a message of happiness or reassurance, but it is the truth and it is a warning." He spoke openly of the nation's wounds—of King's and Kennedy's assassinations, "the agony of Vietnam," and the "shock of Watergate." He recognized his own weaknesses as a leader and the fact that "all the legislation in the world can't fix what's wrong with America." "I realize that more than ever as president I need your help," he intoned. It was a speech of humility and honesty and more.

The *Washington Star* called the speech "remarkable." Carter had, in the words of a journalist at *Time*, written "one of the most extraordinary chapters in presidential decision making." Pundit David Broder, who had visited Carter at Camp David just two days before the speech, said it "will surely go down in history as one of the most extraordinary addresses a chief executive has ever given. What he said was the kind of thing Americans have never heard from a president before." It really was amazing to consider that a president completely down in the polls—Carter stood at just 25 percent approval—told the American people that something was deeply wrong about the nation's soul and that he shared the blame. *Time* admitted that "in the whole history of American politics, there had never been anything quite like it." The writer most responsible for the speech, Hendrik Hertzberg, said, "It was, in the most unorthodox and extraordinary way, the President of the United States speaking truth."[12]

Phone calls and letters flooded into the White House, almost all of them favorable, with some citizens pledging to fight the war against America's reliance upon foreign oil by riding a bike or moped to work, spending less money, or turning down the thermostat. Those on Carter's staff who had doubts about the speech realized it was the right thing to do as they watched Carter's poll numbers skyrocket eleven points, something that hadn't happened for a long time.[13]

It was a speech that reached historic proportions, even if it didn't ring with beauty. It would never become a speech that children might commit to memory, the way some still do the Gettysburg Address. Reading it today will not make tears well up in eyes the way Martin Luther King's "I Have a Dream" speech might. It offers no memorable lines—no "the only thing we have to fear is fear itself," no "ask not what your country can do for you," no bold term like "the Great Society." But it shared with those speeches a view of the nation as a community bonded together spiritually and strengthened by facing adversity. It called on citizens for sacrifice the way John Winthrop's original founding speech for settlers moving to Massachusetts, "City on a Hill," did; the way Lincoln's Gettysburg Address evoked the memory of death in battle; and the way FDR's and Kennedy's inaugural addresses called for sacrifice and civic commitment. Carter's speech resonated, in part, because it touched something in the American subconscious, a worry about falling from our better ideals.

Unfortunately, we *mis*remember the speech today. Most of us know it as Carter's "malaise" speech, even though Carter never used that word. Or, we convince ourselves that as a doomed president, Carter laid the blame of the nation's problems at the doorstep of blameless citizens. Watch episode 80 of *The Simpsons*, where Springfield citizens gather for the unveiling of a statue of Jimmy Carter. Below Carter's pathetic-looking figure are emblazoned the words

"Malaise Forever." The citizens then riot in anger. As usual, pop culture nurtures amnesia.

Our memory of the speech comes from those who reworked it, who twisted its words into a blunt instrument that helped them depose a president. So this book can be read as a historical mystery—how it was that Carter's words received immediate applause and yet wound up ensuring his defeat. The story of Senator Ted Kennedy and Governor Ronald Reagan standing in the wings, mounting political warfare, will help solve this presidential murder mystery in part, while reminding us of what they got wrong about Carter's speech. *How* they twisted Carter's words tells us something about where the country went from that moment.

That the speech could save and destroy Carter at the same time only highlights the question originally asked by the *New York Post* that should now be worded: *What the heck were you up to, Mr. President?*

To explain what Carter was "up to" requires us to open the door and look inside the White House. The story begins in April 1979, when an energy crisis emerged and when Pat Caddell grew more aggressive in pushing the sort of speech that would take another three and a half months to become reality. The lens will have to be widened to examine those who jockeyed for influence and pushed or pulled against Caddell's idea: the frenetic image maker, the staid press spokesperson, the protective future chief of staff, the nerve-racked vice president, the demure first lady, and the stoic policy adviser. But we must also look beyond the White House, to the streets, televisions, popular music, gas lines, movie theaters, and radios of America. The president, after all, felt compelled to give the speech in order to explain the nation to itself. And so the speech serves as a view into the American soul during the last year of one of the country's most troubled decades.

Indeed, it would seem that Carter helped ring out the decade of the 1970s in his speech, a time when shards and ghosts of unresolved crises haunted the country. The past kept torturing the present with memories. The failure in Vietnam, the fears and conspiracies nurtured by Watergate, the assassinations and violence of the 1960s—all these things pressed in on the nation's psyche during the decade. They could not be easily left behind. Carter wanted to confront these legacies, to rebuild confidence while recognizing historical scars, to move the country forward with a sense of humility and fragility that those scars demanded.

Carter's message of moral complexity resonated in the context of the times. His speech aligned with a moment when moviemakers ended an unspoken moratorium on films about Vietnam and its brutal legacy. With a time when the fate of boat people escaping Vietnam changed and complicated the lingering debate about the war's legacy. With a time when a revolution in Iran and its concomitant oil crisis kicked the country in the teeth and signaled that the American century—when the country supposedly dominated the world—was ending.

Carter's speech also deplored cultural currents that worried Americans even as they participated in them. The so-called me decade disturbed as much as entertained. Disco culture, which dominated during the first half of 1979 in record sales and the proliferation of dance clubs, represented, for some, America's hollowness, vacuousness, and self-infatuation. Studio 54, the hippest discotheque in Manhattan— where the glitterati gathered every night to embrace drugs, decadence, and voyeurism—started to face serious troubles during the summer of 1979, its owner already under scrutiny for drug possession and tax evasion. Chants of "Disco Sucks" could be heard throughout the summer, eventually exploding into a riot at Comiskey Park in Chicago during the Disco Demolition Rally of July 12. Some angry young men hungered to blow up a culture of cocaine-snorting glitterati gazing at their mirrored reflections, to revolt violently against the me decade.

Worries about American culture could be gleaned not just in

Carter's speech but in the books he read to help him write it. There were many works of important, self-scrutinizing social criticism that came out in the late 1970s, as the me decade produced both participants and critics. Books about America's "culture of narcissism" sold like hotcakes during 1979. Religious leaders especially worried about Americans losing sight of what bonded them together and ditching the language of the covenant for self-interest. Ordinary Americans panicked as they watched their friends divorce and wreck their own families in increasing numbers. This was also a time when profound questions confronted the grand narrative of technological progress benefiting the country, questions impossible to ignore in light of Three Mile Island's nuclear meltdown and NASA's Skylab catapulting toward earth.

As the speech's moment approached, the times turned truly insane. Angry about rising costs of diesel fuel and limited supplies, truckers prompted riots in America's suburbs, translating angry populism into abject violence. Gas lines erupted with fights and guttural rage. Below the surface of a society supposedly composed of narcissistic, self-absorbed individuals dancing away their worries in discos across the country there lingered angrier elements that could erupt and tear the nation apart. It was a time when a president felt pressed to scrutinize his nation's value system and history to explain why the country seemed to come apart so easily, but also why it might have resources that could chart a better direction.

Which is also to say that the speech stood at a crucial turning point in our past. The year 1979 looks like other transformative years, for instance, 1968 or 1945 or 1932. It was a year in which secular trends bubbled up into crisis points. Most importantly, 1979 was a year in which Carter's patriotism—tempered with humility and critical self-scrutiny—fell to the triumphalism and dreams offered by Ronald Reagan and the larger conservative movement of which he was a part. It was a year when Carter and his religious faith—heeding the warnings of sinful pride that he had learned from the great theologian Reinhold

Niebuhr—collided with the apocalyptic redemption promised by Jerry Falwell, the burgeoning Christian Right, and even, ironically enough, a rock-celebrity-turned-born-again-Christian named Bob Dylan. The speech tells a story of a turning point in the nation's history that we still live with today.

This book offers a cultural and political history of a speech and the context in which it was written and received. Like the speech itself, this book examines the intersection of politics and ideas, the values that frame our national community, and the struggles to interpret those values. To tell this story is to say something about the meaning of contemporary America. Looking back at the speech helps us understand what we became after we turned the corner in 1979, and it reminds us of what we forgot when we put Carter's words of warning behind us.

1

DIAGNOSING A NATION'S HEART OF GLASS

APRIL 1979

And Iran really fell. It's so weird watching
it all on TV; it really could happen here.

—ANDY WARHOL[1]

1.

1979: A good year to pronounce the American century dead. The country's hold on the world had slipped. The Iranian revolution booted the shah, the man America had backed in power as a hedge against the spread of Soviet communism, from his throne. Just as in Vietnam, America felt defeated by a third world country. Except here the damage was harsher for those at home: Iran, the second largest exporter of oil next to Saudi Arabia, shut off its supplies. Reports about an impending gas crisis hit America's newspapers and magazines. The age of limitless, low-priced gas—what better symbol of American power than that?—had ended. As gas supplies dwindled, prices rose, and so would the general inflation rate, *up, up, up*, into double digits. The prosperity of the 1960s—when economic abundance raised tides and floated most boats—had collapsed. The pronouncement one social critic made at the beginning of the decade seemed more appropriate now: "We have arrived" at America's "years of middle age and decline."[2]

Americans looked like citizens occupying an empire in its final days. They were jaded and apathetic. Polls showed that the number of citizens who read or worried about public affairs "hardly at all" jumped upward: 54 percent bothered to vote in the 1976 presidential election, and then 38 percent in the 1978 midterm elections (with lower participation among the most educated). The president's approval ratings crashed around the same time, almost reaching the level of Richard Nixon's during the Watergate scandal and the Arab oil embargo of 1973, even though most citizens thought Jimmy Carter a moral, upright president, the farthest thing from Tricky Dick. They had simply given up on politics, entirely. When Carter went on television to give speeches to his fellow citizens about the issues of the day, few Americans bothered to watch. There were so many bread and circuses that distracted and that constituted the cultural vacuity of the 1970s: disco dancing, roller skating, hot tubs, mood rings, television shows like *Charlie's Angels* and *Three's Company*, a whole slew of fads and mindless diversions.[3]

They could not work forever, though. The energy crisis of 1979 would make itself known in the lives of ordinary citizens. It simmered at first and then finally blew up. On March 28, a nuclear power plant on Three Mile Island (TMI) near Harrisburg, Pennsylvania, almost melted down due to a pump and valve failure. Residents heard resounding booms and watched "puff radiation" clouds released. Reports by the plant's spokespeople were confusing at best. Pregnant women and children evacuated "tens of thousands—even hundreds of thousands—to who knew where and for who knew how long," as one journalist described it. The story line coming out of TMI paralleled, to an eerie extent, the hit movie *The China Syndrome* released just weeks before. In it, a cameraman played by Michael Douglas shoots footage of a nuclear plant melting down, its cooling system rattling away, and then shows the footage to a scientist who says: *It looks like the core almost melted.* If that happened, he goes on, it would "render an area the size of Pennsylvania uninhabitable." The movie audiences who packed Harrisburg's local cinema must have gasped at that line.[4]

Jimmy Carter was especially disturbed by the news at TMI and the fears provoked by the movie and press reports. The president believed nuclear power was one element in a broader solution to America's energy crisis. He had begun his career in nuclear engineering, working with nuclear-powered subs in the U.S. Navy right after World War II. Nuclear power couldn't be used to fuel cars, of course, but, if safe, it might alleviate some of the pressures on other energy sources, or so the president thought.

Carter decided to pay a visit to TMI on April 1. Hands folded behind his back, he shuffled around in the requisite plastic booties while glancing at control panels. Governor Dick Thornburgh of Pennsylvania, a moderate Republican who wanted to temper the panic, hovered close, offering words of assurance. But questions gnawed at the president: What about the gas bubble that remained in the plant's cooling system? Was it dangerous or potentially explosive? What did the near meltdown say about the energy crisis as a whole? What about the levels of confidence that Americans had in the country's ability to solve the impending energy crisis—of which TMI was merely the tip of the breaking iceberg?

The same day he visited TMI, Carter got bad news from Iran. That country had taken the next step in its long-unfolding revolution by declaring itself an Islamic republic. Ayatollah Khomeini—his white beard stretching out his stern face—called his countrymen's declaration "unprecedented in history." Khomeini was right; Shiite Islam had never embarked on remaking a country's entire existence. The Iranian revolution was no longer about toppling the American-backed shah but rewriting all civil laws to follow the Quran or at least Khomeini's interpretation. Theocracy now administered itself at the grass roots: Roving mobs attacked women who refused to wear the *chador* and enforced the ayatollahs' bans on disco dancing, drinking, and watching movies. "Death to America!" chants were heard on the streets of Tehran. Soon American flags would be burned, effigies of Carter torched in Tehran's public squares. For President Carter this wasn't just creepy but bizarre. He had suspected communists might take over the country—this still being the cold war, albeit in a state of détente—but never mullahs and Islamic fanatics. This was new and terrifying all at once.[5]

The *New York Times* reminded readers that the America hating in Iran was bad enough on its own terms but also for its material consequences: "The loss of Iranian oil" would leave "the United States with a gap of 400,000 to 500,000 barrels a day." The Organization of the Petroleum Exporting Countries (OPEC) would constrict oil shipments even further, hiking prices, and eventually generating long gas lines in America. The radical countries within OPEC—especially Libya—wanted to take revenge against the United States no matter what more moderate Saudi Arabia might desire. After all, America under Carter's leadership had just gotten Egypt to recognize the state of Israel and to sign a peace treaty that didn't address the Palestinian question. Even Saudi Arabia had no problem avenging this insult by America, knowing it was one of Carter's most famous and proudest accomplishments.[6]

America-hatred and OPEC retaliation sparked retaliatory backlash within the United States. Henry "Scoop" Jackson, a powerful Democratic senator from the state of Washington who had run against Carter in the Democratic primary and was highly critical of the president's energy and foreign policy, denounced OPEC's move as "a combination of greed and punitive doctrine." Hints were given that retaliation—through either trade or military action—would be legitimate. Jackson had an intellectual fan base growing at the magazine *Commentary*, edited by Norman Podhoretz. The publication was a hotbed of what some now called neoconservative thinking about American foreign policy. Writers there loved to dream of a time when the legacy of the Vietnam War—the defeat of a superpower by a scrawny third world communist country—could be overcome, when America's "confidence" in its military power reasserted. "As for America," Walter Laqueur wrote in the March issue of *Commentary*, "its inability to influence events in the Persian Gulf reflects its diminished stature in world affairs." Overly fearful of another Vietnam, Laqueur went on, Americans fell prey to the "shilly-shallying in Washington."[7]

Even Carter's own secretary of energy, James Schlesinger, thought along these lines (as did sometimes his national security adviser, Zbigniew Brzezinski). Schlesinger had served as defense secretary under Carter's predecessor Gerald Ford, and now he was, in the words of the *National Journal*, suggesting "the United States make its military presence known in the Middle East to safeguard the flow of oil from that region." Such gutsy posturing—an agressive solution to the energy crisis—frightened Schlesinger's own boss, Jimmy Carter.[8]

2.

Carter had to figure out his own solution to the energy crisis and quickly. He had to make a speech about the matter on April 5. Jackson's words, Schlesinger's counsel, and the neoconservatives' bellicose writings were too aggressive and hypocritical for him. After all, Carter had been warning for the last two years that an energy crisis like this should be foreseen and that angry tantrums against the world were childish. Carter's original National Energy Policy (NEP), proposed back in April

1977 and constructed by Schlesinger himself, had aimed to "reduce United States dependency on foreign oil" by emphasizing conservation through an intricate network of taxes and tax credits. But Carter had botched the plan. He had sent Schlesinger off to work in secrecy and to complete the plan in ninety days (Carter himself was confused by Schlesinger's first draft). The president had refused to take any advice from Congress, even though the plan would eventually go there for approval. So when the cumbersome NEP came out of the legislative meat grinder eighteen months later, it had lost most of its punch. Carter continued to warn and push for more action on the energy front, but nothing came from his warnings.[9]

So now in early April of 1979, on the second anniversary of Carter's announcement of the NEP, the president's speechwriters struggled to write something about TMI, the news in Iran, and the gloomy forecasts for a future energy crisis. They passed to the president drafts on which he'd scrawl his inimical slanty handwriting. Speechwriting in the Carter White House was, to be blunt, a royal pain and cumbersome process. Drafts of speeches had to be sent out to anyone with an inkling of expertise in the area. And in the case of energy, there were a lot of experts. Staff members too were pulled in to see this speech as it moved through draft after draft. The final version turned soggy, a compendium of different views. It was becoming, like most of Carter's speeches, uninspiring.

The difficulty in writing wasn't just the bureaucratic nature of composure. It was the president himself. Carter had a split personality when it came to explaining policies. Part of him was a technician, the man with an engineering background who explained the ins and outs of oil import levels, refinery production, inflationary rates, and an allocation system created under President Nixon until inevitably the television viewer's eyes glazed over. Then there was Carter the moralist, the born-again Christian who had taught Sunday school in Plains, Georgia, for years, until he came to the White House. This side of Carter pined to diagnose the end of the American century, to argue that a dream of limitless supplies was a bad idea in the first place, an unrealistic and even sinful way of looking at the world. *This* president didn't want to get technical but wanted to ring warning alarms in public. So the speech he planned to deliver did both things at once, and neither very well.

Warning Americans about the energy crisis came easy to Carter. He had done it throughout his presidency: In his original speech announcing the NEP, he had explained that "the energy crisis has not yet overwhelmed us, but it will if we do not act quickly." Carter also feared that warnings fell on deaf ears. Most Americans thought the energy crisis a hoax: Big oil companies had simply jury-rigged it, holding back supplies to ratchet profits. The words *big oil* rolled off Americans' lips with disdain, conjuring memories of greedy robber barons at the turn of the century watching gushers of oil shoot sky high and their bank holdings along with them. Or, take the current images of *Dallas*, a television show Americans started to watch in record millions in 1978, about a sleazy oil-rich family whose members screwed and screwed over one another. There was legitimacy to such hatred: Oil companies really were making money hand over fist in 1979. When Mobil Oil released an advertisement in the spring of 1979 that equated "increased profits" with higher "productivity," most Americans hearing about an impending gas shortage probably thought "Bullshit." The companies were probably just hoarding gas in underground bunkers somewhere.[10]

Carter's gut raged with anger at the oil companies, but his head rang with complexity. The reality of the energy crisis was more complicated than greedy companies bilking the public. For sure, oil monopolies tamped down production in early 1979 to tighten markets and drive up revenues. But there were also federal policies at play here, and not just price controls. Around the time of the famous Arab embargo of 1973—the last time that Americans panicked on growing gas lines—President Nixon created a gasoline allocation system. It had been intended to "distribute supplies evenly around the country," but like numerous policies, it now backfired and "assured, perversely, that gasoline could not be shifted from an area already well-supplied to one where it was needed." Thus, Carter knew that once the gas crisis really hit, the pain would be maldistributed: Big cities (Los Angeles, for instance) would suffer more than small towns in rural states like Wyoming. He also knew that some oil refineries had recently experienced accidents and thus weren't producing at full throttle. The Iranian cutoff of exports and the aggression of OPEC simply pushed the problem over a cliff, making an already bad situation worse.[11]

So on April 5, Carter gave his speech of policy explanations mixed with moral warnings. "The energy crisis is real," America's greatest I-told-you-so president intoned, recalling his predictions of an energy crisis two years earlier. He calmed fears about TMI, promising an "independent Presidential commission." But he mostly focused on the gas crisis Americans would face soon, knowing that here was where federal action could actually make an impact. Carter called for phased "decontrol" that would raise prices in the short term by repealing ceilings on prices and force Americans to cut back on gas consumption. But worry not about your wallets being drained, he counseled his fellow citizens, for as president he would impose a "windfall profits tax" that would hit oil companies like Exxon and Mobil hard and would generate federal funds that could be used to search for alternative energy sources. This was Carter's famous centrism: Neither over- or under-regulate. In other words, aggravate both conservatives and liberals.[12]

Carter hoped to provide some policy solutions and also show Americans the moral dimension of the energy crisis—how the gas shortage highlighted the country's frailties in a world not under its control. He hoped to dissect those ironies of history in which a superpower watched its power curdle. He pressed for Americans to think of living with limits and making sacrifices. If Americans didn't start cutting back their oil consumption, Carter explained, "we will almost certainly have gasoline shortages as early as this summer." As a prophecy of doom, it was a bit softer than it should have been. The shortages would, in fact, come sooner.[13]

There was a problem with Carter's warnings: The American people didn't listen to them. Roughly 80 million Americans watched Carter's first energy speech back in April 1977 when he announced his NEP and called for a "moral equivalent of war" against the energy crisis; only 30 million watched him on April 5, 1979. The denizens of a declining empire had tuned their leader out.[14]

3.

Pat Caddell thought he knew *why* Americans were tuning the president out, and on April 9 he started to make direct inroads on getting the president to listen to him. Caddell had been paid by the Democratic National Committee (DNC) to provide the White House with numbers about approval ratings, the popularity of specific issues, and strategy. He was a peculiar-looking man, impeccably dressed but shaped like a pear. His jaw caved in, providing him his nickname "the chinless wonder." He hid that feature by growing a black beard that happened to have a white streak running through it. It gave his darker features more intensity and helped hide his youthfulness. He was only twenty-nine. He had spent an itinerant childhood following his Coast Guard father from Florida to Boston. In Florida, Caddell taught himself polling by going door to door in Jacksonville, asking his neighbors questions and then predicting elections—which he did well. He then studied politics at Harvard University where he formed his own company, Cambridge Survey Research (CSR), and joined the growing ranks of professional pollsters, first advising George McGovern's unsuccessful run for president. Along the way to joining Carter's team in 1976, he honed interviewing techniques but also grew fascinated by ideas, avidly reading and arguing about history and politics.

He wasn't just the president's pollster, he was a full-time worrier. He was moody, and his moods shot in different directions. He could be exuberant and confident at times, morose at others. At one point, he'd make doomsday predictions, at another sunny forecasts, believing even the worst situation could take a positive turn. During the famous Middle East peace talks in 1978, Caddell remembered Carter introducing him to Egyptian president Anwar Sadat: "This is my pollster. He brings me a lot of bad news, but I still love him anyway." That's because Caddell had a penchant for seeing silver linings in collecting storm clouds. The situation in April 1979 was no different.[15]

If anyone had asked, Caddell would likely have said that Carter's April 5 speech seemed uninspired, too fixated on energy issues and ignorant of the psychic crisis underlying the impending gas shortage. One day while perusing back issues of *Time* magazine, Caddell came across an article about "disastermania." That's *it*, he thought, that's how Americans would view TMI or oil shortages. As apocalyptic events, not as technical problems solved with policies of decontrol or taxation or whatever. Carter's words on April 5 would go by his few listeners like chattering nonsense. The president thought too much in technical rather than psychological terms. Americans no longer listened because they no longer trusted their leaders. They saw the world as a chaos of conspiracies that no one could control.

Caddell had the statistics to prove this. He could show the number of Americans he considered "long-term pessimists" grew at breakneck speed during Carter's presidency. But stating this case made Caddell look like a highly manic college professor, fishing around in his briefcase for bad news.[16]

The president's right-hand man, Hamilton Jordan, rebuffed Caddell consistently, thinking the pollster's doomsday pronouncements counterproductive. Jordan too was young, just thirty-four. He had thick black hair that stuck to his head like a plastic football helmet and a ten-dency to dress casually at work (white shirt unbuttoned, cowboy boots). Carter trusted Jordan since he had worked for him as far back as 1966 as a student coordinator on Carter's first (and unsuccessful) run for gov-ernor of Georgia and then would be his executive secretary after Carter won the governorship in 1970. Jordan grew up in Albany, Geor-gia, where he had witnessed the civil rights movement as a child, and had left the state to become a civilian volunteer in Vietnam in 1967. He was thought of as a wunderkind strategist and leading member of the Georgia Mafia that crashed the Washington establishment in 1976. That reputation provided Jordan with a problem—a boorish tendency in his personality that the media loved to play up. Stories about his of-fending secretaries with bawdy humor now took backstage to stories about his peering down the blouse of an Egyptian ambassador's wife and saying he wanted to see the "pyramids," and spitting Amaretto and cream on the breasts of another woman who had rebuffed his advances at a bar. The press loved documenting rumors about his piggish ways. He was also known for his brazen attitude toward mem-bers of Congress (Tip O'Neill nicknamed him "Hannibal Jerkin") and for building a fence around the president that some found annoying.[17]

Certainly Caddell found it that way. He was forced to go around and contact the first lady, Rosalynn Carter. As second best, it was a smart move. Rosalynn had the president's trust on issues of politics even more than Jordan. After all, she had grown up in the now-famous Plains, Georgia (population 600), a small town without a library or movie house, just a little school and a Baptist church. Rosalynn was a friend of Ruth, Jimmy Carter's sister, who had introduced the couple to each other. The two married young, when Jimmy was just twenty and she seventeen. Like many women in her generation, she served as a loyal wife, helping Jimmy make his way through his training and first career steps in the navy. When her husband announced that he wanted to move from Norfolk, Virginia, where they lived, back to Plains to inherit his father's business as a peanut farmer, Rosalynn was dismayed. She savored independence from family ties and their small town, but then she did what was expected of her: She moved with Jimmy and their growing family and made the best of it by getting involved in civic activities and the Baptist Sunday School in Plains. She worked with her husband as he rose from state senator to governor to president. Though quiet and demure, she had a better political ear than Jimmy and was able to recognize when he had made political gaffes and bad decisions. The president recognized her gifts enough to invite her to attend cabinet meetings. Many thought she held a great deal of power in the White House.[18]

Caddell thought so too. Recognizing her political gifts, he called her on the phone to work his magic. He had a peculiar charisma built from his sense of assuredness. "I really would like to come and see you. It's very important," he pleaded with her. Then he added, "And I would like several hours." She invited him to the White House for breakfast.

On April 9, Caddell whisked himself from his office to the White House, making a quick five-minute walk. Ignoring his food, he started pulling out statistics and charts from his briefcase and showed his numbers on "long-term pessimists." When Caddell started to explain that Americans were losing faith in their government, their futures, and themselves, she turned ashen. Rosalynn wasn't sure what to make of this. Caddell noted the first lady's bewilderment, leaned across the table, and quoted Napoleon, "Glory comes only in great danger." Caddell saw himself as a warrior charging up a hill in battle, romantically slaying an enemy. If the president talked openly about the crisis and showed that Americans could return to their better civic values of commitment and trust, then the president could solve the crisis. Again: Depressing news wound up producing a happy ending.[19]

Rosalynn went to Jimmy. This time he listened. If his wife believed the issue mattered that much, then Caddell should write a memo.

That's how Carter got all of his information, from the typed page. The president once told an adviser, "I can read faster than people can talk," and his biggest source of pride was a clean desk at the end of the day, all memos read and answered, usually with his trademark "J" signature at the top. Besides, Carter was going on vacation in just a few days so he'd be refreshed and ready to take on something that was likely to be depressing. Receiving the news, Caddell started to write.[20]

4.

Later that evening of April 9, the day Caddell and the first lady break-fasted, millions of Americans watched the Academy Awards. Celebrities strode the red carpet at the Dorothy Chandler Pavilion in downtown Los Angeles. They were greeted by Johnny Carson, who wisecracked that the event would be "two hours of sparkling enter-tainment—spread out over a four-hour show." But this awards celebra-tion was something more, for it symbolized how much had changed in Tinseltown recently. Two films dominated the awards: *Coming Home* and *The Deer Hunter*. Both were about the war that Jimmy Carter and the rest of the country struggled to come to terms with and both ended an unofficial but real moratorium on films about the Vietnam War made in Hollywood. The rest of the evening showed how much Vietnam's legacy was contested and still very present four years after the conflict was officially over.[21]

The crescendo of the evening's event came when director Francis Ford Coppola lumbered onstage to announce that the best director award would go to Michael Cimino, the director of *The Deer Hunter*. The audience heard tension enter Coppola's voice. For eight years, he had struggled to make his own movie about Vietnam, *Apocalypse Now*, and he was just on the cusp of finishing it. When he watched

The Deer Hunter, he recoiled. The film, for him, was naive and jingoistic, seemingly the opposite type of film from the one he was trying to finish at that very moment.

Coppola's disdain wasn't just sour grapes about another director winning a coveted award. *The Deer Hunter* really was a sentimental movie about male bonding and love of country. It opened with a wedding scene in which a group of young steelworkers got drunk and promenaded before a banner that read "Serving God and Country Proudly." The film ended with a funeral scene for a character who had killed himself in a game of Russian roulette in Vietnam. Friends gathered in a local bar and sang "God Bless America" tearfully. Never once did the film ask any questions about the legitimacy or morality of the war.

The movie generated huge amounts of discussions. Jimmy Carter even engaged in the dialogue. He was a true movie buff, watching an incredible number of films at the White House (usually one a week at least). *The Deer Hunter* "deeply moved" him. It did what Carter wanted the country as a whole to do—to recognize, *really recognize*, the war's damage in the lives of ordinary, hardworking men. The final scene left the audience realizing that a member of the community was dead and gone, creating frayed friendships, a broken romance, and sorrow. Or so Carter thought.[22]

Though an avid movie viewer, Carter never understood what movies could actually accomplish. The man now gunning for his job, Ronald Reagan, *did*. While Carter used films to "relax" and rid himself of the pressures of the world, Reagan believed in the ability of movies to alter reality, to speak in emotional resonances and construct dreamscapes and myths that could actually change perceptions of reality. After all, Reagan had cut his teeth not in the political world but in Hollywood. Learning how to provide smooth delivery of lines as a sportscaster in Iowa, he went to Hollywood during the Depression to try his luck. His skills got him into B-movies. But he rose through the ranks and honed his anticommunism as an activist within the Screen

Actors Guild (SAG) trying to purge his union of communists. During the 1950s, Reagan worked as a spokesperson for General Electric, ditched his Democratic Party affiliations, and became a Republican. He worked on Barry Goldwater's infamous 1964 campaign for president and became governor of California in 1966. After two terms, he aimed for the presidency, almost beating Gerald Ford in 1976 for the Republican Party presidential nomination. He was preparing for his second try at the job.[23]

His second try, as of 1979, consisted of making radio addresses, while others worked behind the scenes to build his political organization, Citizens for the Republic (this way, Reagan could continue to make money from his radio broadcasts). *The Deer Hunter* merited Reagan's full attention, because the movie simplified the confusion Vietnam had created by evading judgment about the war's legitimacy and focusing instead on the story of young men who bonded together. It showed working-class men sacrificing for the sake of their country even though politicians forced them to lose. Reagan went on the air and called *The Deer Hunter* a "story of friendship among young men" that was "unashamedly patriotic." Those who criticized it were the same people "who in the 1960s & early '70's saw no virtue in anything America did." Unlike Carter, whose thinking was always a jumble of complexities and ironies, Reagan thought there was no reason to be ashamed of patriotism or the glories of war, even when it came to a war many believed America had lost and had been wrong to enter in the first place.[24]

The neoconservative writers at *Commentary* magazine concurred. "To judge by the surprisingly strong positive reaction to *The Deer Hunter*, the ardent patriotism it expresses is not so dead a commodity in today's America as some might have thought," one writer at *Commentary* explained. Norman Podhoretz, the magazine's editor, blustered to a newspaper journalist that "the film" projected "a lower-class patriotic response to the war protesters." The "silent majority" was ready to kick ass against the protester mentality that held America back. "If the movie makes an unequivocal statement about Vietnam, it is that the war was fought by these people; when the price of being an American had to be paid, they were the ones who paid it." That is, "working class" people from "ethnic stock" fought a war that the liberal elite and the protesters wouldn't let them win.[25]

Problem was the protesters were still around, even at the awards ceremony itself. Angry members of Vietnam Veterans Against the War (VVAW) gathered outside the Chandler Pavilion to oppose *The Deer Hunter* as an "imperialist" farce. Then the protest actually wound up inside the theater itself, when Jane Fonda accepted the Best Actress award for her role in *Coming Home*. She had called *The Deer Hunter* "a racist, Pentagon version of the war." She believed her depiction of Sally Hyde in *Coming Home* offered a different political message about Vietnam's legacy. *Coming Home* was just as sentimental as *The Deer Hunter*, showing men—Sally Hyde's husband (Bruce Dern) and a paraplegic vet she falls in love with (Jon Voight)—destroyed by the war. The film's pacifist conclusions were clear. When the two men confront one another in a climactic scene, Voight yells at Dern, "I'm not the enemy. The enemy's the war." The movie closes with Voight lecturing a group of kids who are considering military duty. War's "not like the movies," he warns.[26]

Fonda was still known as "Hanoi Jane" to many. She had visited North Vietnam in 1972, launching her protest career from Saigon and marrying Tom Hayden, the radical leader of the 1960s New Left, a year later. Neoconservatives abhorred her. "If an entertainer could volubly and profanely take on the President, Congress, the Army, and other sacred institutions of the country," a writer at *Commentary* intoned, "and still win an Academy Award, things had clearly changed" for the worse.[27]

But Ronald Reagan and neoconservatives had little to fear, for soon after Jane Fonda left the podium, on came Reagan's close friend, John

Wayne, to accept a lifetime achievement award. Wayne was Fonda's counterweight in Hollywood, a reminder that Tinseltown wasn't populated solely by radicals. He championed his conservatism in the swagger of cowboys and military men he played on the screen but also in his own political statements. Wayne's biggest accomplishment came when he made *The Green Berets* in 1968. It was a warmongering movie that hit theaters just as antiwar protests tore through the country, and it depicted a lily-livered journalist who doubted the merits of the Vietnam War only to take up a gun himself against the Vietcong by the end of the movie. Wayne intended the movie to piss off the "Eastern liberals" he derided.[28]

The Academy Awards would be John Wayne's last public appearance. He was battling cancer, something he claimed to have licked years before but which had come back to emaciate his body. The tough guy now looked pale and thin. But he screwed himself up and told the audience: "I came to Hollywood the same time as the Oscar, and we plan to be around a long time to come." Wayne was wrong. He would die not long after saying this. And his death would cause more resonances than he could have imagined. For some, including Reagan, he stood for the nation's dreams.[29]

5.

Jimmy Carter was getting prepared for his forty-seventh press conference on April 10. He held about the same number of press conferences as Richard Nixon but was trying to remain more open to inquisitive journalists, even if he distrusted them. He eschewed secrecy. Carter wanted to be the anti-Watergate president, giving the press unscripted chances to scrutinize him rather than brazenly attack the press the way Nixon did. Indeed, Carter's press secretary, Jody Powell, called the president "excessively candid" with the press, an especially bad trait now that in 1979 journalists had turned against him, depicting him as weak and ineffective. No matter, though, for Carter could still go in front of them with confidence, deploying his gift for thinking on his feet. He'd point to a journalist, flash his grin, and then answer the question succinctly and clearly.[30]

This day, he received typical questions about his energy decontrol plan, inflation, the federal budget, and Three Mile Island. Then a peculiar one was shouted out about his religious faith and Senator Jesse Helms, a Republican from North Carolina: "As a born-again Christian, Mr. President, what is your position on prayers in public schools?"

The issue at hand was the Helms amendment. Senator Helms had been fighting for the right to reserve time for voluntary prayer in public schools ever since he had been elected to the Senate in 1972. Winning reelection in 1978 only emboldened him. Helms had fought just about all of Carter's policies in the Senate as he advanced his New Right agenda with zeal and aplomb. He didn't expect to win on the specific issue of school prayer, but he did expect to drive a wedge into politics and force politicians to play their hands (embarrassing liberal members who might find themselves out of step with their more conservative constituencies back home). He would thereby gain traction for a conservative movement he was leading, a movement that was fast drawing religious leaders and grassroots political activists into its fold. Indeed, the question asked of Carter at the press conference showed just how much influence Helms was having at the time.

Carter responded. He suggested Congress shouldn't act on the Helms amendment, because the Supreme Court had already ruled against prayer in schools. He ruminated on his own views about religion: "I happen to be a Baptist. I believe that the subject of prayer in school ought to be decided between a person, individually and privately, and God." Carter's worldview was clearly structured by the teachings of his church and his own Sunday school lessons, but he was also a pluralist who understood that politics must have a secular basis. Carter admitted to praying every day, often more than once, but he also believed the presidency had no "religious connotations." The president was both a born-again and a rationalist, as he was a moralist and a technician. He refused to make absolutist claims that stymied rational debate. Besides, Carter believed that Helms had placed too much emphasis on this-world behavior—prayer itself—rather than thinking of God's judgment as something beyond human influence. In all these ways, Carter was fast becoming one of the last *liberal* Southern Baptists in America, or so some, including Helms, believed.[31]

Carter's argument against the Helms amendment captured a rift opening in America. Helms viewed religion as distinctly public, not private, and as something that should be institutionalized lest society fall prey to what the senator from North Carolina labeled "secular humanism," a belief system that placed man above God's teachings, that elevated rationality over a literal interpretation of the Bible. Helms once explained that "the banishment of the Lord from the public schools" resulted in "a permissiveness in which the drug culture has flourished, as have pornography, crime, and fornication." Without religion in the public square, decadence and decay would triumph. It was that cut-and-dried.[32]

The press conference awakened Carter to the changing landscape of American politics, but it also, more simply, helped him wrap things up in order to take a much-deserved vacation. After a few meetings the next day, Carter flew to Brunswick, Georgia, on April 12 when his ten-day vacation started. He spent most of it on Sapelo Island off the coast of Georgia. Evenings found him on the beach, barbecuing steaks; days found him reading Hemingway and fishing.

It was relaxing for sure, but the mean ways of the world still pressed in on him. On April 20, Carter left Sapelo Island for his hometown of Plains, Georgia. On this, his last full day of vacation, he paddled a canoe out onto a small pond near his house and threw in his fishing line. Out of nowhere swam a vicious-looking animal, its teeth bared, hissing and growling as it approached Carter's canoe. The president slapped the water with his paddle. The creature kept coming. Suddenly Carter thought to himself: Oh my God, it's a *rabbit*. He swung again just as the animal paddled away. He told his press secretary Jody Powell about the incident after his return to the White House, and Powell just guffawed, believing rabbits couldn't swim. Carter inquired if White House photographers had been around and taken pictures. He was thinking of using them to show that in fact a rabbit tried to attack him and his canoe. The incident would come back to haunt Carter a few months later.[33]

6.

While Carter vacationed, Caddell worked on his memo. He would come into the office and dictate to his assistant who typed frantically. Caddell poured through books, examined notes, and paced. Sometimes he would talk out loud, his words tumbling over one another as he raced to keep up with his thoughts. The memo was becoming a book. It aimed to accomplish something that has challenged political observers and historians ever since: To get a handle on the meaning of a very strange decade, the 1970s, and the problem of governing in a country grown cynical.

Caddell set the stage for the president with what he had at hand: gloomy statistics. A year ago, Caddell had warned the president: "Even if you are reelected I think the ability to govern is now the most serious issue. I fear, and the data suggests, that the public has begun to tune you out." The number of listeners for his April 5 speech should have made that clear already. Caddell pressed the reelection issue, playing upon the president's insecurities. He cited Ted Kennedy, the liberal senator from Massachusetts, pondering a run against Carter for the

Democratic Party nomination for president. Kennedy's name evoked jitters in the White House, and Caddell knew he was pushing buttons. Especially considering his conclusion: "Can you be reelected?" "Maybe at best" was the depressing answer.[34]

But Carter wouldn't listen if Caddell only played upon reelection fears and polls. The young worrier latched onto the engineer and moralist sides in Carter's personality, both at once. For the engineer, Caddell offered statistics and charts that graphed out loss of faith in government and public leaders. Carter could trace his fingers across lines going up and then down to show the growth of "long-term" pessimism. There were numbers stacked up over one another, showing changed responses to questions over several years. It would later be called malaise, but what Carter saw in Caddell's memo was hard-boiled math.*

Caddell had something for Carter the moralist too. If he had stuck with polls, Caddell would have lost his boss. Carter didn't like thinking in terms of popularity contests. So Caddell started dissecting the nation's soul. He moved from doubt about the president to doubts about citizens' own sense of individual efficacy and social trust. All indicators showed a crisis. "This crisis," Caddell explained, was "in many ways dwarfed by what Lincoln and Roosevelt faced, yet in many ways the reverse is true, for there are no armies to be dispatched or millions to be given jobs." Not a Civil War or Great Depression but a "great funk," as one historian would later call the 1970s. This explained why cutting through the din would be difficult for Carter, why a "break-through" hit rock solid walls. There was the defeat in Vietnam, the embarrassment of Watergate, the pains of inflation. But more than that, there was the mixture of these things into a sickening stew, into a

---

* A funny story about the technical side to Carter's personality: Once when he grew confused by a Dylan Thomas poem that he loved, he decided to break the poem down into component parts and diagrammed each line. Only then could he figure out why the poem resonated emotionally for him.

full-blown psychic crisis at the national level that made people tune out the president.[35]

Add the energy crisis to the mix, and a perfect storm emerged. The very thing that Carter was trying to get the American people to face reminded them that the world's richest superpower was, at least on this front, at the mercy of the third world. It spoke to a feeling of falling from grace, a sense of living in an empire in decline.

This sort of fear—what some called "doomsday chic"—became omnipresent during 1979. Stories about America's decline had been told since the country's founding. It was an easy tale of civilization falling into barbarism, a story that traced its roots back to antiquity and traveled up to the present, and one that became especially potent in a year like 1979. How else to explain the popularity of the year's best-selling book, Barbara Tuchman's *A Distant Mirror*? Tuchman's story about fourteenth-century Europe and the bubonic plague wouldn't seem a natural topic for a bestseller. The historian documented in great detail how medieval chivalry descended into barbarity, illustrating how civilization was a thin veneer and war a constant in Western history. By the time that Caddell started to write his memo, Tuchman's book had enjoyed bestseller status for twenty-five weeks in 1979. Americans were fascinated by stories of decline into decadence and ruin.[36]

Caddell himself was partial to William Shirer's *The Collapse of the Third Republic* (1969). Written by a journalist who had firsthand accounts of France's fall to the Nazis in 1940, Shirer's story fit in with Caddell's ideas about America: the story of a corrupt republic, a political elite out of contact with the realities of ordinary life, a dangerous right poised on the brink of gaining power, a left corrupted by bad ideas and demagogues. Shirer showed how the media whipped up a hatred of elites only to allow ordinary citizens to rage. He even compared Leon Blum, the leader of France's Popular Front and one-time premier, to Adlai Stevenson, the two-time Democratic Party candidate during the

1950s who seemed uncertain about his leadership capacities. The comparison must have made Caddell ponder: Carter was looking more and more like Stevenson, that is, uncertain, timid, and unwilling to dirty his hands with political compromise. Shirer's story ended, of course, with Hitler. Caddell considered the possibility that "America could yield to a 'man on horseback'"—an eerie premonition—but suggested that "more likely" a "spiritual crisis" would lead "society to turn inward," making the United States "a shadow of its former self." Not that that was good news.[37]

Caddell was striking chords that reverberated, especially in the head of a president insecure about his own country's future. Like Jesse Helms, Carter worried about the country's civic morality (he just didn't think school prayer would help the matter). And 1979 was a good year for worrying: A number of social critics believed they were getting a better handle on the changes that Americans had gone through during the decade of the 1970s. The sense of decline Caddell believed he saw added up to a general withdrawal from politics and the growth of "me-ism," a reclusive drawing inward to the self. "Selfishness seems to pre-dominate everywhere," Caddell worried. All he had to do to confirm this suspicion was gaze out at his country's cultural horizon.[38]

7.

Caddell couldn't have invented the "Awareness Extravaganza" even if he had wanted to. Held in the auditorium of Julia Richman High School, a public school on the Upper East Side of Manhattan, as Caddell was writing his memo, the event symbolized the pathological obsession with selfhood that he wanted to document. Consider the event's emcee: Jerry Rubin. He was the quintessential 1960s radical who shucked protest for self-exploration. He had joined with Abbie

Hoffman during the 1960s to create the Yippies (the Youth International Party), which used guerrilla theater and confrontational protests to oppose the Vietnam War. He was arrested along with other activists for illegally protesting the Chicago Democratic Party Convention in 1968. But soon after, he grew disillusioned. As the protest movements he once engaged in started to fizzle, Rubin decided to give up on political activism and focus instead on a search for inner peace through "est, gestalt therapy, bioenergetics, rolfing, massage, jogging, health foods, tai chi, Esalen, hypnotism, modern dance, meditation, Silva Mind Control, Arica, acupuncture, sex therapy, Reichian therapy." He drew up this list of self-awareness crazes with pride rather than shame.[39]

Rubin wasn't alone in his search. Numerous 1960s activists had moved from protest politics to self-awareness. Rennie Davis, a close friend of Tom Hayden, the leading activist in Students for a Democratic Society (SDS), had also been arrested in Chicago and then grew disillusioned especially after a large protest against Vietnam held in the nation's capital in 1971. By 1973, he turned to the child guru Maharaj Ji and the practice of meditation, pledging his life to the Divine Light Mission. Consider too Tom Hayden's first wife (before he married Jane Fonda), Casey Hayden. She had been engaged in the civil rights and feminist movements of the 1960s, but her own disillusionment led her to a commune in Vermont during the 1970s. There she "met a self-styled yogi and helped create the Integral Yoga Institute in San Francisco." Numerous activists found Eastern religion's meditation a healthy substitute for the raucous world of political engagement. Looking inward seemed more fulfilling than changing the world.[40]

Jerry Rubin just made a bigger, self-promotional splash of his conversion to me-ism. All of the different experiments he engaged to discover his true self fit under the title of the "human potential actualization" movement that he now hoped to promote at the Richman auditorium (the way he once promoted the movement against Vietnam).

Those entering the event paid sixty dollars and received free Perrier water and a bounty of advice about a variety of self-help practices. Arnold Schwarzenegger, the celebrity muscleman who liked to prance around on stage and show off his pumped-up body, spoke, as did other gurus of self-love. One stand sold couch pillows that were pink satin and read I LOVE ME.[41]

The event epitomized what the social critic Tom Wolfe called the "me decade." A journalist turned pop sociologist, Wolfe wore an immaculate white suit wherever he went to jot down notes about the state of America's soul and to come up with catchphrases about social trends. In this case, he visited "encounter sessions" and "new age" therapy meetings where people claimed to overcome hemorrhoids through meditation. Wolfe believed that some time after World War II Americans had grown fat with prosperity and were thus freed to pursue the collective process of "changing one's personality—remaking, remodeling, elevating, and polishing one's very self . . . and observing, studying, and doting on it. (Me!)"[42] Americans threw off tradition and family and explored their selves through Eastern mysticism, crystals, New Age music, or whatever else they could find. The me decade and its cult of self became the second most important "sign of the crisis" that Caddell listed in his memo—next to political apathy and the decline of voting.

Throughout the 1970s, Americans checked out quick-and-easy practices to find themselves. Jerry Rubin had celebrated Erhard Training Seminars (est), a process in which people locked themselves into a room to face the abusive rants of a trainer who knocked down their old selves in order to create newer, happier ones (sometimes people would adopt a different first name in the process). Michael Rossman, a New Left activist who grew appalled by the numbers of protestors drifting toward est in the 1970s, called it "the most potent short-term mass-consciousness-changing technology to go public during the 1970s." There was also transcendental meditation (TM), a process that took only twenty minutes twice a day but promised prompt self-renewal. Self-help was offered in numerous bestselling books of the 1970s with titles like *I'm OK, You're OK, Looking Out for Number One, How to Be Your Own Best Friend*, and *When I Say No, I Feel Guilty*, as well as the founding of the popular magazine with the all-telling title, *Self*. Even President Carter's favorite activity of jogging was reimagined more as self-exploration of inner peace than exercise. Or so James Fixx argued in his bestselling book, *The Complete Book of Running* (still on the charts in 1979).[43]

The hope to discover one's real self had a flip side, what Wolfe called "the great Divorce Epidemic" and "wife shucking." The year 1979 witnessed the tenth anniversary of California's famous no-fault divorce law, which alleviated the burden of those seeking a divorce to explain their rationale for separation, making the process easier, quicker, and less guilt-provoking. The law spread east from California over the next ten years, doubling the divorce rate as it spread. The results were obvious: Single-person households increased 60 percent by the end of the decade. "Joint custody" entered the American lexicon. And in 1979, companies started to market do-it-yourself divorce kits, perhaps the quintessential symbol of the me decade, promoting an instant, presto way to shuck and renew.[44]

Divorce sunk into the crannies of America's pop culture. The comic strip "Splitsville" was invented in 1979; it depicted a bumbling father who shuttled his daughter around, read dirty magazines, and sought a replacement for his wife. America's best-known novelist, John Updike, collected a series of stories about his fictional Maple family into a larger novel entitled *Too Far to Go* that was published to fanfare in 1979. Updike felt ambivalent about divorce (as he did about many things), having gone through one himself. He explained in the introduction to his stories: "Though the Maples stories trace the decline and fall of a marriage, they also illumine a history in many ways happy, of growing children and a million mundane moments shared. That a marriage ends is less than ideal; but all things end under heaven, and if temporality is held to be invalidating, then nothing real succeeds." In the television-movie version of *Too Far to Go*, broadcast nationally the month before Caddell wrote his memo, the husband acted nonchalant, even blasé, about his impending divorce until he had to break the news to his son and daughters at the dinner table. There he burst into spasms of uncontrollable crying. Americans felt torn between believing divorce was just another part of the human condition—the journalist Gail Sheehy labeled it a new "passage" in midlife—or an abject emotional catastrophe. The me decade created a sense of freedom mixed with the ambivalence that freedom often accompanies.[45]

Caddell had witnessed the damage done by divorce in his own circle of friends. His town house in Georgetown became a rotating bachelor pad for members of the Carter administration who divorced while working at the White House. Ham Jordan, Gerald Rafshoon, and the president's chief political liaison, Tim Kraft, lived there after their own divorces. Caddell himself was single and about to turn thirty, a perpetual bachelor who seemed to delay commitment in light of the failed marriages around him. He dated Hugh Hefner's daughter, brought Lauren Bacall to the inaugural ball, and drove a gold Mercedes in classic swinger style. But his Catholicism made him uncomfortable about his late-in-life single status and his workaholic nature.[46]

He also knew how perturbed his boss had grown about divorce. During the first few days of his presidency Carter had told a group of staff members: "I have asked my own White House staff, and I've also asked cabinet members to protect the integrity of their own family life . . . Those of you who have left your spouses, go back home . . . I think it's very important that we have stable family lives." Like Carter's National Energy Plan announced around the same time, the president's advice and warning went unheeded. And it suggested how extensive the problem was. In the president's own circles, the culture of divorce had taken hold. Caddell could have paraphrased the cartoon figure Pogo: We have diagnosed the me decade, and the problem is us.[47]

8.

Caddell could simply turn on the radio in April to get a sense of how the me decade had transformed Americans' views about commitment to long-term relationships. The disco hit "Heart of Glass," by the new wave rock group Blondie, was being played all over the airwaves, racing to number one on the charts at the time. The song reflected a growing survivalist ethic concerning romantic relationships and also showed the pervasive nature of disco during the decade. Blondie's song could have served as the sound track for Caddell's memo.

"Once I had a love and it was a gas," Blondie's lead singer Debbie Harry crooned over the pumping disco beat, "soon turned out to be a pain in the ass." She prettied up that line for the radio version and thus created the song's title. Her message was: Love is a pain, better to cocoon oneself from attachments, and love yourself instead. Lester Bangs, one of America's greatest rock critics and a friend of Blondie (before the band went disco), believed the song captured "the emotionally attenuated" feel of the 1970s. He argued that it was symbolic not only of disco's pervasive hold on popular music (*everyone* was going disco, it seemed) but also of the decade's ironic distance from romantic love and the growing impact of what he labeled "Andy School."[48] Meaning Andy Warhol, the man who delighted the most at Blondie's success and who was already a cult figure of the 1970s. Knowingly or not, he was the band's guru on postmodern love.

Still known as a pop artist of the 1960s who suffered an attempt on his life in 1968, Warhol was shifting career tracks then by focusing on producing his fanzine, *Interview*, which served as a gossip rag about fellow celebrities in New York City (and would soon inspire the glossier magazine *People*). Warhol was attuned to the cultural feel of the 1970s, being a public philosopher of vacuousness. He believed in skating on surfaces, snapping Polaroid shots of his fellow celebrities and calling them art. Warhol found his own views on love echoed in Blondie's song. The artist had explained in his 1976 book, *The Philosophy of Andy Warhol*: "Love affairs get too involved, and they're not really worth it. Fantasy love is much better than reality love." Blondie simply provided the music for that message. When the song broke big, Warhol planned to put Debbie Harry on the cover of *Interview* and mapped out a celebration party for her at Studio 54, the cultural capital of Andy School.[49]

Studio 54 had been New York City's primo disco club for the last two years and an institution that captured the feel of the decade. It was "housed in a former opera house and television studio" and run by Steve Rubell, a fast-talking man addicted to quaaludes who had a knack for promotion that exploited gossip networks and gimmicks. The club blasted disco music onto its dance floor, where Warhol's celebrity friends gathered. If people made it past Rubell's scrutiny at the front door, they might find Halston, the upscale fashion designer who dominated the 1970s; Elizabeth Taylor, the plumped-out movie star and wife of Senator John Warner; Truman Capote, the impish writer who wrote very little then but sported an expensive face-lift; Margaret Trudeau, the pot-smoking wife who had separated from her husband, Canadian prime minister Pierre Trudeau; or Bianca Jagger, ex-wife of the Rolling Stones' lead singer Mick. The glitterati danced, chatted, and snorted cocaine in the halls below the club's main floor. When asked if the place was like "ancient Rome," Diana Vreeland, the former editor in chief of *Vogue* and another member of Warhol's circle, responded, "Darling, isn't that what we're aiming for?"[50]

Though the club was on its last legs when Warhol planned his celebration for Debbie Harry (Rubell faced charges of tax evasion and drug possession), it had become a place that fascinated not just those who wanted to get in every night but also those cultural and social observers who were trying to make sense of the American scene in the 1970s. Consider the observations of the music critic Albert Goldman, one of the best writers about the relation between disco and American values. Goldman noticed how the club rejected traditional rock performances in order to assemble dancers on the floor to marvel at one another and see their reflections in the large mirrors behind the bar. The message was obvious to Goldman: "In an age when physical appearance and conditioning have become obsessively important, disco provides a perfect arena for the exercise and display of all those carefully nurtured and cultivated bodies." Goldman highlighted the club's voyeurism, the evenings of random contacts between preening individuals who masked their detachment in exquisite concern for outward appearance. "The real thrust of disco culture," Goldman explained, "is not toward love of another person but toward love of the self, the principal object of desire in this age of closed-circuit, masturbatory, vibrator sex. Outside the entrance to every discotheque should be erected a statue to the presiding deity: Narcissus." That too seemed the message of Blondie's song, Warhol's philosophy, and Caddell's growing set of worries about the country.[51]

Disco's vacuousness and love of the self, like new age religion and the divorce epidemic, represented an undercurrent in American culture that Carter's young pollster was trying to explain. Long-term pessimists were now fast pursuing a life of detachment and rejecting commitment to others. Love of the self was replacing more traditional values of sacrifice. The nation's heart of glass needed diagnosing, so Caddell kept writing as Blondie's hit played in the background.

9.

While "Heart of Glass" climbed the charts, so did a book that tried to explain the song's infatuation with individualism, withdrawal, superficiality, and narcissism. The last week of March saw Christopher Lasch's *The Culture of Narcissism* enter the bestseller lists; during April, it rode a wave, becoming the most discussed, if not necessarily read, work of serious nonfiction. *People* magazine decided to run a story about the book and dispatched a reporter to interview the author. Americans were hungry to figure out why they were becoming self-obsessed and shallow and perpetually unhappy and cut off from one another. The book's opening line explained why it would get a wide readership in 1979 that included Caddell: "Hardly more than a quarter century after Henry Luce proclaimed 'the American century,' American confidence has fallen to a low ebb."[52]

An academic historian, Christopher Lasch was stunned by the fame and celebrity his book achieved. No one would have expected a bestseller from his pen, least of all him. He was a shy Midwesterner who lived in what he called the provinces in upstate New York, where he taught American history at the University of Rochester. He had been a "radical" and supported the 1960s student protest movements until they became enamored with violence and confrontation. The counterculture never interested him. After all, he was a family man, married with four children, and lived in a quiet suburban setting. He was also a worrier by nature, someone who felt the pain of others. By the 1970s, he had noticed a growing number of his friends divorcing and splitting from their families. Unlike Updike (whom he had roomed with at Harvard University as an undergraduate years before), he was saddened by divorce, and it propelled him to read psychological theory and books on the history of modern love and the family.

The Culture of Narcissism served as a more serious version of Tom Wolfe's pop sociology merged with a moralistic sensibility. While Wolfe offered anecdotes about encounter sessions, Lasch employed history, sociology, and psychoanalysis to draw his story line back in time to the nineteenth century. The book became famous for esoteric theories buttressing sweeping judgments about American politics, culture, and character. Voter apathy—something Caddell worried about—was for Lasch a "healthy skepticism about a political system in which lying has become endemic and routine." Permissiveness had overthrown puritanism and the work ethic. Experts dominated every element of life, including parenting, as people rushed to buy self-help books. The result was the "proletarianization of parenthood" and "a managerial, corporate, bureaucratic system of almost total control." Lasch enjoyed drawing broad strokes such as this one that helped explain Jerry Rubin: "After the political turmoil of the sixties, Americans have retreated to purely personal preoccupations. Having no hope of improving their lives in any of the ways that matter, people have convinced themselves that what matters is psychic improvement."[53]

One thing hadn't changed since the 1960s for Lasch. He was still a man of the left who used historical materialism to explain cultural matters. He traced the roots of narcissism back to the industrial revolution and the rise of advertising during the 1920s. Higher productivity and credit induced self-love, not innate selfishness. With a surplus of products to move, corporations nurtured synthetic demand through advertisements that used psychological appeal rather than material need. This was not a particularly innovative insight, but it posed difficulties for Caddell whose gaze went back only as far as Vietnam and Watergate. Was the crisis to be driven back to the late nineteenth century and into the sinews of capitalism? That would make the present crisis seem insurmountable.

Caddell hadn't read Lasch's book closely, if at all, by April. He glossed it, calling it a work about "personal gratification," and even getting the title wrong (it became *Narcissism in America* in the memo he was writing). Caddell shared this misreading with others. Critics and reviewers quickly leaped over the book's complexity and turgid arguments to emphasize its polemic against selfishness and its "apocalyptic" tone. One reviewer said Lasch's name sounded "Dickensian in the context." *Newsweek* shouted out, "Awake! Reform! thunders Christopher Lasch." But the book didn't thunder; it stewed in its strange mix of psychoanalytic theory, social history, Western Marxism, and democratic theory.[54]

Most critics treated the book as a sermon against selfishness. This was partially Lasch's fault since he seemed to suggest personal involvement had replaced political activism in the 1960s. But if readers cut through the difficult meanderings in psychoanalytic theory, they found the book arguing that the problem wasn't selfishness, it was the *diminishment* of the self. Take Lasch's treatment of Andy Warhol. He describes Warhol standing before a mirror and struggling to erase a pimple on his face. "The sense of security provided by the mirror," Lasch explains, "proves fleeting. Each new confrontation with the mirror brings new risks." The self is uncertain, "obsessed" about its projection of images outward; the self is beleaguered by the world that reflects back upon it. Warhol's superficial obsession with surface reflected the self's larger collapse into insecurities and withdrawal. The artist's views on love simply highlighted his fear of commitment. Lasch agreed with the philosopher Shirley Sugerman, who described narcissism as "survival" and "a defensive maneuver against the fateful perception of man's lovelessness and rejection."[55]

Even though Caddell misread Lasch's book, he was onto something. Lasch was struggling to merge his own cultural conservatism—disdain for divorce, selfishness, and consumerism—with leftist politics. Such an amalgamation of ideas matched up, at least partially, with Carter's worldview. Here was a president who deplored abortion and divorce, and also the selfishness of capitalism. Lasch recognized this set of concerns in the president. In 1976, he had written his friend and fellow historian Eugene Genovese, "I'm more and more convinced that" Carter is "the most intelligent politician to have risen to national prominence in a long time." But little could he expect when writing those words that he might be invited to the White House. And little could he foresee this: a president being advised to read a left-wing social critic who thought voter apathy a legitimate form of protest. That spoke volumes. Friends came to Carter from very strange places indeed.[56]

10.

Armed with statistics, his reading of Lasch and Wolfe, and a set of observations about American pop culture, Caddell put the last touches on his memo. It was now officially more like a book; Part I stood at seventy-five pages. Caddell tossed it with a resounding thud into Carter's in-box on April 23. Fresh from vacation, Carter applied his speed-reading skills to the tome and was taken aback. Staff members were quick to joke that "Of Crisis and Opportunity" (Caddell's own title for his memo) should have been called "Apocalypse Now"—a double entendre, since it referred to the tone of the memo and the fact that Caddell had provided advice to Francis Ford Coppola about the best way to market and promote his upcoming Vietnam film with that title.[57]

Dismay, disastermania, and deadly poll numbers explained the staff's rewording of the memo's title. But what about the fourth word in Caddell's original title—"opportunity"? That represented the pollster's own personal hope that always sat in tension with his gloominess. The majority of the memo included bad news but then shifted to a simple premise: "The American people want to restore greatness in America." A discerning reader might have said: *Really?* Wasn't this a nation mired in infantile self-love and consumer indulgence, incapable of imagining a civic rebirth? But Caddell knew he couldn't leave the president with doom and gloom. He traced out an alternative by referencing "covenant language"—talk of community—that existed throughout America's past. He included long quotes from the African American civil rights leader Reverend Jesse Jackson (another figure who merged cultural conservatism and uplift with left-wing politics) about "spiritual regeneration." Caddell had made a case for the president to deliver a jeremiad to the nation, to tell his fellow countrymen how they had fallen from better times but could return to national greatness.[58]

The silver lining in all of this was an idea of James MacGregor Burns, a political scientist who had once run for Congress but now taught full-time at Williams College in Massachusetts. Burns began his academic career by studying the presidency of Franklin Delano Roosevelt. Then he abstracted this study into a general study of politicians in which he distinguished between "transactional" and "transformational" leadership. The first envisioned the politician as a trader with the American people, as someone who said, *vote for me, and I'll deliver you the goods*. The latter "recognizes and exploits an existing need or demand of a potential follower" and "seeks to satisfy higher needs, and engages the full person of the follower." This idea stuck in Caddell's brain.[59]

That there were transformational leaders in America was certainly true. That the list included Jimmy Carter wasn't. But the president did have his own style of leadership. He could recognize the severity of a crisis and speak truthfully. Honesty and forthrightness were two of Carter's strongest attributes (and why, though Americans might have doubted his presidency, they never doubted *him*), and perhaps they could help him shatter Americans' growing distrust over the rhetoric of the political class that Caddell criticized. Carter would have to embrace a sense of humility about his own leadership—to warn about the energy crisis with honesty and toughness and to admit his own challenges as a leader. And perhaps that might get the country into a better place to confront the crisis that Caddell had outlined in his memo. It wasn't necessarily transformational, but it was the closest Carter could come.

11.

On April 25, Carter got his chance to test out this style of leadership. He held a town hall meeting in Portsmouth, New Hampshire. This format of citizen-president exchange had become one way to get Carter's message out without the filter of the media. Caddell, for one, liked the idea. It also just so happened that New Hampshire was a state whose Democratic primary came early in 1980. Carter knew he would face a challenge from California governor Jerry Brown and maybe Massachusetts senator Ted Kennedy. He was ready for some early campaigning—shaking hands, kissing babies, and cajoling. But he wanted to do it differently.

The dearth of trust in leaders that Caddell had outlined became apparent quickly as the meeting started. Hecklers showed up. The crowd seemed feisty and unruly. But Carter didn't flinch. Instead, he told the crowd, working his way into talking about the energy crisis, "I'm not going to sugar-coat it for you. The energy future will not be pleasant for you or for me or for other Americans." That was the sort of tough language—talking seriously about the crisis in order to prepare citizens for sacrifice—that Caddell could hope for. The toughness flowed from his April 5 speech but took on a different feel in a setting where cynicism became vocalized.[60]

Carter took questions about inflation, energy, and home mortgages. And then came an odd moment. A person asked if the president's daughter Amy, who went to a public school, bragged to kids about her dad being president. "Ordinarily, Amy, being the daughter of a President, probably does more apologizing than she does bragging." The crowd laughed.[61]

Carter seemed ready to answer critics by admitting his own faults in a self-deprecating manner. But he wouldn't let people off the hook in the process. He was moving toward humility without losing sight of the responsibilities of political leadership. And the town hall meeting made him more aware of the problems his pollster had outlined: the challenge of governing in an increasingly cynical country that was trying to shirk its problems. His own challenge as a leader would have to include cutting through the cynicism and the sound of hecklers.

12.

The next day Washington, D.C., witnessed a transformational leader of a wild and apocalyptic kind. Reverend Jerry Falwell stepped forward to lead the nation's first "I Love America" rally. Similar events had occurred at numerous state capitals but never at the nation's. The choreography was straightforward: American flags were placed in rows, and the I Love America Singers, most of them college kids, gathered around, decked out in red, white, and blue costumes. The men wore identical ties, the women white billowy dresses. They started by singing "Faith of Our Fathers": "We will strive to win all nations unto Thee; And through the truth that comes from God, We shall then be truly free." They followed that with "America the Beautiful."[62]

Falwell's purpose in organizing this event and others at state capitals was to ensure America's redemption. For quite some time, he had been a born-again, Bible-thumping Baptist, building his Thomas Road Baptist Church in Lynchburg, Virginia, practically from scratch. But he began to recognize that the sins plaguing America were *national* sins. He had conceived "I Love America" rallies in 1976, during the country's bicentennial celebration. If Americans could confess their collective sins in public and then pledge to remake their laws to follow conservative Christian teachings, Falwell believed, God might pass kinder judgment on the nation.

Taking his show to state capitals and now to D.C. reflected Falwell's growing politicization. Back in 1964, when he was still just a local minister and the civil rights movement was at its height, Falwell gave a famous sermon entitled "Ministers and Marches" in which he condemned preachers who engaged in politics. Falwell didn't just disagree with the civil rights movement, he believed evangelicals should stay out of all politics, lest the word of God be tainted. But now Falwell watched as the president of the country gave the go-ahead for the IRS to deny private Christian schools tax-exempt status (that would include his very own Liberty Baptist College). He watched government support a woman's right to abortion, feminists and politicians (including the president) work to pass (unsuccessfully) the Equal Rights Amendment (ERA), and courts try to make it easier for Americans to divorce. And so he knew the time for political engagement was now. The "I Love America" rally was his political solution—galvanizing evangelical anger at existing laws of the land and seeking redemption and reform.[63]

So now Falwell was on the Capitol steps, waiting for the I Love America Singers to finish "America the Beautiful." He stepped to the podium, Bible firmly clenched in his hand. He was a well-built man (having played football when younger) but slightly tubby now that he was forty-five years old, with a strange resemblance to Barney Rubble, the cartoon buddy of Fred on *The Flintstones*. Falwell had a "mellow voice," with a light southern twang, just right for jeremiads that didn't repulse listeners (one journalist described his voice as that of a "car salesman").

"In 1776," Falwell explained, "fifty-six men signed a document called the Declaration of Independence. They pledged their fortunes, their lives, and their sacred honor to a document that four times specifically refers to the dependence of this nation upon God." People would scream out, "I love America!" as he said this. Falwell then derided the sick realities of a Christian nation fallen from its founding: everything from the ban on prayer in public schools that his close friend Jesse Helms fought to television shows like *Charlie's Angels* (what some called the tits-and-ass formula). Falwell built up steam and then lashed out at "materialism, self-centeredness, and pride" at home and godless communism abroad. And then he closed with 2 Chronicles 7:14: "If my people, which are called by my name, shall humble themselves, and pray, and seek my face, and turn from their wicked ways; then will I hear from heaven, and will forgive their sin, and will heal their land." There it was: the assurance of salvation so long as the laws were reformed, new legislation won, and sinful ways corrected.[64]

A crowd of supporters recruited from his *Old Time Gospel Hour* gathered around Falwell on the Capitol steps. The fastest-growing Christian television show on the air was filmed at his Thomas Road Baptist Church in Lynchburg, Virginia, where he had preached every Sunday for years, now more to television cameras than those sitting in the pews. Falwell's viewership grew throughout the decade, making his show televangelism's greatest success. At the moment, numerous politicians stood close to Falwell, their heads bent in prayer. There was Harry F. Byrd, a southerner who bolted the Democratic Party back in 1970 to become an independent, and John Warner, another senator from Virginia who had the impeccable conservative credential of having married the multiply divorced Hollywood star Elizabeth Taylor. And, of course, looking dour as ever, stood Senator Jesse Helms. They were all on the march, and they seemed at the moment to hang on Falwell's every word.[65]

One man about to enter the White House was also listening, though not present at the event. His name was Robert Maddox. He too was a Southern Baptist who had grown up in Atlanta's suburbs and then attended Baylor and Emory universities. After graduating, he ministered at the First Baptist Church in Calhoun, Georgia, where he met Carter's son, Jack, and his wife, Judy. Jody Powell had heard about Maddox's interest in becoming a speechwriter and invited him to join the White House. The minister leaped at the opportunity and even before being hired started to write drafts of speeches for the president, usually the sort given at gatherings of Southern Baptists or the National Conference of Christians and Jews. They weren't great speeches, but Maddox's religious background made him of interest enough for some on Carter's staff to invite him to the White House in April 1979 (he'd actually occupy his White House office in mid-May). Maddox was still in close contact with a number of Southern Baptists, a group who had voted for Carter in large numbers in 1976. But Maddox was starting to note that Falwell was making inroads among these believers (especially on the issue of abortion). He wanted to build a case that the president take Falwell seriously and perhaps somewhere down the road throw him a "sop." So he started to build a file on Falwell and hoped to present the president with a report about the skills of this rotund televangelist on the steps of the Capitol. Though Maddox could see the future, he didn't get the audience with Carter he hoped or deserved for some time.[66]

There's an interesting irony to note about Falwell and Carter at this juncture. When writing his inaugural address back in 1977, Carter had wanted to use the exact words Falwell took from Chronicles. His speechwriter at the time, Patrick Anderson, thought it "overly pious," and Ham Jordan counseled him against anything that provoked the "weirdo factor." So Carter, begrudgingly, gave it up and settled for a milder, less judgmental passage from Micah. Chronicles—with its harsh judgment and assurance of redemption—fit Falwell's worldview just fine, while making Carter's advisers and, by way of them, Carter himself nervous. Falwell believed America to be a Christian nation; like

Helms, the reverend believed the only way to save America was to push religion back into the public square. Either that or decadence would win. It was that simple. And for Carter, it wasn't.[67]

13.

The day after Falwell had shuttled his singers into buses to drive to another state capital, Caddell, Rosalynn, and Jody Powell met with Carter. It was the meeting that Caddell had hoped for, and he used it to press for the president to give a "breakthrough" speech, as he was now calling it, one that could cut through the din of narcissism and make Americans aware of the profound crisis they were living through. His words tumbled out over one another again, he waved his hands around and made large pronouncements backed up with the assuredness of studying the public's attitudes. His intensity dominated the meeting.

Jody Powell, the president's press secretary, listened but didn't speak. He had a sharp face and a full head of sandy brown hair, which made him look intense, seemingly a man on a constant, low-boil simmer. Like Jordan, he was deeply loyal to his boss and a member of the Georgia mafia. Raised near Plains, Georgia, he had been born poor and scrappy. Expelled from the Air Force Academy for cheating, he eventually graduated from Georgia State University. He grew more and more interested in politics and decided to pursue graduate studies at Emory University where he wrote a paper on George Wallace and the populist tradition in American history (an interest he shared with Pat Caddell). He immediately joined up with Carter in 1966, seeing him as a candidate who understood the power of southern populism minus its lingering racism. He started as a driver on Carter's first and second governor's race. In that capacity he became very close to Carter, sometimes feeling that his best service was to protect the future president from criticism. He therefore made an excellent press secretary (some claimed him one of history's best).[68]

Part of Powell's skill at his job was his capacity to avoid judgment, especially in the course of background conversations about policies. He could sit back and listen, even though he often held personal judgments. This capacity built trust among those he worked with. Part of that also came with his understanding of his job: He wasn't supposed to make judgments about policies before announced, because he would have to go out and justify them later (and some might doubt his sincerity if they had seen him argue the opposite during staff meetings). But that day, as he listened to Caddell pontificate, he grew nervous. It sounded dangerous for the president to think about a speech around Caddell's themes, and he could only imagine how the press might react. But he remained silent, ready to see what the marching orders would be.[69]

Rosalynn was starting to think, ever since she breakfasted with this young pollster, that Caddell was onto something, that there really was a crisis in America that her husband needed to address. She thought about her work with the respected activist and social critic John Gardner. Gardner had served in the Johnson administration and then formed Common Cause in 1970, an organization that worked for campaign finance reform and other "good government" causes. Now, Gardner consulted with various nonprofit and philanthropic organizations. He had grown alarmed at declining rates of volunteerism among Americans during the 1970s and had joined with Rosalynn to examine ways to revitalize the voluntary sector of American society, nourishing grassroots and civic participation. In Caddell's warnings, the first lady saw the rationale for her work with Gardner.

Then there was the president. He couldn't commit to Caddell's speech, not yet at least, but with Rosalynn in the young pollster's corner, he started to take the whole thing more seriously. He would soon call Caddell's memo a "masterpiece," even though he could still grow shocked at its apocalyptic tones. Noncommittal during this meeting, Carter told Caddell that he'd do some speed-reading, books by Christopher Lasch and James MacGregor Burns (and even Alexis de Tocqueville's old classic, *Democracy in America*). Let's see where this goes, he seemed to suggest. But it would require something more than reading and polling data to push him all the way, and that was fast in coming.[70]

2

MAKING FRIENDS AND ENEMIES
IN A TIME OF CRISIS

MAY 1979

*The United States—and its people—is a searching nation. We are
a free nation, not afraid to face defects, not afraid to expose problems,
not afraid to debate differences, not afraid to correct mistakes.*

—JIMMY CARTER, MAY 29, 1979[1]

1.

On May 1, the editorial page of the *Washington Post* rang out with the
headline "Hair." The piece didn't discuss the movie by that title about
to hit theaters but rather President Carter's recent haircut. Reporters
noticed Carter had changed the part in his hair from right to left. "Just
about everyone," the *Post* wrote half-mockingly, was talking about the
political "significance" of the matter. Did the president's haircut symbolize a political move from right to left, a hope to steal some of Senator Ted Kennedy's liberal thunder?[2]

The person most believed to be behind the haircut was Gerald
(Jerry) Rafshoon, the president's key image maker. He was a bundle

of energy with curly locks and crow's-feet that formed around his eyes when he smiled, giving him an impish look. Born in Brooklyn, New York, he moved with his family, which was Jewish, to Texas. His childhood experience made the boy tough and a bit of an outsider. After attending the University of Texas, where he majored in journalism and advertising, Rafshoon moved to Atlanta in 1959 to work for a department store and Twentieth Century-Fox, eventually forming his own advertising agency. One day in Atlanta, he was driving and heard a radio advertisement for Jimmy Carter's run for governor in 1966. Rafshoon thought the ad stunk (it was lousy) and called the campaign to tell them so. He was immediately invited to help with advertising and then permanently hitched to the Georgia mafia. He created ads for both of Carter's gubernatorial campaigns and the 1976 presidential run.[3]

Rafshoon drifted in and out of Carter's circles. He wanted to return to his own business and career after the president was inaugurated. But Rosalynn, having picked up on Carter's political tin ear and thinking that Jerry had a talent for spin, wanted him back on board. So in July 1978 Rafshoon came to the White House to "save the President's ass," as he put it, by improving his "style." He soon conceived Operation Rescue, a plan to respond to Carter's critics in the media. And he was put in charge of speechwriting, a task until then under the control of Jody Powell. Rafshoon counseled Carter constantly about his appearance in public, telling him to speak more forcefully, wear darker suits, and even "fire some people" on his staff (a premonition of things to come) in order to look tougher. The term "Rafshoonery"—a constant massaging of presidential image—now rolled off the lips of D.C. pundits. One Ohio newspaper ran a cartoon that depicted Rafshoon approaching Abraham Lincoln and saying: "Frankly, Abe, sweetheart, you've got an image problem. Dig?"[4]

The real explanation behind Carter's recent haircut wasn't Rafshoonery. It was that the president's hairline was receding, most likely due to job stress, and the haircut, the president's own personal decision, made him appear younger. Still, Carter had fun with inquisitive journalists. At first refusing explanation, he then freewheeled. This, he said, pointing to his hair, "is only for the primaries. For the general election—right down the middle."[5]

The *Washington Post* editorial highlighted the fractious relationship between the press and White House in 1979. Journalists scrutinized every detail of the president's life for political implications. No matter how little Carter cared about imagery—a disregard that drove Rafshoon nuts—the press *did* care. This too: The haircut commentary symbolized the death of the "imperial presidency" diagnosed by the historian Arthur Schlesinger Jr. a few years before. The presidency was no longer feared the way it had been under Nixon; it was laughed at. Carter's predecessor, Gerald Ford, was perhaps the most mocked president in American history, memorialized in Chevy Chase's pratfall imitation that ran regularly on *Saturday Night Live*. (Dan Aykroyd was now doing imitations of Carter on the show.) The popularization of the term Rafshoonery made clear how the president's actions and statements were refracted through a lens of cynicism and jokes. Political consultants like Rafshoon had already made citizens more suspicious; they figured that what the president said had been placed there by his handlers.

Ironically, Carter was reminding Americans of his own moral seriousness right at the time the press was riffing about his haircut and image. On May 1, Carter gave the customary Law Day address as part of a celebration of the Constitution and the rule of law (the holiday had been founded by President Dwight Eisenhower). Carter opened by defining justice for his audience as "the highest goal." But then he warned: Justice is "a pursuit which is never completely realized. There are always challenges to it brought about by the fallibilities of human beings, the intense pressure of competition in a free society, the constraint of liberty where freedom does not exist."[6]

That remark might have sounded banal, but it showed the president's debt to one of America's most important theologians, Reinhold Niebuhr, and thus the moral seriousness that Carter could muster. On numerous occasions, Carter described Niebuhr as one of the most important figures in his own intellectual development. The theologian had been at the height of his influence during the early cold war when he taught at the Union Theological Seminary in New York City and wrote both scholarly and popular pieces about sin and self-love. Niebuhr was indebted to Saint Augustine, who emphasized that selfishness was an ineradicable part of human nature, that is, that "self-love" was grounded in "the self's abandonment of God." But Niebuhr wasn't a conservative; in fact, he was a key figure in Americans for Democratic Action and other liberal organizations. He had an enormous influence, for instance, on Martin Luther King and the struggle for civil rights. Niebuhr warned his fellow progressives and liberals that hoping in justice was legitimate, but that believing in the perfection of human nature wasn't. To create a more just world required tempering hopes with a sense of humility grounded in the deep-rooted nature of self-love and selfishness. Humble yourself, Niebuhr counseled, against "the pride and self-righteousness" that too many do-gooders suffer. Only an ironic and more chastened attitude could allow society to achieve justice. "Idealism" needed to come "to terms with the limits of all human striving, the fragmentariness of all human wisdom, the precariousness of all historic configurations of power, and the mixture of good and evil in all human virtue." Carter drew these lessons about limits and sin close to his heart.[7]

In fact, it was the 1974 Law Day speech that Carter gave in Georgia in which he made clear his debt to Reinhold Niebuhr—and, oddly enough, at the same time, to musician Bob Dylan. That speech won Carter grudging respect from Senator Ted Kennedy, who was also to speak, as well as from the wild, drug-addled Hunter S.

Thompson, America's famed gonzo journalist, who was covering the event. Thompson kept slipping back to his car to refill his "iced tea" glass with Wild Turkey bourbon and then listened as Carter pontificated about humility and spoke off the cuff about justice, poverty, and sin. Carter reminded his listeners that those dedicated to public service had to pay attention to their own egoism and self-love, accept the "fallibility of man" and the fact that "the sad duty of the political system is to establish justice in a sinful world." Thompson concluded that Carter was "one of the most intelligent politicians I've ever met."[8]

Niebuhr's theological ponderings about sin and self-love served Carter especially well in May 1979. It wasn't hard to see the impending gas crisis as a larger moral crisis, a debilitating blow to the selfish desire to live unbounded. And to break the trance of self-love required a leader who could challenge the naive ideal of perpetual abundance. Less than two weeks after the Law Day speech, Carter told a gathering in Iowa that "the Federal Government has no secret scientific miracle tucked away that will suddenly produce a cure for our long-standing overdependence on foreign oil." Thus, the energy crisis prompted more than a change in policy but rather an end to narcissism and childishness. There are "thousands of smaller steps by individual people, by scientists, by researchers, by local officials, business" that can "lead to an eventual goal of energy self-sufficiency for our country." Carter hit upon the ideal of a nation bonded together in common mission to tackle the crisis, a nation that recognized limits and its own vulnerability. He was on the cusp of shedding his inner-technician for his inner-moralist.[9]

2.

"Goddamnit, Jim," Jody Powell screamed into his telephone receiver. He had just read about an advanced copy of a story that James (Jim)

Fallows had written about the president and that was about to appear in the *Atlantic Monthly*. "This is the kind of thing you send as a letter to the president. You don't publish it." Powell didn't add, as he might well have, *as an article in one of the most read magazines in America*. Powell moved from low-boil simmer to full-blown explosion at times like this. After all, he had hired Fallows before Rafshoon was brought in to run the speechwriting department. Powell had grown weary of staff members providing leaks to the press. Now here was Fallows writing a particularly mean-spirited article that was the talk of the town in D.C. even before it had appeared. Just the president's luck, Powell thought, betrayed by one of those people who really knew how his mind worked, or at least how his rhetoric didn't.[10]

"The Passionless Presidency" was Fallows's title. Those words would stick to Carter like glue as few others did. Having been Carter's speechwriter for two years, Fallows seemed to know of what he wrote. His insider's confession was harsh: Carter had "profound ignorance" about the job he assumed. The president might be smart "in the College Board sense," but he lacked boldness. The most famous line that would be repeated in numerous stories about the article read: "I came to think that Carter believes fifty things, but no one thing." This was the complaint of a speechwriter who couldn't find ways to tie Carter's disparate thoughts together into coherent rhetoric. Fallows complained that Carter had numerous "problems as an explainer." He had gotten distracted with minute details, like scheduling the White House tennis courts for employees. Powell rolled his eyes when he read that complaint: The president tries to do something nice for his employees and gets slammed. Jesus, Powell thought, Carter couldn't win with anyone.[11]

Much of what Fallows's article suggested wasn't new, and much seemed to reflect a cliché, the narrative of a young idealist grown disillusioned and then venting his anger. Fallows had lived a sweet life before coming to the White House. He grew up in Redlands, California, in the attractive San Bernardino Valley, and attended Harvard University, where he edited the student newspaper, the *Crimson*. He won a Rhodes Scholarship (a prize that Jimmy Carter had coveted but didn't win) and then went to work with Ralph Nader, finally winding up at the neoliberal *Washington Monthly* magazine. As he entered his twenties, Fallows moved from the left to the political center. He was drawn toward Carter because he believed the president could "look past the tired formulas of left and right and offer something new." Fallows figured that helping out in speechwriting was the best way to push the country toward that vision.[12]

Fallows recognized the problems of speechwriting soon after joining the White House. First of all, he hated the bureaucracy. An array of specialists checked his speeches, which created editing nightmares. Carter also had a "wooden ear" and would cut out rhetorical flourishes that Fallows would try to put back in. With all of this work, Fallows found himself at the White House 24-7, which exasperated his young family. The president who chided employees to spend time with their loved ones had no idea of what work life at the White House was really like. And so Fallows did the only thing he could, he left—and then wrote about leaving.[13]

This was a pattern of speechwriters who preceded Fallows. After all, Jimmy Carter was something of a control freak when it came to his public rhetoric. And he hated flourishes or pompous phrases. In fact, while governor of Georgia, he didn't have a speechwriter and composed all his speeches himself, sometimes by hand on large yellow notepads. When he found it impossible to do that in the White House, he hired Robert Shrum, who left after only a few weeks, publicly blasting Carter for not being liberal enough. Then there was Patrick Anderson, who, in the words of the *National Journal*, "seemed more intent on gleaning material for a novel" than writing speeches. Fallows was the next and the longest-lasting speechwriter up to that point, leaving in November 1978.[14]

Fallows's departure had left the reins to Hendrik (Rick) Hertzberg, the man who could be considered Carter's final and best speechwriter. Hertzberg had been in the White House since February 1977, hired originally by Fallows. Though not officially promoted to chief speechwriter, by 1979 everyone working at the White House saw him that way. He never quite fit in, though, having been raised the son of an "unbelieving Jewish father" and a "Quaker mother," both of them avowed socialists. Hertzberg was much further to the left than Carter (in fact, Hertzberg recollected that he hadn't voted for Carter in the 1976 Democratic primary, thinking Carter too southern and centrist). During the 1960s as Hertzberg came into adulthood, he enlisted in the navy but then found himself appalled by the Vietnam War (long before Jimmy Carter ever did) and applied for conscientious objector status. "Quite by chance, a medical difficulty developed, and I was hastily mustered out" of the navy rather than having to suffer punishment, so Hertzberg recalled. He then turned his journalistic skills into a career at the *New Yorker*. When offered a speechwriting job by Fallows and Powell, he jumped at the opportunity, having been fascinated by the White House for a long time.[15]

Hertzberg brought with him some important personal traits. First, he had a good sense of humor, often accentuated by a grin that showed off his large teeth, enhanced by his circular eyeglasses. Humor was a necessity, being a democratic socialist working for a centrist president, especially since Jordan and Rafshoon loved to call him a "pinko" and laughed at how he still rode a bike to work. But Hertzberg also managed to keep his ideals in perspective. Other staff knew that they needed Hertzberg, since here was a man who could write. And besides, the loss of another speechwriter would be disastrous. They also knew that Hertzberg believed, unlike Fallows, that the president could deliver good speeches if they were written the right way. He hoped to prove his contention.[16]

As Hertzberg took over, he hired his friend Gordon Stewart.

Stewart had graduated Phi Beta Kappa from Oberlin College and then earned a master's in history from the University of Chicago and one in drama from Yale. He had written Hollywood scripts and directed plays, including the *Elephant Man.* A collapsed lung had prevented Stewart from being at the scene of production for the play, and he decided to quit (only to watch it become a smash hit on Broadway that year). Hertzberg knew that Stewart had written some speeches earlier for Midge Costanza, the mayor of Rochester, New York, who had helped introduce Carter at the Democratic Convention in 1976 and eventually became a public liaison at the White House under the president. What Hertzberg might not have considered at the time was one of Stewart's greatest strengths—his background in directing made him attuned to the drama of delivering speeches as much as how to write them. In any case, the two of them worked together well.[17]

There was talent in the speechwriting team of 1979, but still, Carter remained suspicious about speechifying. He hated the oratory of southern politicians who would demagogue their way into public office by making absurd promises and using flowery language. Hertzberg understood Carter's fear and found the president still striking rhetorical flourishes from drafts, keeping speechwriting a battle of back and forth. (The April 5 speech, for instance, had been seen by at least twenty staff people before completion.) It was especially difficult when done in the back of a presidential car, banging away on a Selectric typewriter, as Gordon Stewart found himself doing in early May on the freeways of Los Angeles. He was riding with Carter, who was about to confront the reality of the gas crisis he had predicted a month earlier.

3.

The gas crisis of 1979 almost *had* to begin in California, the sunshine state of the future and, of course, the automobile. "California dreaming" turned nightmare by May, especially in Los Angeles. It wasn't just the federal allocation system that tightened supplies to the area. It was the city's slavery to the automobile. This was a city with no center, a city of strung-together suburbs and freeways where a car was a necessity of residency, a city whose shared experience was the isolation of driving. The writer Joan Didion, who lived in L.A., once tried to explain the "rapture" of driving freeways. "The mind goes clean," she wrote. "The rhythm takes over. A distortion of time occurs, the same distortion that characterizes the instant before an accident."[18] And in May 1979 the biggest accident of all came—a gas crisis.

Though polls reported that 69 percent of the public still didn't believe in an "energy crisis," L.A.'s residents pulling up to the pumps thought differently. Service stations would shut down early if they ran out of gas, creating even longer lines at stations remaining open. Panic buying set in. People rushed out to get gas even if they didn't need it, generating more lines in the process. Families set up breakfast tables next to gas lines so fathers could wait in line to fuel up while the kids ate. One person burned himself alive by siphoning gas with an electric pump that emitted sparks.[19]

And of course there was violence. The line cutter became the leading symbol of greed and retaliation on California's gas lines. One man avenged a line cutter by placing "his locking gas cap on her gas tank," locking it, then driving "away with the key." Another person attacked a pregnant woman mistakenly thought to be cutting into line. One gas station attendant dressed up in "Arab garb" and strapped a pistol to his side to entertain customers but also to settle conflicts.[20]

The state of California became a panic zone, forcing "Governor Moonbeam" to enter the situation. Jerry Brown was the sprightly forty-one-year-old governor of the state, who often referred to "the cosmos" and the glories of space exploration in speeches (hence, his nickname). He was the son of the state's previous governor Pat Brown, whom

Ronald Reagan had defeated in 1966. (It was Reagan that Jerry replaced in 1974.) Brown had shown little interest in politics during childhood, deciding to study in a Jesuit seminary in order to become a priest. But then, like many of his generation, he engaged in the civil rights movement and the antiwar protests that erupted during the 1960s. So he decided to enter politics; the governorship of California was, he hoped, the first step toward the presidency. He had run against Carter in the Democratic primary of 1976 and was getting ready for a repeat performance in 1980.[21]

Brown's desire to dethrone Carter was strange because the two shared political sentiments. Like Carter, Brown believed in political decentralization and loved the neo-counterculture book *Small Is Beautiful*. Both were fiscal conservatives, and Carter would have nodded when Brown decried the "politics of overpromising." Brown differed with Carter on nuclear power (he hated it) and in his belief that America should hold a Constitutional Convention to pass a balanced budget amendment. The latter belief seemed inspired by the success of California's Proposition 13 limiting property taxes, which passed in 1978. (Brown hated the proposition at first but then changed his mind soon after it passed.) Besides these disagreements, though, when Brown criticized President Carter as "sort of strange," the words seemed to bounce back and stick to Governor Moonbeam himself.[22]

One key to Brown's long shot for the presidency was his celebrity status, or at least his tendency to date celebrities. When the gas crisis hit, some newsstands still carried the issue of *People* magazine with Jerry Brown and Linda Ronstadt, the bestselling rock star, on its cover. Brown had taken her along to Liberia in April, hoping to show off his foreign policy credentials. The nature of their relationship remained ambiguous and something of a mystery, especially weird because Ronstadt was purported to have a drug problem and to have gone through a string of boyfriends that included Mick Jagger. The trip turned disastrous, with press photographers hounding the couple and breaking into fistfights on the plane to Africa as they vied to get the most telling photo.[23]

After that botched trip, the governor faced the panicked gas crisis at home. Talk of small is beautiful and the cosmos wouldn't put gas in people's cars. The new politics needed to be ditched for the old. Brown renewed a policy his predecessor, Governor Ronald Reagan, had instituted during the gas crisis of 1973—namely, rationing in the form of an odd-even system of gas purchases (a policy Reagan was now trying desperately to disown). Odd numbered licenses got gas on odd numbered days, while even numbered licenses waited for even days. Brown prevented topping-off and panic buying by requiring people to purchase a minimum amount of gas at each filling. In addition, he did what any other governor would do: He asked Washington for help.[24]

Jimmy Carter listened, even though some counseled him not to. Other governors argued against favors for California. Carter's own secretary of energy, James Schlesinger, concurred with that argument, once again contradicting and annoying his boss. Other politicians went one step further, saying that California *deserved* the mess it was in. Senator Daniel Patrick Moynihan quipped, "There's something about the state of California. They're a funny bunch. They've panicked." Carter knew better than this. This wasn't about California; it was a national crisis made worse by an allocation system. So Carter issued a statement and got on a plane to California, arriving May 5.[25]

After morning meetings in Los Angeles about economic development, Carter headed off to public speaking events. He witnessed block-long gas lines and told reporters: "I don't want to mislead you. It's going to get worse. What we need is a massive effort at conservation." Then he addressed downtown crowds for the occasion of Cinco de Mayo. Organizers noticed that two thousand people gathered for the celebration, when last year it had been ten thousand, another sign the gas crisis was forcing people to stay home. Carter spoke Spanish to the crowds. He thanked them for their VIVA CARTER! signs, but winced at STOP GAS LINES! signs.[26]

It was here that Carter faced the strangest and creepiest moment of his trip, one that conjured dark memories of recent American history—the assassination of JFK that occurred sixteen years before and that Congress was now reinvestigating via its Select Committee on Assassinations (its report about possible conspiracies was due out some time in the summer of 1979). Just fifty feet away from the podium where Carter spoke lurched Raymond Lee Harvey—a man who shared two names with JFK's assassin, Lee Harvey Oswald—who happened to be holding a starter pistol. He planned to shoot it, thereby causing a distraction and allowing snipers to take out the president. One of the illegal aliens he figured would help kill the president was Osvaldo, a name that conjured freakier connections to the Kennedy assassination. Fortunately for Carter, a Secret Service agent spotted Harvey looking suspicious and arrested him, and the event passed like a scene from the film *Taxi Driver*.[27]

After his speech, Carter took a short detour to Room 946 in the University of California Hospital, where he visited John Wayne to wish him well. Carter was shocked at how sick Wayne looked.

4.

Jerry Brown shadowed Carter back to the White House for an antinuclear rally held May 6 at the Capitol. Carter was in church while masses of people descended on the nation's capital to protest against nuclear power, holding signs that read NO NUKES.

Later in the evening, Carter greeted almost one hundred people at the White House movie theater. The film they watched began with an author describing a book he was writing about the "decay of con-temporary culture" and a "society desensitized by drugs, loud music, television, crime, garbage." These were the opening lines from *Man-hattan*, a movie that fit the culture of the 1970s like a glove, touching on the themes of divorce, narcissism, and midlife crises. Carter liked it enough to schedule another viewing on May 23, just as the film be-came the hit of the month.[28]

The plot centered on a forty-two-year-old man (played by the film's director and writer, Woody Allen) divorced from his first wife and sep-arated from his young son. He hitches up with a high school beauty, in an almost stereotypical midlife crisis. Suffering from "mere narcis-sism," in the words of his ex-wife, his friends are all highly educated, self-absorbed, and in psychoanalysis. Allen eventually rejects his young girlfriend for a woman closer to his own age (played by Diane Keaton) who is, unfortunately, in her own words "all fucked up" and incapable of long-term commitment. She dumps Allen to continue an affair with his married friend, which drives Allen into a state of jeal-ousy and inexplicable moral anger. The final scene shows Allen run-ning back to his young girlfriend who's leaving for Europe. She tells him to wait for her return and "have a little faith" in people. At this, Allen looks wistful and uncertain, as if having faith in others is pre-cisely the thing he can't do. The narcissist had been diagnosed.

The movie represented Woody Allen's desire to "advance in the di-rection of films that are more human and less cartoon." The film critic Stanley Kauffmann believed *Manhattan* was "a serious comedy about a man trying to live by moral principles in a world of gratification-as-ethics." Since most Hollywood fare had turned silly and superficial in an age of blockbusters, *Manhattan* became easy to oversell. Allen found boatloads of public praise. The *New York Times* touted the movie's "ten-derness," "hilarity," and "virile muscle," without explaining that strange last term. The movie captured "what it means to be a vulnerable, selfish, innocent, corrupt, hollow, harried, loving, frightened, and terribly mixed-up human being." Andrew Sarris, the *Village Voice* critic not known for praise, simply called it "the one truly great American film of the 70s."[29]

Allen played up the impression that his film was an intellectual master stroke by giving interviews about the movie's themes. His tone was that of a social critic whom Jimmy Carter could have been reading just then: "It's not a good time for society," Allen explained. American culture was "desensitized by television, drugs, fast-food chains, loud music and feelingless, mechanical sex." Allen condemned the "immediate, self-gratifying view. We've got to find the transition to a life style and a culture in which we make tough, honest, moral and ethical choices simply because—on the most basic, pragmatic grounds—they are seen to be the highest good." But Allen failed as a preacher. He recognized his own narcissism: "My character" in *Manhattan* "says that the metaphor for life is a concentration camp. The real question in life is how one copes in that crisis. I just hope I'm never tested, because I'm very pessimistic about how I would respond. I worry that I tend to moralize as opposed to being moral."[30]

5.

On May 11, Congress rejected Carter's plan to have the power to ration gas in case of future emergencies. What Carter saw in Los Angeles reminded him of why the option of rationing was imperative. If another region was especially hard hit with shortages in the future, he wanted the ability to take fuel from other areas that had more. But Congress balked. Some feared the president didn't have the power to carry through the plan. Others feared angering oil companies. Some worried that if the president imposed rationing, consumers might panic and try topping off at the pumps, making the situation worse.

When Carter pushed for a compromise with a bit less power granted the presidency, representatives rejected it outright. Many viewed Carter as an early lame duck president undeserving of assistance no matter how bad the crisis got.[31]

Carter couldn't hide his frustration, believing this would ensure that the future gas crisis would be even worse. "I was shocked and embarrassed," he said. Members of Congress had "put their heads in the sand" and played a game of denial. "Parochial interests" and "timidity" pushed aside the long-term national interest. Carter felt neither transactional nor transformational at this moment. He felt like the anti-imperial president, stymied by Congress and a victim of his own frustration.[32]

Carter's secretary of energy, James Schlesinger, didn't help matters. Though appointed "energy czar" early on in Carter's presidency after serving as secretary of defense under Gerald Ford, Schlesinger never worked well with the president or Congress (his original work on the National Energy Plan that was done in full secrecy had already made that clear). Schlesinger was haughty and gruff, puffing a pipe during cabinet meetings and aggravating just about anyone. He consistently contradicted the president in public, suggesting to Jerry Brown, for instance, that Carter's promise to provide more gas to California in May was just talk with little substance. One congressman complained that Schlesinger "couldn't sell beer on a troop ship" much less to Congress. Everyone recoiled at his arrogance and wished that Carter would just get on with it and fire the man. But Carter hesitated.[33]

Stuart Eizenstat, Carter's domestic policy adviser, was starting to elbow Schlesinger aside. His roots went further back than Schlesinger's, at least when it came to Carter. He was born in Chicago to a Jewish family, who moved to Atlanta when Eizenstat was young. He studied political science at the University of North Carolina and then received a law degree from Harvard. Soon afterward, he entered the White House in the last year of the Johnson administration and worked as

Hubert Humphrey's research director during his failed run for the presidency in 1968. Eizenstat then returned to Atlanta and private practice. His legal circles soon intersected with Carter's. With his background in political science, he took up the challenge of writing issue papers for Carter in 1970 during his second run for governor. When Carter announced his decision to friends to run for president in 1974, Eizenstat was asked for a repeat performance as in-house wonk. The transition to domestic policy adviser proved seamless.[34]

Eizenstat was stoic and hardworking. His short hair, horn-rimmed glasses, and suit and tie made him appear the nerd, and his mind worked like a wonk's, able to craft elaborate policies on short notice. But most important in this case, he had a deep loyalty to Carter and was growing convinced that displacing Schlesinger was the right thing to do. Positioning himself closer to the president, he was just about to get the chance to write up a full-fledged energy plan. His thinking had drifted recently to how energy was carefully preserved during World War II. Eizenstat started to wonder if this was a model for how to conserve energy in the future and if war analogies provided the right language to push the country in that direction.[35]

As Carter lost on standby rationing, he also learned how bad things were on the foreign policy front. He faced an upcoming battle over SALT II, an arms control treaty he was painfully working out with Leonid Brezhnev, the elderly leader of the Soviet Union. That the Senate would approve SALT II after Carter signed off on it with Brezhnev was looking less certain. Senators raised questions about verification. Hawks associated SALT II with détente, thus weakness; doves saw it as too little too late. Carter faced opposition from the hawkish Senator Scoop Jackson, who was able to forge alliances with Senator Jesse Helms, at least on this issue.

More annoying was the state of the Panama Canal Treaty, the breakthrough agreement over the "great ditch" that America had built through Panama during the early twentieth century, providing a waterway to connect the Pacific and Atlantic oceans. Carter had inherited the treaty to cede the canal back to Panama from Gerald Ford, and Carter made it his personal responsibility to help pass the treaty, unpopular though it had been. The treaty was signed after a long and troubled battle in March 1978. But not without creating enormous backlash. In 1976, catching wind of Ford's support for the treaty, Ronald Reagan had won the state of North Carolina during the primary by arguing that "we bought" the Panama Canal, "we paid for it, we built it, and we intend to keep it." Reagan persevered in that cause and now in May 1979 found that the senator from North Carolina, Jesse Helms, was making headway by slowing down the treaty's implementation. Helms and his colleagues in the Senate still referred to it as "*our* canal." Meanwhile other new right activists, especially in the American Conservative Union, were publicizing Helms's initiative, raising money, and aiming their sights at a number of liberal Democrats who supported the treaty and whom they now hoped to defeat in 1980.[36]

It seemed no matter where Carter turned, he faced enemies who were not just well organized but who also used bold and declarative language that could make him flinch, even if it did not change his mind.

6.

To escape the depressing world of politics, Carter hid out in the White House theater. Films still allowed him a way to circumvent reality for a brief time—on May 10, for three hours. That day, Carter welcomed around twenty staff people and the director Francis Ford Coppola to the White House. Coppola was an old client of Pat Caddell and Jerry Rafshoon, who had both advised the director on issues of marketing and promotion. The director now wanted to test out *Apocalypse Now* even though he hadn't figured out an ending. En route to the Cannes

Film Festival for another early showing, Coppola brought bottles of wine from his own vineyard and explained to his White House viewers: "My invitation to you" is "to help me finish the film." It wasn't the first time Coppola had sought assistance from the president of the United States. He had written urgent notes to Jimmy Carter two years ago, pleading for a Department of Defense helicopter. As he explained, "All out cooperation was granted John Wayne's film *Green Berets*," the war-whooping film that Lyndon Johnson had begrudgingly aided. Coppola pleaded that his film would "help America put Vietnam behind us, which we must do so we can go on to a positive future." He never explained how it would do this, and Carter ignored the request.[37]

Coppola was a man in a hurry. Making the film had taken almost ten years, and the process was as mind-boggling as the film itself. Coppola shot it in the Philippines amid guerrilla war and typhoons. Most of his actors were stoned on pot and LSD. Martin Sheen had a heart attack during filming, and Coppola himself suffered a nervous breakdown. And Marlon Brando, the prima donna of all time, refused to read the script before showing up and kept asking for more money. When reporters inquired about the film, Coppola blurted out in megalomaniac form: "It is not *about* Vietnam. It *is* Vietnam. It's what it was really *like*—it was *crazy*. We went insane."[38]

Like *Manhattan*, the movie seemed to address issues Jimmy Carter was pondering at the moment, especially how the legacy of Vietnam had accentuated a broader crisis of confidence in the country. The movie was based loosely on Joseph Conrad's *Heart of Darkness*, as it followed Captain Willard (Sheen) traveling up river to find Walter Kurtz (Brando), an "insane" and "corrupted" military leader who has moved beyond the military's "timid, lying morality." Willard discovers Kurtz's compound, a small empire full of native peoples who perform animal sacrifices and seemingly worship Kurtz. Before Willard kills Kurtz, he listens to his confessions about war turning men into killing machines.

"It's judgment that defeats us," Kurtz explains. And when he dies, Kurtz simply mutters the words "the horror" over and over. Coppola intended his "operatic" movie to make clear the permanent damage war did to men's psyches.[39]

The reaction at the White House was mixed. Rafshoon offered advice, promptly ignored by Coppola. Others turned away or grew bored. Carter's response is unknown (he wrote a short note of thanks for the film and the wine), but the movie certainly fit Carter's own thinking about Vietnam's legacy. As Coppola explained, "The film is about moral ambiguity." He had wound up making a film that was closer to Carter's own feelings about Vietnam's legacy than *The Deer Hunter*. Moral ambiguity: Those two words summed up the president's sense about Vietnam perhaps better than any others. Though Ronald Reagan never spoke of *Apocalypse Now* in a radio address, the way he had *The Deer Hunter*, it's hard to imagine the California governor seeing very much redeeming in the film. When it came to Vietnam as with most other issues, ambiguity was not one of Reagan's natural feelings.[40]

7.

Ted Kennedy was fast becoming Carter's enemy number one. The senator from Massachusetts was driven by the legacy of his family's name and by his own liberal beliefs to challenge Carter. In late April, he called the president's windfall profits tax proposal—the center-piece of Carter's speech on April 5—a "token," "no more than a fig leaf over the vast new profits the industry will reap." Carter retorted that Kennedy's comment was "a lot of baloney." Kennedy rejoined: Raising gas prices via decontrol would only hurt the poor, those whom he felt a responsibility to speak for. Jerry Brown had been battling Carter from all over the political spectrum, but Kennedy waged a clearer war from the left. The stage was set for a good old-fashioned fight: the centrist president versus the liberal senator.[41]

Democratic Party activists, and especially those liberals within its ranks who despised Carter's centrism, started to take note of the clash, ignoring Kennedy's public claim that he wouldn't challenge Carter in the fast-approaching Democratic primary. By May there was a "Draft Kennedy" movement on the ground in New York, Florida, Wisconsin, California, Rhode Island, and Illinois. In Iowa, the movement became known simply as "Anyone But Carter" (ABC). Most important, though, was Ohio, a key swing state that Carter knew he'd have to win to hold the presidency in 1980.[42]

In Ohio the movement found a fierce ally in Tim Hagan, a stocky and impetuous young man who had grown up in Youngstown and now chaired the Cuyahoga County Democratic Party. In early May he too ignored Kennedy's statements about not running and started pressing for the county party to endorse the senator. Ohio's state Democratic chairman C. Paul Tipps and Senator John Glenn both condemned Hagan, arguing that his efforts threatened to divide the party. Hagan burrowed ahead and called a convention where Tipps's and Glenn's warnings manifested themselves. Pressing to endorse Kennedy, those delegates who gathered in Cleveland engaged in fistfights on the floor. The vote was close but favored endorsement of Kennedy. The convention soon ended, but not before one dissenter at the meeting warned: "We turned our back on Harry Truman and got Eisenhower. We turned our back on Lyndon Johnson and got Nixon. If we turn our back on President Carter, we'll get Nixon's best friend, John Connally," one of the lead contenders in the Republican primary. Replace that name with Ronald Reagan and the claim made sense.[43]

That liberal activists flocked to Kennedy was remarkable, considering he seemed more a tragic than hopeful figure. Certainly the family name reminded activists of a better time for Democrats in the past, but the "last brother" (as he would be labeled by some) and "Kennedy imprisonment" (as the critic Garry Wills would soon call it) reminded Americans of the legacy of assassination that had gunned down his two more famous siblings. It was especially eerie to note how Ted Kennedy's life followed that of his brother Robert: They had both been mediocre undergraduates at Harvard and law students at the University of Virginia (some people had even asked Ted to run for president in 1968 soon after Bobby was killed). Worse was how Ted Kennedy now faced rumors and criticisms. He was suspected of drunken philandering. His wife, Joan, was a recovering alcoholic, his marriage on the brink of divorce, and his relations with his daughter Kara quite sour. Even worse, the country was fast approaching the tenth anniversary of Chappaquiddick—the 1969 accident when Kennedy drove his car off a bridge and swam to safety, leaving his passenger, Mary Jo Kopechne, a young legislative aide, dead in the water. The tenth anniversary would certainly evoke debates about Kennedy's ethical behavior that evening. It would not be pretty.[44]

Some of Carter's advisers were quick to write off Kennedy. The senator was damaged goods, they argued. One explained to the press, "You know," Kennedy's "really all over the place. About the only thing we know for sure about him is that he can swim."[45]

But this was a false front. The inner circles worried. Pat Caddell understood that the Massachusetts senator had what Carter lacked, namely, "boldness." In his April memo, he noted "Edward Kennedy's rising appeal." The senator "stands as a symbol of Hope, of a past which was America's high water mark." Caddell saw in polling numbers that a majority of Americans rejected Kennedy's left-leaning liberalism on actual policy matters. That just made his "rising appeal" all the more troubling—a dead set of ideas in a questionable candidate could still inspire more than Carter.[46]

Rafshoon concurred. For him, of course, it was Kennedy's "style." One of Kennedy's foibles was that he never learned how to speak into a microphone, so he yelled while making speeches. Rafshoon reflected,

"People love it when he stands up and raises his voice and says that, goddamit [*sic*], we're going to do something about this problem. They don't even listen to what he's saying." He's "forceful," you're not, Rafshoon complained. It didn't matter that Kennedy was "completely out of step with the mood of the country," what mattered was that he was "tough."[47]

Tim Kraft, the president's chief political liaison, worried about the Draft Kennedy movement enough to consider calling Dennis Kucinich, the boy mayor of Cleveland who now wavered in his earlier support for Carter. Kraft thought he might persuade Kucinich to get Hagan to back down. But he decided not to make the call. "It would go public and inflate Hagan tremendously (White House joins maverick mayor against him) and generate core support for him" from grassroots activists. So Carter would just have to deal and watch out for his soft political underbelly.[48]

8.

The headline news during the second half of May was depressing: Inflation was recalculated to be closing in on 13 percent. New auto sales plummeted 25 percent. There were riots in San Francisco—cop cars torched, the windows of City Hall smashed—after a lenient sentence was granted the killer of Harvey Milk, an openly gay council member.[49]

Then on May 24, disastermania struck again—271 people died in the worst plane crash in United States history. As people scurried into airports and onto the highways to start their Memorial Day weekend, a DC-10 flew out of O'Hare airport in Chicago, bound for Los Angeles. It didn't get very far before it lost an engine, spit fuel, and then plummeted into a field bordering Highway 90. Flames shot five hundred feet into the air. The next day all DC-10s were grounded.[50]

Carter was suffering through his own personal disaster when the news hit. His former director of the Office of Management and Budget, Bert Lance, had just been indicted on May 22. The investigation had been going on for some time and had discovered that before and after coming to the White House, Lance defrauded the government by acquiring illegitimate loans. Though Lance would never be convicted, the op-ed writer William Safire quickly concocted the term "Lancegate."[51]

The term was especially ironic considering that Safire had been Richard Nixon's speechwriter. In a short period of time, Watergate became less an event and more a political instrument for attack politics. Whenever someone placed the word "gate" after an event, the actual event of Watergate itself seemed to grow foggier in Americans' memory. Conservatives especially enjoyed arguing that *everyone* was corrupt, that Nixon's criminal presidency wasn't all that exceptional. There seemed a little bit of Watergate in each and every one of us, or so this line of reasoning went. With Lancegate, Carter's image as a squeaky clean outsider grew scratchier. One writer believed Lancegate "tarnished the post-Watergate good government image of the Carter Administration and robbed the President of some of the early magic and moral authority with the public."[52]

At the time all this bad news poured in, Caddell was writing a memo for the Democratic National Committee (DNC). He argued that Carter was losing to Kennedy and that his presidency was now strongly associated with its "failures." Echoing Fallows, Caddell wrote, "Nearly two thirds of the American public say that, because of the flurry of programs emanating from the Administration, they are confused about what the President is trying to achieve." He went on: "Our data indicate that on measures disassociated with his performance in office—personal warmth, trustworthiness, dedication—the President continues to do fairly well. However, pluralities of Americans feel he has been ineffective, indecisive, and generally not in control of things." The memo was tough and a reminder that Caddell's paycheck came from the DNC, not the White House. The young pollster seemed intent on using his outsider status to come clean to the president and the DNC both. He was growing impatient that his warnings were not having much impact.[53]

9.

Carter didn't need Caddell's memo to remind him that the regular spring meeting of the DNC would be a tough audience on May 25. That day, he entered the Sheraton Hotel in downtown D.C. armed with a speech that seemed risky. He started by explaining his lateness, "I would have been here earlier, but my carpool was late." The audience laughed. Then he added: "When I arrived, I noticed that my free parking place had been taken away." The audience laughed again.

Carter then started to speak in tones of raw honesty. "I want to speak to you this morning in kind of a rare way for a politician, for a President speaking to his own party leaders and his own personal friends." If Caddell had listened he might have grown a bit less frustrated, for Carter was starting to employ some of the young pollster's language: The president talked about how the American people were "doubtful" and "uncertain about the future." He worried openly about "paralysis, stagnation, and drift," as he bemoaned the challenge of moving legislation through a recalcitrant Congress. He condemned the me-first attitude encroaching on America and the growing sense that politics was "spectacle" for most citizens.

Then he paused to shift directions by placing some of the blame on his own shoulders. "As President, I've made mistakes." But his fellow Democrats need not worry, for he wasn't afraid to make "unpopular" decisions in the future. That would require, though, a collective sharing of power between president and citizens. The leader would promise honesty, the citizens, to face reality. The energy crisis would not be solved if Americans continued to "wring our hands" or hope "for some kind of miraculous deliverance." In the question period that followed, Carter summed things up by talking about the need to face "unpleasant facts" rather than think that "somehow or another a miracle is going to occur and a lot of oil is going to be released from secret hiding places."[54]

The next day, the *Washington Post* reported that Carter's speech seemed "sermon-like." More remarkable was its favorable reception. Some of his darker lines received the most applause. Carter figured he was onto something.[55]

Two days later, Vice President Walter "Fritz" Mondale embarked for Wisconsin to give a commencement address to students graduating from the University of Wisconsin. The speech alluded to but essentially hid a growing rift opening up between the vice president and Carter. Mondale and Carter had gotten along extremely well for most of the administration's history (they shared a "rural, small town background," though Mondale's was spent in the northern Midwest). But now, the relationship faltered. Mondale had been picked as vice president, in part, because he was a more traditional Democrat than Carter (what might be called a "base" candidate today). He had cut his teeth working for Hubert Humphrey during the Minnesota senator's rise to power and influence more than twenty years earlier. Mondale embraced his mentor's liberalism—especially his support for labor unions, the civil rights movement, and the Great Society that Lyndon Johnson would eventually construct. Mondale was an optimistic liberal who believed in the power to make society more just through government action, and he now found himself chagrined by the president's fiscal conservatism and Niebuhrian pessimism. He was especially flabbergasted by the rise of Ted Kennedy's popularity. He felt that his liberalism was losing out to Carter's centrism. And he experienced a growing "sense of futility," in his biographer's words.[56]

When Mondale stepped to the podium to give what most students expected to be a bland commencement speech, they listened to him talk about the virtues of the SALT II treaty. They applauded him when he offered standard praise for the University of Wisconsin, citing the state's famous progressive governor Robert La Follette. But the most important line from the speech came early in what might have appeared an insubstantial comment: "I'm going to give a short speech, because I have a long-overdue fishing trip I'm going on right afterwards."[57]

That became a historic fishing trip into the famous Boundary Waters of northern Minnesota. Here the vice president would paddle and ponder the question: Should I quit my job? It was shocking to consider the idea that he might quit. The last time a vice president departed office was when Spiro Agnew left the Nixon administration, but that was because of scandal. Mondale had simply become alienated from the president's policy decisions. He asked his wife, Joan, at one point what he should do. *Quit*, she suggested, "it'll be better." But at some point while canoeing, he decided to stay. If he quit, that would become a major crisis and the media would go crazy with it. To be controversial just wasn't Mondale's style. Besides, he figured he could become Carter's liberal conscience, and so he returned to Washington, D.C., on June 2, ready to get back to work.[58]

While Mondale found personal resolve to bolster his own liberalism, Ronald Reagan continued to act as the president's conservative conscience. He was using his radio addresses to firm up the vision of his future run. This time, he addressed the energy crisis head-on in a way completely different from Ted Kennedy's condemnation of Carter. Reagan spoke to "Californians sitting in long lines," who "are angry" and not "certain as to who they should be mad at," those same Californians Carter had recently visited. Well, the anger of his fellow Californians, Reagan insisted, should be directed not against oil companies but against the Department of Energy, which kept regulating gas production through a bureaucratic allocation system. The enemy was the government. Deregulate *entirely*—not the way Carter wanted to, slowly and cautiously—and problem solved. Bountiful supplies of oil would be found for all, Reagan promised.[59]

10.

Carter had proclaimed the week of May 28 to June 1 Vietnam Veterans' Week. This was a first. It reflected how Vietnam vets had moved to the center of America's conscience. It wasn't just the films about Vietnam that reminded Americans of the lingering effects of the war. There were increasing reports about psychological problems among vets in addition to stories about increasing unemployment, drug abuse, and violence. There were new allegations that the chemical Agent Orange had done profound physical damage to vets who breathed it in after it had been sprayed down onto villages as an exfoliant. Memory about a difficult war was worn on the face of each paraplegic veteran and in each Veterans Hospital busting at the seams.[60]

To initiate the week, Carter invited numerous veterans to the White House where he revealed a stamp the postal service would issue honoring Vietnam vets. The act seemed small, but Carter followed it with a larger speech about Vietnam's legacy. In an editorial printed just two days after Vietnam Veterans' Week, the *Wall Street Journal*, following the lead of neoconservative writers, insisted the term "hero" be applied to vets in order to show that the war was noble. Carter couldn't go that far. The situation was too morally complex—Americans had done some horrible things in the jungle both to others and to themselves, as Coppola's movie reminded him. But those horrors had not turned Americans into monsters. Vietnam vets were neither John Waynes standing with pride and assuredness nor Walter Kurtzes warped into cynical, nihilistic violence.[61]

The president called Vietnam "the longest and most expensive" war "in the history of our country." The results were "human suffering" and a "highly divisive" form of politics. Unlike World War II's veterans, Vietnam's suffered from "people back home" refusing to support them. Carter himself opposed the war late (turning against it in 1971) and now felt responsible to address the war's moral legacy. He embraced the "basic right" to protest but recognized that protest made the postwar return of veterans more difficult, the price paid for defending the interest of a constitutional republic. A moral quandary.

This made coming to terms with the war more difficult. Carter closed by quoting Philip Caputo, a veteran and author who was at the gathering. Caputo had written on the memory of a friend's death: "You were a part of us and a part of us died with you, the small part that was still young, that had not yet grown cynical, grown bitter and old with death." Caputo had been not just a vet but also a protester, so the ambiguity in his words was more pronounced: "Whatever the rights or wrongs of the war nothing can diminish the rightness of what you tried to do. We loved you for what you were, and what you stood for." Carter was drawn toward Caputo's attempt to recognize sacrifice and death without elevating them to pristine heroism—a challenging balancing act in the larger project of remembering a controversial war.[62]

But there was a problem with this argument: When Carter spoke of a "divisive" politics in which protesters cursed the vets, he seemed behind the times. By 1979, the clarity of the protest left had blurred. Angry sign holders and chanters had vanished. Replacing them was confusion. Now the damage of the war and the horrors of the society born thereafter—the totalitarian system anchored in Hanoi—were impossible to ignore. America's entry into the war could still be remembered as unjust or mistaken, but America's enemy now appeared truly barbaric.

Witness the boat people. Anyone watching television news in 1979 saw chaotic and heartbreaking scenes of Vietnamese and Cambodian families scurrying onto rickety crafts, floating out to sea, and drowning. From 1977 to 1978, numerous boat people escaped Cambodia and the horrors of Pol Pot's regime, but many were Vietnamese. By January 1979 Pol Pot's regime in Cambodia collapsed, and soon China invaded Vietnam. Carter turned his back on the problem, hoping, at the time, to normalize relations with China. But the results weren't easy to ignore: a massive increase in communist repression and refugees hemorrhaging out of Vietnam.[63]

Most families fled to Malaysia or Thailand, but these countries started to refuse them entry (by June, Malaysia's government shot refugees on the spot). So the refugees did the only thing they could: They got onto boats and floated to points unknown, many of them drowning or dying from malaria and dysentery. The lucky few made it to the United States, entering Los Angeles and moving east from there.[64]

The boat people pressed in on America morally as well as geographically. In January 1979, CBS aired a documentary on the refugees. Journalist Ed Bradley got onto boats to interview people only to find himself pulling victims out of the water to save them from death. As much as Americans hoped to put Vietnam behind them, the boat people disallowed it.[65]

One celebrity made the transition from protesting the Vietnam War to protesting the Vietnamese treatment of its own citizens quite easily. Right in the middle of Vietnam Veterans' Week, Joan Baez created a stir. She had been a leading light in the civil rights and peace movements of the 1960s, lending her lilting voice and strumming guitar to numerous causes. She had refused to pay taxes in opposition to the Vietnam War and organized an institute that taught the principles of nonviolence. In 1972, she followed in the footsteps of Jane Fonda and visited Hanoi. Baez witnessed the infamous Christmas bombings and wrote home angry letters decrying America's actions. Now, seven years later, she found herself singing concerts to benefit the boat people and drafting a letter to protest the genocide of the Socialist Republic of Vietnam.

The letter appeared May 30. It was reproduced in major newspapers across the United States. Its message rang out: "Thousands of innocent Vietnamese, many whose only 'crimes' are those of conscience, are being arrested, detained and tortured in prisons and re-education camps." She connected previous protests to this one: "It was an abiding commitment to fundamental principles of human dignity, freedom, and self-determination that motivated so many Americans to oppose the government of South Vietnam and our country's participation in the war. It is that same commitment that compels us to speak out against your brutal disregard of human rights." Baez had gathered signatures of fellow peace movement activists. For her, justice was justice, no matter what side of the political divide it fell on.[66]

The letter landed like a bomb in the circles of the remnants of the 1960s protest left. William Kunstler, a radical lawyer who sprang protesters from jail during the 1960s, refused to sign the letter. He charged: "I do not believe in public attacks on socialist countries, even where violations of human rights may occur." He even suggested that "the American government manufactured" Baez's letter. Abbie Hoffman, underground now while dodging cocaine trafficking charges, agreed. Jane Fonda refused to sign and said that Baez "aligns" herself "with the most narrow and negative elements in our country who continue to believe that communism is worse than death."[67]

These accusations showed how difficult it was for some to move beyond the simple dichotomies of the 1960s. But in their illogic, they hit upon a truth: The realities of postwar Vietnam were starting to bolster the right more than the left. One frustrated citizen wrote to the *New York Times* a week after it had published Baez's letter as a paid advertisement: "The 'hawks' of the 60s predicted exactly what Miss Baez now condemns. They said we were in the war to defend the South Vietnamese from just this sort of treatment . . . I believe we lost the war because the doves destroyed our resolve." That same day the *National Review* praised Baez: "We used to think Miss Baez was a hopeless naïf. We were wrong. She is living in the real world, and honorably." And then Ronald Reagan gave a radio address about Baez: "By her own admission it took some time for her to accept the reality of what was going on. The first horror stories out of South East Asia found her trying not to believe them but she didn't close her mind. She sought the truth." Reagan had waited to address the topic almost a month after the original letter was published, hoping Jane Fonda would respond to "2 letters" Baez had sent her after Fonda's original blistering counterattack. It would have been fun for him to blast Hanoi Jane while siding with flower child Baez. But he settled for knowing that his belief in the Vietnam War as just and decent no longer sounded so bizarre. The right's own protest against protest was starting to bear fruit.[68]

11.

Baez's biggest accomplishment in music history—introducing Bob Dylan to a national audience—was also making news in late May. Baez and Dylan had been lovers and co-performers in the early 1960s, the cute couple of coffeehouse folk, his nasal voice playing well against her lilting soprano. Dylan rode Baez's coattails to fame. But their paths diverged, hers merging easily with the protest circles of the 1960s that she now found herself battling and his turning into the standard cliché of the fried-out rock star.

By 1978, Dylan's life had hit the skids. Recently divorced, he slept around with groupies and indulged in drugs while touring and recording his live album *At Budokan*. Some labeled him a "washed-up relic from the 60s" who recycled old material. Others called his 1978 performances "The Alimony Tour."[69]

But in 1979 Bob Dylan met Mary Lice Artes, a member of the Vineyard Fellowship, "a small but growing evangelical church in the San Fernando Valley of Los Angeles." The Jewish rock star converted to evangelical Christianity. Reverend Ken Gulliksen of the Vineyard Fellowship baptized him and gave him books by his favorite theologian, Hal Lindsey, a close friend of Jerry Falwell.

Lindsey had written the bestselling book of the 1970s, *The Late Great Planet Earth*. He had a special knack for making Christianity hip—for instance, calling Antichrist the "Weirdo Beast"—and for interpreting current events in light of apocalyptic stories from the Bible. The movie version of the book came out in mid-1979. Orson Welles narrated it, and Hal Lindsey took center stage throughout to explain his ideas about Armageddon and the rapture. The signs were everywhere, he told his audience: natural disasters, pollution, nuclear weapons, killer bees, wars in the Middle East. Soon after making the movie, Lindsey turned his attention to writing a another book about the forthcoming 1980s that portrayed events in Iran and OPEC's rising power as signs of "end days." He had a capacity to say things that Jerry Falwell was saying, just making them sound hipper and more appealing to younger audiences, in part due to his more apocalyptic tones.[70]

Dylan now took as his charge the translation of Hal Lindsey's ideas into rock 'n' roll. He hit the studio in late May to make his comeback album, *Slow Train Coming*. Its hit single would be the autobiographical "Gotta Serve Somebody": "You might be a rock 'n' roll addict prancing on the stage," Dylan sang, but "you're gonna have to serve somebody, yes indeed." On the title track, Dylan blasted out Lindsey's teachings by deriding "foreign oil controlling American soil" and "sheiks walking around like kings." He argued that a "slow train" was coming to save Americans from their impending end days and energy slavery.[71]

If Baez's call for action on the issue of boat people showed how much things had changed since the 1960s, Dylan's born-again recording session nailed the coffin shut on that decade. The hippie rock star had pushed rock 'n' roll from celebrating love and drugs to providing apocalyptic Christian warnings about decadence. Rock star lust gave way to born-again devotion. Jimmy Carter's favorite rock musician now refused to sing the songs the president most enjoyed (they were written before Dylan found Jesus) and sang only about Hal Lindsey's end-times. The rock star had found salvation, and Christianity no longer sounded dour as it cranked itself out of a guitar amplifier. The times were certainly changing, even if the end of days hadn't come.

12.

Pat Caddell knew that some in the White House didn't take him seriously. "There is a tendency without visible or tangible manifestations," he once explained, "to dismiss the urgency and to brand the heralder as an alarmist." Ham Jordan would have certainly nodded his head at this comment. But what if Caddell brought more alarmists to the table, perhaps his case could become stronger. So the young pollster planned a dinner party. It was to be held on May 30.[72]

The dinner invitation list was impressive. It included Daniel Bell, a sociologist at Harvard University. A child socialist during the 1930s, Bell drifted to the political center during the 1950s and was labeled a neoconservative during the 1970s. That wasn't accurate. He described himself as a socialist (still) in economics, a liberal in politics, and a conservative in cultural matters. Caddell had finished reading *The Cultural Contradictions of Capitalism* in which Bell argued that consumer capitalism produced values inimical to the work ethic. "The rise of a hip-drug-rock culture on the popular level undermines the social structure itself by striking at the motivational and psychic-reward system which has sustained it." Bell had an advantage at dinner parties: He was not only a sharp thinker but an impressive talker who mixed ideas and funny stories in lightning fashion.[73]

Bell was joined by Charles Peters, editor of the *Washington Monthly*. Peters was a southern-born journalist with a quiet voice but raspy wit; he had written some seminal articles about the future of progressive politics that impressed Carter. Peters argued for a "rebirth of patriotism" by reinstituting the draft and promoting public service among young people. His magazine became a center of neoliberal political thinking, as it was sometimes called, meaning a liberalism not so enamored with Senator Kennedy and willing to take some of the teachings of conservatism seriously—such as a belief in individual responsibility and a distrust of federal bureaucracy. This too: Peters believed in the need to cultivate civic virtue and a feeling of patriotism, not exactly the sort of things most Americans associated with liberalism at this time. His monthly magazine was also, ironically enough, where James Fallows had gotten his start in journalism.[74]

One of Peters's friends was also present: Bill Moyers, a man who worked as press secretary in the Johnson administration and was now a television journalist with a talent for in-depth interviews with politicians and intellectuals. He had talked with Carter on numerous occasions and was actually considered to head the CIA (Peters himself thought he would be a good candidate for Carter's chief of staff, an idea that went nowhere). Carter and Moyers shared a Southern Baptist background, but Moyers distrusted the president as too taciturn and rigid.

John Gardner, like Moyers, was another refugee from the Johnson administration present for dinner. He served as the secretary of health, education and welfare under Lyndon Johnson. Afterward, in

1970, he formed Common Cause, an organization whose "good government" causes and especially campaign finance reform got a boost
from Watergate. Caddell knew Gardner mostly for his book *Morale*, in
which he worried that America's "shared purposes" were "in doubt."
Like Peters, he believed "voluntary association" and "citizen action
groups"—grassroots participation—might cure an ailing democracy.
He had already worked on those issues with the first lady.[75]

One of the more talkative guests was Jesse Jackson. He had cut his
teeth in the 1960s civil rights movement. When Martin Luther King
Jr. was assassinated in 1968, Jackson was there; some in the movement thought him a grandstander who wanted to seize King's legacy
for his own purposes. By now, though, Jackson had moved out of
King's shadow by forming PUSH (People United to Save Humanity),
an organization that worked against poverty especially in northern
urban areas. He gave "uplift" speeches littered with one-liners like,
"It's my attitude that will determine my altitude" and "Down with
dope, up with hope." He was fresh from a series of Excel-A-Thons in
Los Angeles when he attended dinner at the White House.[76]

Journalist Haynes Johnson was the dinner guest whose presence was
most curious. He wrote for the *Washington Post*, a newspaper that drove
Carter's administration insane (it was that paper's "Style" section where
nasty stories about Ham Jordan had appeared). Somehow Carter had
taken a liking to Johnson, providing him an open door to the White
House, perhaps hoping for honest reporting and trying to get out of the
antimedia attitude that had marked the Nixon administration.

The final guest was Christopher Lasch. By now Carter had speed-
read his way through *The Culture of Narcissism*. The president was interested in what "political implications" he might draw from the book, or
so Jody Powell explained to Lasch when he called with his invitation.[77]

This was an impressive list of participants. It showed that Carter
hoped to bring ideas into the White House. And the list of invitees

had more coherence than might first appear. Besides Johnson (whose political views were less clear), all dinner participants shared a peculiar constellation of ideas: They were liberal or left on economic issues but culturally conservative. This was not so far from Carter's own tangle of beliefs. In an infamous interview he gave *Playboy* magazine during his campaign for president, Carter refused to put himself in a "box." He was, for instance, "personally opposed to abortion" yet wouldn't outlaw it. He had profound doubts about the selfishness ingrained in capitalism but wasn't a socialist. Or consider his views on Helms's pressure for school prayer: Carter respected religion's role in public life but didn't want to have government imposing it on civil society. So when he looked around the table on May 30, he saw allies.[78]

Powell called the invitees while Caddell wrote up a memo that served as a menu for conversation. Its central question was: If we "agree" that "the problems are rooted in culture, social structure, and economics," then "what is the role of the President, the government, the political system in what is essentially a non-political cultural/societal problem"? Caddell followed with other questions, such as how can we marry "concrete concerns like energy, inflation, etc. with more abstract concerns like goals, values, moral regeneration, volunteerism/community participation"? In the end, Caddell had thirty-two questions, which suggested a plan for a lengthy rambling evening. And so it would be. The fact that the participants didn't know of Caddell's list of questions before attending the dinner only added to the confusion.[79]

Around seven P.M., the guests arrived. Drinks were served on the Truman Balcony, and then there was a dinner of lamb chops and asparagus. Carter had a conversation with Bell about the possibility of a religious revival in America and then asked him about his own faith. Bell explained he was a "believing" person but not a "practicing" one. Carter laughed and then pressed him on how America's consumer culture generated wants rather than needs, a distinction the president fixated on throughout the evening, or so Bell noticed.

After raspberry ice cream, petits fours, and coffee, Carter asked for everyone's attention, suggesting the separate conversations end and a more inclusive discussion begin. The president started by explaining that he was worried about something wrong in America and then turned the floor to Caddell who fumbled around in his briefcase for his statistics. Peters looked at the numbers and immediately championed truth-telling in politics, while Jesse Jackson and John Gardner worried that the media would trivialize whatever the president said (Carter nodded at the point). Perhaps there was a way to do a run around the mainstream media.

The conversation turned incoherent, and Carter asked Bell to take command. The sociologist started to argue that the president had been bogged down in details and needed to articulate a broader framework for citizens to understand. He suggested Carter address the civic crisis in a series of letters to the American people. Powell argued the idea seemed silly, and Bell started to wonder if he had misspoken, realizing that he wasn't sure *what* was going on or what exactly Carter hoped to accomplish.

Carter then turned to Lasch who had been quiet, somewhat "overawed" by the conversation. Just then, a butler interrupted, and Carter whisked himself away for a phone call. So Rosalynn took over. She said she wanted to start up a discussion on "values" and how they could be rebuilt. Bell worried that such a project would fail, arguing that government had no role to play in nurturing values. As he pointed out, government couldn't empower civic institutions—they had to remain free by definition. Gardner said that he and the first lady were working on the problem already by seeing if government could find ways to aid voluntary associations without becoming too intrusive.[80]

The president's daughter, Amy, scurried into the room dressed in pajamas, and then Carter returned from his phone call. He asked Lasch again for his advice. Lasch worried that talk about civic sacrifice during an energy crisis would fall flat. "Many people had turned down the heat in their houses" last winter "only to find that utility companies proceeded to raise their rates," he pointed out. The president grew impatient. He had heard all of this energy-crisis-as-hoax stuff before. And so he turned to the historian and said: *Well, what would you do to solve the energy crisis, Mr. Lasch?* Lasch responded timidly, "I don't know." Those words destroyed any future he might have had as a political consultant.[81]

By ten thirty, the conversation flagged. The president asked Bill Moyers for his thoughts. Moyers argued that the president had to move the country back to the "consensus of 1963," before the Kennedy assassination, Vietnam, and Watergate. That sounded overwhelming, even more impossible than the idea of government aiding civil society institutions. Then Moyers averred that Carter might not win a second term. Carter's jaw tensed up. Moyers told Carter that he had been an exceptional campaigner but not an exceptional president. There was a nervous hush at that. Then Carter asked Moyers for advice. Invite people to the White House and open up to ordinary citizens, the journalist suggested. Carter thought the idea stale, but Caddell duly noted it.[82]

The clock struck eleven. Carter herded everyone onto an elevator. Daniel Bell hitched a ride with John Gardner back to his hotel and asked if Carter would listen and take their advice. Gardner didn't think so but also blamed the participants since "we failed to come up with the right answers" or even "the right questions." Meanwhile, Peters, Johnson, Caddell, Lasch, and Powell went to a bar and talked politics. Lasch was surprised to hear Powell call Kennedy a "demagogue" who'd be easy to beat in 1980. He might have noticed Caddell remained silent on the point.[83]

If Caddell's intention was to provide some intellectual bolstering to his arguments, perhaps he succeeded. But the dinner hardly offered clarity. Just how could the president ever be expected to talk about all of these problems? Nonetheless, Caddell remained even more certain that he was on the right road. He had new ideas about the loss of public faith from Daniel Bell. Moyers's suggestion of reaching out to ordinary people also sounded good. The young pollster was making mental notes about the speech he was certain the president would eventually give and that he hoped he could help write.

13.

The next day, May 31, the *Los Angeles Times* ran an editorial about what had happened since Carter's energy speech on April 5, including his prediction of the energy crisis and his visit to the paper's city to see the gas lines. When he predicted the gas crisis, the editors argued, Carter had "in this matter at any rate" been a "prophet, however unhonored." Those words suggested that at least some seemed ready to listen and that the energy crisis was recognized for what it was: a reality that could grow worse. Better yet, the American public hadn't fully tuned out its I-told-you-so president.[84]

The same day the editorial appeared, twenty-eight big-rig trucks double-parked outside the White House at dawn in order to block traffic and bring attention to the shortage of diesel fuel. The organizer of the event, Mike Parkhurst, spokesperson for the Independent Truckers Association, explained, "This was just a little landing party to kind of let people know the trucks are out there." That sounded ominous. When a group of truckers had taken similar action at the Los Angeles City Hall two days before, they blew their horns, flashed their lights, ran red lights, and jammed traffic. There were hints of scenes from Sam Peckinpah's crazy movie *Convoy*, in which yahoo truckers wreaked chaos out west by driving through multiple states and rolling over police cars. (The 1978 movie got a small revival at the Olympia Theater in New York City in late May 1979.) Everyone knew that if they wanted, truckers could raise hell.[85]

Hell was just around the corner. And it would provide an answer to the question Pat Caddell pondered: How to link the broader themes of cultural pessimism and the energy crisis? Answering this question would come in the form of chaos, anger, and breakdown.

3

"THE WORST OF TIMES"

JUNE 1979

Civilization is thin ice.

—JOHN GARDNER[1]

1.

Pat Caddell had struggled to read America's mood back in April. It seemed diffuse, "nearly invisible" and "intangible." When he fumbled in his briefcase for statistics at the White House dinner in late May, many participants scratched their heads. But by June 1979, the mood of the country was easy to diagnose. The country was *pissed*—in a state of outrage. June became a month of violent gas lines, trucker shootings, riots in American suburbs, and visceral hatred of the president. Narcissism turned to anger as the dam of civilization burst. *Now*, Caddell thought to himself, now is time for the president's *breakthrough*. It's no longer simply the moral thing to do, it's necessary for our nation's survival, let alone the president's.

Caddell watched the president's poll numbers slip further than even *he* could imagine. The *New York Times* showed Carter's approval rating move from 42 percent in March to 30 percent in June. That's "staggering," Caddell wrote the president. It would seem that "frustration" with you was "moving toward personal hostility as opposed to indifference or disappointment." Caddell was growing more annoyed that his warnings didn't seem to reach the president or at least that the president didn't seem to do anything about them. To add to his misery, the DNC was behind on its payments to his polling firm, Cambridge Survey Research (CSR), forcing "senior employees" to go on "half salary all year."[2]

Just as his poll numbers tumbled downward, Carter faced a rebuff from Iran. That country's foreign minister, Ibrahim Yazdi, rejected Carter's selection of Walter L. Cutler as ambassador to Tehran. Cutler had served as a diplomat in Africa, which suggested to the Iranians a connection to the United States' legacy of imperialism in the third world. Iran's rejection sent a chilling diplomatic message: Anti-Americanism was rising in Iran. Then came reports about more roving mobs and political murders in the country.[3]

Carter responded to bad news the only way he knew how: He started issuing warnings that sounded graver than the last ones he offered. Notching up his own Nieburhian emotions in early June, he addressed the annual Jefferson-Jackson Day Dinner sponsored by Indiana's Democratic Party, an event where party regulars raised money and listened to guest speakers. Carter thanked the party's activists for his primary victory in the state during 1976. Then he turned more morose: "One of the most immobilizing fears among our people is the fear of being cheated and misled," he warned. "As much as anything else, this keeps our people from making a small, personal sacrifice to solve the problems of inflation and energy." Denial of the energy crisis—a recent poll showed that 65 percent of the American public *still* thought it a fiction—could not be solved by promising "magic cures." Rather, the country needed "some pain and some sacrifice." A few days later, speaking to the United Food and Commercial Workers

International Union, Carter continued building this theme by condemning the rise of "me first" attitudes and "the politics of selfishness" in America. He might have wondered if these words would reach the nation as a whole.[4]

2.

On June 6, Reverend Jerry Falwell, fresh from his recent "I Love America" tour that had landed him on the Capitol steps in late April, announced the founding of the Moral Majority. "This non-profit organization," its press release read, "was created to give a voice to the millions of decent, law abiding, God-fearing Americans who want to do something about the moral decline of our country." The group's formation was a breakthrough, an entity that could galvanize evangelical Christian anger at the decadent culture of the 1970s—a culture of pornography, abortion, the ERA, and what Jesse Helms had labeled "secular humanism."[5]

The Moral Majority was also a result of Jerry Falwell's growing political frustration. The problem with the "I Love America" rallies he had been doing was their episodic nature. Falwell would roll into town, recruit audience members at churches and evangelical colleges, and then perform his orchestrated event. After the fanfare, though, there was nothing left. How could he receive true national redemption from collective sin if there wasn't something that bolstered these events, that provided an outlet for those ready to organize and push back against secular humanism? Falwell had worried about this problem throughout April, and to his good fortune, he was contacted in May by a group of new right activists who noted the reverend's growing popularity at the rallies and on his regular television show, *The Old Time Gospel Hour*. They approached Falwell about creating an organization that could provide more political heft.

Robert Billings had placed the original call to Falwell, telling him he wanted to form an organization that could "save America." Billings had a potent group of activists assembled already: Ed McAteer, a successful businessman who managed sales for Colgate-Palmolive and then decided to go into politics by forming the Religious Roundtable (an organization that recruited James Robison, another televangelist who shared a great deal with Falwell); Howard Phillips, executive director of Conservative Caucus, a group that lobbied hard against the Panama Canal treaty and then prepared for future grassroots battles against congressional legislation; and Paul Weyrich, chair of the Committee for Survival of a Free Congress (CSFC), an organization that raised money and support for conservatives running for political office.[6]

The man who came to this meeting and offered the most was the man who made Falwell uneasy. Richard Viguerie was now known as the kingpin of the "new right." Falwell distrusted Viguerie. Sure, the man had a Bible on his desk at all times, but he was raised Catholic, and he seemed more a political wheeler and dealer than a religious man. He looked intimidating, with a big bald dome of a head and piercing eyes. Afraid to ask people for money in person, Viguerie had pioneered "direct mailing," a crucial advance in the new right's strategy. It worked this way: Identify a foe—abortion, the Equal Rights Amendment, a ban on prayer in public schools, gun control, busing—and then carve out a niche of people angry about the issue. Deluge them with computer-generated letters that asked them to write their congressman about impending legislation and pony up money for the cause. Direct mailing was populism made easy. It helped conservatives portray liberals as "the party of the large contributor" and themselves as the party of "small donations." Viguerie enjoyed walking through rooms full of computers and watching letters stuffed into envelopes. It made him feel powerful, a one-man message machine. "You can think of direct mail as our TV, radio, daily newspaper, and weekly news-magazine," Viguerie explained. "Our" meant those who agreed: the right wing message machine that ran on its own.[7]

Like Pat Caddell and Jody Powell, Viguerie had an interest in contemporary political history, specifically in working-class whites who voted for George Wallace in 1968. Viguerie had concluded that the "blue-collar worker in America is right of center." His political ambitions were bold: If the new right could emphasize social over economic issues, it could win working-class whites away from the Democrats and toward the Republicans (and push that party farther to the right simultaneously). The language Falwell used—cleaning up America, redeeming the country—could ensnare these people. Viguerie himself outlined the need for a "National Commission to Restore America." But how could he get the white working-class evangelicals in the fold? He figured that Falwell's televisual charisma could be combined with his own organizational strategy to draw evangelicals into the burgeoning new right.[8]

When Viguerie joined the others to discuss forming a new organization, they grew surprised by their shared enemies—abortion, the ERA, and smutty television shows. But still Falwell worried that his comrades were activists rather than men of God. Besides, he had warned against preachers entering politics back in 1964. But Viguerie would remind him about how the IRS had tried to change the tax-exempt status of private Christian schools, or how Anita Bryant successfully defeated gay rights in 1977 in Florida, or how ordinary citizens had recently battled sex education in West Virginia's textbooks a few years back. Christian evangelicals were realizing they had to organize politically, if only to defend their way of life. Falwell had to agree. As the participants in the meeting talked about the issues that angered them, Weyrich came back to the question of forming an organization and said in passing, "What we really need is a moral majority of Americans with a name like . . ." McAteer cut him off and asked Weyrich what term he just used. That was *it*, that was the name of the organization they would form. Falwell loved it.[9]

Soon after it was founded on June 6, the Moral Majority started to build its membership, raise money, and mobilize members to get behind specific legislation and to fight liberal politicians. It felt like a movement was gelling, since the Moral Majority joined ranks with Christian Voice, a group founded six months earlier to issue "report cards" about politicians based upon a "morality scale." Christian Voice's statement of purpose sounded a lot like Falwell's: "We believe that America, the last stronghold of faith on this planet, has come under increasing attack from Satan's forces in recent years . . . that the standards of Christian morality (long the protection and strength of the nation), the sanctity of our families, the innocence of our young, are now under the onslaught . . . launched by the 'rulers of darkness of this world' and insidiously sustained under the ever more liberal ethic." But Christian Voice had one problem: It was housed in Pasadena, California. The Moral Majority intentionally set up shop in Washington, D.C., and made Robert Billings, the man who initiated the original call to Falwell and who happened to have numerous political connections, its executive manager.[10]

Falwell was especially pleased: He wouldn't have to give up ministering and could allow people with more political savvy than he had to run an organization completely in synch with his values. He could rely upon the good work of Senator Jesse Helms, who was already trying to obstruct the IRS's attempt to crack down on religious schools. He could recruit new members to his cause of national redemption by simply ministering weekly on his television show. And he could fight a president who believed religion was more a private matter of the heart than a public tool to remake society. In other words, he could push a nation toward redemption.[11]

3.

Meanwhile, on the other side of the political spectrum, liberals who hoped to nominate a presidential candidate other than Carter in 1980 were getting their act together and pushing harder than ever, growing giddy with the president's sagging poll numbers. On June 10, the largest Draft Kennedy meeting to date convened in Minnesota, organized by George Mische, a city councilman from St. Cloud. A relic from the 1960s protest left, Mische raged against defense spending and convinced himself somehow that Carter—no matter how hard the president pushed for SALT II and resisted attacking Iran to seize the oil fields there—would lead the country into another war. He received help from Representative Rich Nolan (D-Minn.). Nolan's and Mische's work paid off: Around 260 people turned out and chose for their organization the name Minnesotans for a Democratic Alternative. They pushed Kennedy to run, just as Tim Hagan had in Ohio. When Vice President Mondale caught wind of the meeting, he was mortified: His home state, a hotbed of prairie liberalism, was abandoning him. Mondale's decision to stick it out with the president was looking more and more embarrassing and less and less effective.[12]

Kennedy continued to dodge the question of whether he would run for the nomination. He seemed to be "winking his way to the White House," as one journalist quipped. This got on Carter's nerves, and it started to show. The night after the Draft Kennedy meeting in Minnesota, the president held a dinner for sixty members of Congress, an attempt to shore up dwindling support. At one point, Thomas Downey (D-NY) asked Carter how he felt about 1980. Toby Moffett, a young Connecticut congressman who rode the wave of Watergate to win office in 1974 and who now opposed Carter's energy plans, listened in. "I'm ready for 1980," Carter claimed. *What about Kennedy?* Moffett asked. Carter shot back: "If Kennedy runs, I'll whip his ass." Another congressman turned and asked, "Excuse me, what?" "If Kennedy runs, I'll whip his ass," Carter repeated. When asked about the comment the next day, Kennedy said the president must have been "misquoted." He hadn't been.[13]

Carter's belligerence didn't change anything in the burgeoning anti-Carter movement; it just gave the movement more steam. Nor did Carter's new health care plan, which called for hospital cost containment and some other regulations. The plan was intended to diffuse Kennedy's monopoly over the issue of national health care, which he had worked on since 1966. Carter's secretary of health, education, and welfare, Joseph Califano, was dispatched to Kennedy's office to try to garner support for the administration's more centrist reform of health care. If anything, the president's attempt to mollify Kennedy just angered liberals more.[14]

On June 23, Americans for Democratic Action (ADA) met in the Mayflower Hotel in Washington, D.C., to voice their rage. The organization had started back in 1947, and it remained the most important liberal group around. An independent organization, it positioned itself to the left of the Democratic Party. In its early days, members had argued against the militaristic elements in Harry Truman's "containment" policies. In 1960 the organization pressed John F. Kennedy to take a more principled stand on the issue of civil rights. And in 1968 ADA endorsed Eugene McCarthy against Hubert Humphrey to protest the Vietnam War. In Carter, the group saw a dangerous centrism and betrayal of liberalism, and so they protested.[15]

The White House dispatched Stuart Eizenstat to calm members of ADA. Walter Mondale would probably have been a better choice, but that would have suggested the administration cared more than it did. Besides, Eizenstat was drawing closer and closer to Mondale, bonding around their shared liberalism and their rational approach to interest group politics. As the quintessential wonk, Eizenstat knew policy well enough to argue with those who would consider themselves experts on the floor of the ADA convention. In addition, Carter's domestic policy adviser had witnessed what a split within the Democratic Party had done to the man he once worked for, Hubert Humphrey.

As Eizenstat mounted the podium, the audience mumbled that he looked "unhappy." Why wouldn't he be? He was amidst friends turned into a pack of wolves. The audience hissed when he tried to explain Carter's decontrol plans. He responded with silence or "ho-hums." And then, out of frustration, Eizenstat launched into his history lesson: He reminded the organization's members of their fight against Humphrey in 1968 and the resulting split in the party. The outcome had been Richard Nixon's presidency. *Do you want to repeat that awful mistake?* Eizenstat asked pointedly.[16]

But nothing could break the collective delusion mounting in the room. The historian Arthur Schlesinger Jr., a lifetime member of the organization whose roots went back to the battles with Truman, decided to play upon the delusion and press a hard line. He approached the podium, looked out at the sea of gray hair, and then launched into his speech. While endorsing Kennedy, he promised fellow ADAers that good times were just around the corner: "We can be confident that sometime in the 1980s the dam will break, as it broke at the turn of the century, in the 1930s and in the 1960s. Our sense of adventure will revive. Our blood will start flowing again. There will be a breakthrough into a new political epoch, a new conviction of social possibility, a new demand for innovation and reform, new efforts to redeem the promise of American life." The dam would break, for sure, but not in the way Schlesinger dreamed. The historian was a poor political forecaster. He had been closer to reading the future of the country when, just a few days earlier, he disparaged "long gas lines" full of "screaming and fighting" as "a disgraceful spectacle." That was the present, and as the present it foresaw the future more than liberal dreaming ever could.[17]

Nonetheless, Schlesinger's case had been made. ADA's members deliberated. They decided quickly, as most knew they would, to endorse Kennedy.

4.

John Wayne died June 11 after the final stages of fighting the "big C," as he once called cancer. Richard Nixon's favorite movie star and Ronald Reagan's close friend now became even more mythological in death than in life. Jimmy Carter, who had communicated with Wayne throughout his presidency, issued a statement: "In an age of few heroes," John Wayne was "the genuine article." Wayne was a "symbol of many of the most basic qualities that made America great." This was a remarkable blind side of Carter's, considering just how many young men took inspiration from Wayne's movies and enlisted in the army only to be killed in the jungles of Vietnam. Or, considering how conservative most of Wayne's views were. Nonetheless, Carter had had a good correspondence with the actor and felt him to be a friend.[18]

Carter's sentimental reaction was echoed in the funeral oration that followed Wayne's death. To speak poorly of the dead would, of course, have been inexcusable, and a chorus of celebration sang Wayne's praises. Republican Senator Robert Dole from Kansas extolled, "He provided all of us with convincing evidence that America was like the frontier itself: Youthful, brimming with potential, self-assured, a bit headstrong." "He was one of America's great mythological heroes," glowed the *Wall Street Journal*.[19]

The realities of Wayne were much more complex. This beacon of conservatism and traditional values was twice-divorced and at the time separated from his third wife. He had never served in the military yet implored young people to go to war—especially in his film *The Green Berets*. But such realities about a movie actor interrupted dreams, and during bad times like June 1979, Americans wanted dreams, no matter how fanciful. Movie acting as patriotism, celebrity worship as heroism: These were not strange things to take hold in a country where Hollywood was the nation's capital as much as Washington.

This is why Wayne's legacy, much like *The Deer Hunter*'s message, belonged more to Ronald Reagan than to Jimmy Carter, no matter how Carter might have wished the opposite. Reagan knew Wayne from his early days in the 1940s as an activist in the Screen Actors Guild, and they had remained fast friends since. Though they disagreed on the issue of the Panama Canal treaty (Wayne supported it), they agreed on much more—on patriotism and a shared animosity toward "Eastern liberals" who, they believed, had betrayed the country. So Reagan could get on the radio at the end of June and seize Wayne's memory for his own, ensuring listeners that the actor was "about what you saw on the screen." Wayne was a tough guy who "refused sedatives" at the end of his life, Reagan pointed out. Reagan's intention, more than Carter's, was to erase the divide between reality and image. *I knew him*, Reagan suggested, and he was good, honorable, and a true sign of the best America offered. He was also what you saw projected on the screen, he insisted. Reagan embraced more than Wayne; he embraced the legitimacy of dreams. That's why Wayne's legacy was Reagan's more than it was Carter's.[20]

5.

On June 14, Carter left the United States to meet with Leonid Brezhnev. They would discuss and sign SALT II treaties that placed "limits on the numbers of missiles and bombers that each side might have" and that they had worked on for the last number of months. All of his hard work on this issue during the last few months now seemed to be paying off. Carter was a man obsessed, committed to halting the arms race but also hoping a foreign victory might lift his own spirits and the country's. He got so giddy about meeting Brezhnev in person, he even called Richard Nixon to find out how to handle the man. Nonetheless, this was the easiest part of the process—just a formal signing ceremony—that hid the difficulties Carter would face in getting SALT II through Congress.[21]

Carter's first meetings with the Soviet premier went well, even though Brezhnev was ill. He couldn't get up and down stairs and appeared to be in a haze of medications, which might explain why he got along so well with Carter. On June 18 the two parties picked up their pens and signed. Carter was thrilled and flew back to D.C. to announce his great accomplishment to a joint session of Congress and to national television audiences. Two hours after stepping off his plane he was making his speech. Mondale was thrilled too, realizing that this was the sort of legislation that he wanted to help promote as part of his attempt to emphasize Carter's liberal side.[22]

Carter's return to America to give the speech was a momentous event that portended an inevitable letdown. Agreeing with the Russians might come easy to Carter, but working with Congress and the Senate to ratify SALT II would be hard. There was, for instance, Senator Scoop Jackson, who would stand firmly against any policy that encouraged détente between the two superpowers. He opposed Carter on numerous domestic issues from the left—including decontrol of gas prices—but forged alliances with the right on foreign affairs. Jesse Helms had already joined Jackson's battle. He saw opposition to SALT II as a logical extension of his opposition to the Panama Canal treaty. The evangelical right, including the Moral Majority and Christian Voice, worried that SALT II would weaken America and make it more susceptible to future blackmail from the force of godless communism.[23]

So when Carter returned home, his spirits sank as his hopes faced realities more squarely. The idea that machines of death could be checked by the stroke of a pen seemed unreal, just as his hopes to get standby rationing powers seemed back in May. On June 19, a day after his address to Congress, the *New York Times*, usually a paper that would celebrate diplomatic victory, reminded Carter: "A good portion of the president's prime television audience" when he addressed Congress about SALT II "was sitting home against its will while a portion that wanted to watch him was out on the gasoline lines." The public cared more about the gas crisis than the proliferation of or limitations on missiles. They were especially aggrieved that the president was spending so much time abroad on diplomatic matters when the real problem—long gas lines—should have been right under his nose at home.[24]

6.

America had become one big gas line during June. Like new-age religion and no-fault divorce, the gas line gestated in California, then spread across the country. When fistfights broke out in early June at a Washington, D.C., gas station, an attendant called it "California east." But really it was *America* as a whole, or at least large swaths of the country.[25]

Ensuring that a car had sufficient gas went something like this during the month of June in New York, Washington, D.C., and the suburbs of New Jersey: Search for an open gas station (95 percent of stations in New York City were closed), wait in a long line for up to six hours (they ran for miles in New Jersey), get to the pump and then find out that there was no gas left. An attendant might say a truck was on its way with resupplies, prompting a further wait. Those who saw the "Last Car" sign on the back window of an automobile (placed by a harried gas station attendant) panicked or thought of stealing the sign and putting it on their own car. Idling during a wait in a gas line wasted even more gas. "One estimate," the historian Daniel Yergin later explained, "suggested that America's motorists in the spring and summer of 1979 may have wasted 150,000 barrels of oil a day waiting in line." Others ran out of gas before getting into line, coasting or pushing to the pumps.[26]

With summer temperatures inching upward, those in gas lines who were afraid to turn on air conditioners that would waste more gas suffered heat stroke. Some avoided this by sleeping in their cars overnight to be first in line the next morning, getting fitful nights of sleep to the sound of passing traffic. In Bethesda, Maryland, a gas station that opened at seven A.M. had a few cars in line by two thirty A.M., thirty cars by five thirty A.M., and then a mile-long gas line by opening time. Conversations at work during June focused on where people found gas or didn't as drivers topped one another's horror stories.[27]

And then there was the violence. When the gas crisis hit California, Daniel Patrick Moynihan, the senator from New York, asserted that Californians were prone to panic and irrationality. Such behavior ran in Californians' blood, Moynihan suggested. But how would he explain the twenty-two-year-old man shot to death in front of his pregnant wife the last day of May in New York in what was a rather short line? How would he explain shotguns and hand grenades pulled on station attendants in D.C.'s gas lines? One angry customer broke the ankle of a gas station attendant, while another armed himself with a machete and charged an attendant, yelling "I'm going to cut your ass up!"[28]

Too much might be made of this breakdown in civilized decorum. For sure, many Americans took things in stride and managed to remain cordial. "Breakfast clubs" started to form at gas station lines, and some people played Frisbee while waiting. Public libraries and some bookstores handed out free reading material. A liquor store in the D.C. area, in a strange and perhaps dangerous move, provided free beer to those waiting for gas.[29]

But such stories ignored the predominant psychic state that gripped people waiting for gas in June. It was the psyche of frustration, mixed with conspiracy and paranoia. Most in line believed the gas crisis to be a big con. "It's just a bunch of fat cats waiting for the price to come up some more so they can make more profit," said one person in a gas line. In Queens, New York, many waiting were convinced that "abandoned service stations in their area" were "being used as secret gasoline storage spots by major oil companies."[30]

The gas line became a sociological microcosm of Pat Caddell's bigger worries about the state of the American psyche. The me decade fully bloomed on gas lines. The gas line cutter or crasher became a key symbol of the summer of 1979. In Fairfax City, Virginia, a woman zoomed to the head of the line. Her belly bulged, and she asked if she could cut in since she was pregnant. News of the pregnant woman beaten in a gas line in Los Angeles still resonated, so others in line said, "yes, of course." "I was shocked when two pillows suddenly fell out from under her dress," one motorist recounted. "We chased her back out of the line." Lies, distrust, and self-interest kicked into high gear at the pumps. One D.C. resident wrote to the *Washington Post*: "Stories of gun toters, line crashers and the like make one wonder about our own civilization." America, the letter went on, had become a nation of "savages."[31]

Hoarding and black market practices exemplified the survivalist ethic that Christopher Lasch had analyzed in *The Culture of Narcissism*. Two bestselling items of 1979 were siphon hand pumps and gas tank locks, their sales rising in tandem. Gas poisoning cases shot up, as Americans used hoses to suck gas out of neighbors' cars. Large gas cans sold like crazy to those who wanted to hoard (one van in New Jersey blew up after an accident since it was stocked with numerous tanks of gas). Then there was the person so desperate he tried to tap directly into a "pressurized gas pipeline."[32]

National fragmentation also showed up on gas lines. Wealthy Americans seceded from the suffering of middle- and working-class Americans. The rich had others buy gas for them, with businesses like

Chauffeur-Gofers popping up. Or they bought, as strange as it might sound, the Elizabethan sedan chair with a cushioned glass booth and four wooden poles used to carry occupants if they happened to live in a place like New York City.[33]

Regional balkanization grew like the class divide. By mid-June, things were worse in the East but better in California. So now western-ers turned the tables on easterners. The *Los Angeles Times* ran a front page headline in late June: "Shoe's on the Other Foot and New York Has a Fit." Just a year earlier, a bumper sticker showed up on many Texas cars that read, DRIVE FAST, FREEZE A YANKEE, which alluded to the fact that heating oil reserves could be depleted by consuming gaso-line (another sign of how the national allocation system worked). Tex-ans were now busily peeling these stickers off, as the 1979 gas crisis ironically wound up hitting the oil-rich state.[34]

In the short term, rationing solved the problem. State after state passed even-odd gasoline sales like California's. But this policy gener-ated unintended consequences. One resident of Washington, D.C., calculated the months that had even days versus odd days and found out that it was disproportionate: "7 months have 31 days . . ." Further-more, the day following the thirty-first is the first. The odds therefore had an advantage. It went without saying that the person who pointed this out had an even number license plate.[35]

All of which suggested that anger and frustration boiling up on gas lines would never be easy to quell. One group of citizens in Brooklyn, New York, organized the American Gas Party and called for protests against "price manipulation by the oil companies and for alternative sources of power." They planned to dump gas in the harbor at Eighty-sixth Street and Shore Drive to simulate the Boston Tea Party. It would be fake gas, in part because protestors worried about environmental damage but also because the real thing was too expensive.[36]

So gas lines inspired collective action and protest. But more worri-some to those in the Carter administration watching (and waiting in) gas lines was the spirit of individual selfishness turning into vindictive violence. The gas line was the energy crisis come home to roost, for sure, but it was also Caddell's civic, moral, and psychological crisis.

7.

America's independent truckers mounted the loudest protests against the gas crisis during June. They watched as their ability to work for themselves melted in the face of dwindling supplies and skyrocketing costs (prices for diesel fuel shot up 34 percent during the first half of 1979). Owning their own rigs and paying their expenses (gas, highway tolls, and fines) made these independents, in the words of *Overdrive* magazine (the only publication that spoke for them), "the last of America's pioneers." They were a large sector of the trucking population as a whole (the latter included union members), claiming they could mobilize around 60 percent of "the national total of long-haul interstate trucks." John Wayne's children, they might be called, the gut-bulging equivalents of America's yeoman settlers on the old frontier.[37]

Trucker culture was full of contradictions but tilted in a conservative and populist direction. There were long hair, tattoos, and flannel shirts. Independent though they were, many suffered from drug dependency, especially amphetamines to keep them awake on the road. Truckers busted on the law—"smokies," they labeled the cops—in citizen-band radio (CB) conversations and stashed rifles in sleeper cabins. Radical individualists, they weren't conservative prudes. *Hustler* magazine, one of the raunchiest porn publications ever, was created with the trucker in mind. *Overdrive* featured photos of large-breasted women in swimsuits next to big rigs. The independent trucker seemed to symbolize a peculiar strain of American conservatism—independent, libertarian, and rowdy all at once.[38]

Independent truckers were the kind of people who worried Pat

Caddell. Those truckers raising hell in 1979 likely voted for George Wallace or Richard Nixon in 1968. They listened to country music—for instance, Merle Haggard singing about welfare chiselers and hippies—while the country danced to disco. And now Caddell worried that they hated Carter, which most of them did.

The spontaneous trucker protests that erupted in May had become more organized by June. The Independent Truckers Association (ITA) despised the government and the Teamsters Union but now saw their only chance in collective action. They demanded more diesel fuel supplies and lower costs as well as nationwide load limits. Mike Parkhurst, president of ITA and editor of *Overdrive*, was spokesperson for the organization; he had begun driving trucks at age eighteen and bought his own rig at twenty. He combined the rare skills of being tough and brilliantly articulate. But even he was surprised by how anger galvanized into a strike: By June 14, 60 percent of independent trucks in America had stopped operating. American consumers started to feel the pinch, with fruit and vegetables rotting in farm fields rather than making it to grocery stores.[39]

The White House responded quickly, even though Carter was rarely around (some, of course, might have thought that the central reason). The Carter administration looked into defraying fuel costs, and energy secretary James Schlesinger sought to reallocate more diesel fuel to truckers rather than farmers. Eizenstat, his influence growing as the crisis mounted, moved to the center of negotiations by arranging a meeting with Alexander Carlucci Jr., president of the Council of Independent Truckers of New Jersey, on June 16 to start discussions. Though both sides seemed ready, they couldn't reach resolution.[40]

So truckers notched up their protests. William J. Hill, president of the Fraternal Association of Steel Haulers (FASH), advocated a 100 percent nationwide shutdown and formed a new organization called the Independent Truckers Unity Coalition (ITUC). The group demanded that the Interstate Commerce Commission (ICC) pass a 10 percent surcharge to defray rising gas prices and that the Department of Energy give top priority to truckers for diesel fuel. Others demanded a 65 mph speed limit (no matter that 55 mph was more fuel efficient) and an increase on the weight limits of trucks.

Stuart Eizenstat played behind the scenes, as was his style, to win a compromise. He coordinated the work of the departments of Transportation, Labor, Energy, and Justice, and the ICC to come up with policies that might tamp down trucker frustration. Working the bureaucracy was difficult, and Eizenstat worried that his efforts wouldn't succeed, believing that "among some truckers the attitude seems to be, 'We won't get all we want until we really create havoc.'" There was "demagoguery" among the leaders and "increasingly emotional responses from truckers talking to each other in truckstops and by CB radios."[41]

Eizenstat knew of what he spoke. Truckers had started to take their rifles out of their sleeping compartments as vigilante violence took hold. On June 18, a man was shot and wounded in Crossville, Tennessee, for refusing to join the strike. A few days later, Florida and Wisconsin governors declared states of emergency because twenty-nine trucks had been shot up, their windshields smashed and tires flattened by bullets. On June 19, Minnesota Governor Albert H. Quie declared a state of emergency in face of a "violent 13-day strike" that "shut down all gasoline and diesel fuel terminals in Minnesota." These blockades became more popular and rowdy simultaneously. The White House asked the FBI to police highways and quell violence, but this couldn't stop the shootings. Truckers who bucked the strike found their tires shot out, making them skid and careen off highways. One driver who blew past striking truckers was warned over his CB radio that he was losing his right wheel. He stopped to get out and check and then was promptly shot.[42]

These actions worked. For instance, with no trucks to transport their products, meatpacking plants in Omaha, Nebraska, and Council Bluffs, Iowa, shut down. Interstate 90 in Montana was barren of trucks, further hurting the meatpacking industry. *Newsweek* noted that truckers had successfully "blockaded refineries and distribution centers with their eighteen-wheelers, and roving bands shot at the rigs of non-striking truckers in 23 states." *Time* reported that "in California, thousands of acres of ripe lettuce and potatoes were plowed under for lack of trucks to ship them east, a loss that is calculated at $15 million to $25 million."[43]

All of which brought independent truckers back to the White House on June 22 to meet with Eizenstat. Schlesinger and Eizenstat had gotten permission from the president to repeal Rule 9, an obscure part of the allocation system created earlier by the Department of Energy to ensure larger quantities of diesel fuel for farmers especially around harvest time. Repealing Rule 9 meant more fuel for truckers, making Eizenstat a master of transactional leadership—taking from one interest group to give to another. Farmers were deeply aggrieved by the news, of course, but they decided that since their crops weren't moving from fields to grocery stores, they would reluctantly accept their fate. Meanwhile, Jack Watson, a White House assistant on intergovernmental relations, drew up federal legislation that created a "uniform national standard on weight and length during a period of declared energy emergency," removing hassles for truckers traveling across state lines. Eizenstat worked with Vice President Mondale to make sure the final negotiations with the truckers went smoothly. The most challenging job belonged to Jody Powell, who had to explain that the White House realized the legitimacy of the strikers' claims without suggesting that violence had worked.[44]

William Hill of the Independent Truckers Unity Coalition expressed caution in the face of this victory: "Statements by the President of the U.S. alone will not end this shutdown, because the independent truckers have learned from past experience that they cannot trust the government in these situations." But the White House had done more than issue words. By June 22, though there was still some lingering violence, most truckers went back to work, victors of spoils in the good old-fashioned world of interest group politics. Eizenstat and Mondale had something to show for their rationalistic approach to politics, for the moment at least.[45]

8.

On June 23, the day the White House planned to announce a peaceful resolution to the truckers' strike, the nation witnessed its first bona fide gas riot. Levittown, Pennsylvania, a tranquil suburban community, erupted into flames.

Just a few days earlier, Governor Dick Thornburgh bragged that Pennsylvania had avoided the gas crunch and could avoid New York's and New Jersey's rationing plans. Sounding like Daniel Patrick Moynihan when the New York senator lampooned Californians, Thornburgh praised his fellow Pennsylvanians for not panicking. But the next day "three out of four" gasoline stations in Lower Bucks County of Pennsylvania "were closed." The lines appeared immediately, and so too did panic. Then, something far worse.[46]

It started with a man named Bo Weaver, a disc jockey at WTTM in Trenton, New Jersey, a station that broadcast to numerous Bucks County residents. Angry at the gas crisis, Weaver rushed inside the studio. He took a sledgehammer and rusty nails and barricaded the door. Then he started playing the song "Cheaper Crude or No More Food" over and over, for three hours straight. Station owners pounded on the door while listeners called in and urged him on. Fans ordered him a pizza that delivery boys shoved under the battered door. Truckers called in thanks.[47]

Radio host Paul Harvey had popularized the song "Cheaper Crude or No More Food" earlier in the year. It was sung by Bobby Butler, an otherwise obscure country artist, to the sound of twanging guitars. Its lyrics hinted at global trade wars, warning that if the "Middle East countries" didn't "lower gas" prices then America should "lower the boom." Butler pointed out that America's farmers "fed the world." "Forget the Golden Rule," Butler sang. Stop shipping food to the Middle East until there was "cheaper crude."[48]

The song and the defiance in playing it over and over fueled Levittown's anger, but it took beautiful weather to get the citizens of Levittown out to riot on June 23. That day, truckers, not yet aware of the successful negotiations at the White House (or just not caring), started to descend on Five Points, the town's central intersection. Crowds of men in shorts and women in bikini tops gathered around four thirty P.M. to support truckers in their demand for lower diesel prices. By six thirty one trucker drove his rig into the central intersection and halted traffic. The police moved in and ordered the trucker to leave. He refused, and the police had to pull him from his truck by his legs. Fights broke out. A policeman drove the truck out of the intersection as crowds of spectators jeered. Some started to toss beer cans at the police. Suddenly, crowds surged into the intersection, and the police moved in to drag them out.[49]

The next day something even worse happened: Hordes of stoned teenagers took over Five Points. They pushed mattresses and sofas into the intersection and lit them on fire. Tires from gas stations were thrown in—flames shooting thirty feet up into the air. Kids danced and whooped. Truckers egged them on as they crashed through a police barricade. An unidentified tow truck dragged a junk car into Five Points. Kids set it aflame and then tossed watermelons from a nearby farm stand into the intersection along with rocks that smashed through the windows of a gas station and post office. Rioters descended on a

Texaco station and pushed a parked van into the intersection and torched it. They stole oil from the gas station and sprayed it everywhere. The air filled with billows of smoke, beer bottles, rocks, and firecrackers. Then the police moved in, flailing their billy clubs. The beatings started. While disorderly conduct charges were issued, hospitals filled with injured rioters.[50]

One family returned from a weekend fishing trip only to be rerouted. When the father asked what was going on, a cop whipped around and told him to get his "fucking" van out of the area and then smashed his windshield. The nineteen-year-old son jumped out and found himself walloped by a billy club. The mother tried to help her son, only to find herself in a choke hold. In whole, there were 117 arrests and many more injuries that evening. Levittown, once a place of orderly suburbia, looked like a "battle zone."[51]

A state of emergency followed. Loiterers in the Five Points area were nabbed and arrested the next day. Most of Levittown's residents were aware it was dangerous to mill around. Smokie was out, truckers told everyone on their CBs. Cops lined up at the gas stations at Five Points, keeping close watch in front of boarded-up windows. The riots had been quelled.[52]

As peace returned to Levittown, Governor Thornburgh instituted even-odd gasoline sales, admitting now that Pennsylvania wasn't that different from New Jersey or New York or California. Still, it dawned on observers that the country had witnessed a painful episode of civilizational breakdown. The *Wall Street Journal* editorialized that "the social fabric of this society is stretched tauter than anytime in a decade." Perhaps most frustrating, President Carter witnessed none of this. Levittown's local newspaper printed these words just a few days after the riot: "Meanwhile, our president looks inscrutable as he goes about his sightseeing and partying in Japan." The country was falling apart, and the president was distant, figuratively and literally.[53]

9.

The day of the riot, Carter flew on Air Force One to Japan for an economic summit with world leaders. The president wanted to build a united front among industrialized nations against the growing power of OPEC. He might have rejected the neoconservative idea of applying unilateral and military action, but he certainly didn't shun diplomatic initiatives. Before departing, he explained that what transpired in Tokyo would "affect the daily life of every American." That's not how it looked back home, and Carter's own words sounded more defensive than sincere.[54]

Carter was no more satisfied with the summit than Bucks County rioters. He would describe its first day as "one of the worst days of my diplomatic life." Valéry Giscard d'Estaing of France and Helmut Schmidt of West Germany resisted Carter's pleas for unity. France wanted warm relations with OPEC and believed America had done little to conserve energy. When Giscard d'Estaing alluded to the fact that America consumed 30 percent of the commercial energy in the world and that gas was still much cheaper in the States, Carter got angry. The German chancellor then piled on, becoming "personally abusive." Knowing that European criticism was at least partially legitimate, Carter felt paralyzed and intimidated.[55]

The relationship between America and Japan was at least more cordial but no less disturbing for Carter. The president was well aware that Japan's car manufacturers were outperforming America's. During June, Toyotas and Datsuns sold like hotcakes in the United States. The president seemed to pine for Japan's balance between industrial output and love for community and family. When asked at a press conference to reflect on what he had seen while in Japan, Carter said: "One of the great things that Americans admire about" the "Japanese is the very close-knit family and community relationships you enjoy in spite of a very great technological change that you've accommodated in your

own lives." He praised "a special grace and civility and gentleness in
your relations with each other despite the noise and the pressures of an
industrial society." These words sounded especially sad in light of
Levittown's riots.[56]

So Carter grew depressed during his overseas trip. This was devas-
tating since he usually thought diplomacy—like his successful trip to
sign SALT II with Brezhnev—could help him escape the growing
nightmare of domestic politics and the gas crisis. His only success on
this trip was to cajole the advanced countries to limit oil imports, begrudgingly in the case of France and Germany. And even those agree-
ments were soon to become moot.

10.

As the economic summit lumbered along, thirteen of OPEC's leaders met in Geneva on June 28. A debate broke out: Should the organization protest the United States' support of Israel? Muammar
al-Qaddafi of Libya said yes, threatening to cut off his country's oil,
about 7 percent of OPEC's supplies. Saudi Arabia objected, worried
the move would alienate the West and generate trade wars. A compromise was reached: OPEC would hike prices by 24 percent.[57]

The consequences for America were obvious: OPEC, after all, sup-
plied more than 80 percent of U.S. oil imports. Thus, Americans would
pay five cents more for a gallon of gas, and that gas would become
harder to find. Carter's blood boiled at the news. All the tepid hopes
coming out of the economic summit he was attending had tanked.[58]

Carter's advisers back home flipped out. Jody Powell and Jerry
Rafshoon contacted the president: Condemn OPEC *now*. Build the
drama up a bit, they suggested, as the tension back home was already
severe. Carter drafted a short message and sent it to them. Rafshoon
and Powell told him to toughen it. "It should be done with force and

a little anger. Dark suit," Rafhsoon counseled, with his usual detail to style. And so the president told the press on June 29: I will cancel my vacation after the summit, return home, and get to work on the energy crisis. *Immediately*.[59]

Before going home, Carter got his European allies to issue a statement against the price hikes. It started out with red-faced American anger: "We deplore the decisions taken by the recent OPEC conference." But then French equivocation could be heard: "We recognize that relative moderation was displayed by certain of the participants." And then the statement turned fateful: "The unwarranted rises in oil prices are bound to have very serious economic and social consequences."[60]

Carter knew just what the price hike meant for America's soft underbelly. As the White House news summary of June 27 stated: "Energy costs fuel 13 percent inflation rate." That number had a double meaning, bad luck but also just plain bad news. Inflation was killing Carter, and he knew it.[61]

Outrage at OPEC and higher oil prices had already bubbled up from the grass roots. The International Association of Machinists brought an antimonopoly lawsuit against OPEC, a complete long shot case that made members feel good rather than accomplishing anything. Ralph Nader—once Carter's ally but now angry at the president's energy policies—organized a consumer strike against higher gas prices. The people's advocate called his new organization Consumers Opposed to Inflation in the Necessities (COIN), not exactly a sexy title but adequate. But consumers were even harder to organize than independent truckers. The organization vented rage but fizzled quickly.[62]

Nonetheless, the anger was palpable, ready to boil over with the news of OPEC's price hike. Carter had gotten the message. He was homeward bound.

11.

One organization was not terribly upset about the current situation: the Republican Party of the United States. Just two days before the OPEC price hike, the GOP finished a five-day summer meeting in Minneapolis to assess the party's mood. The *New York Times* described it as "optimistic." The gas crisis was happening under Carter's watch, and now the opposition party was in an even stronger position than it could have imagined.[63]

One reason for optimism was the party's front-runner for president. The elite of the Republican Party placed their hopes in John Connally, once a Democratic governor from Texas who had headed up "Democrats for Nixon" in 1972 and then switched party affiliation and worked as the secretary of treasury under Richard Nixon. But no matter Connally's credentials and appeal across the political aisle, polling showed clearly that the grass roots of the Republican Party wanted Ronald Reagan to run for president. Reagan was believed to be more authentically conservative and had come close, after all, to deposing Gerald Ford back in 1976. He had also received the "true conservative" imprimatur from such figures as Jesse Helms.[64]

Reagan got a boost throughout May as his stiffest competition for the new right's loyalty—Philip Crane—took a nosedive. Crane was a conservative congressman from Illinois who had fought the Panama Canal treaty with verve. Crane also battled the IRS's threat to eliminate tax exemptions for private (usually religious) schools—the cause dear to Jerry Falwell's heart—and called for the full deregulation of the oil industry—a cause dear to Ronald Reagan's heart. But in May 1979, his proponents on the right started to jump ship. Richard Viguerie and Paul Weyrich, both early supporters, bolted the campaign, believing Crane had moved too far to the center. After all, Crane had refused to sponsor a human life amendment to outlaw abortion, and Viguerie knew that this could alienate the evangelicals he was trying to bring into the party in the next election. Crane's staff started to leave and his debt started to pile up.[65]

As Crane's campaign crashed, Reagan's rose. The biggest threats the governor from California faced (besides his old age) was Senator Howard Baker's run and the possibility that Gerald Ford might enter the race. By June 1979, though, Reagan was beating Ford in the polls by 5 percent. Reagan was also nineteen points ahead of Baker, who seemed too busy in the Senate to run much of a campaign. Polls in June barely registered Connally and Crane, let alone George Bush or John Anderson, two other candidates. Republican Party activists could safely label Ronald Reagan the front-runner now. Pat Caddell knew that Reagan was the man his boss would have to beat.[66]

Throughout 1979, everything seemed to fit in place for Reagan: His Citizens for the Republic was organized and active, allowing his supporters to continue to map out strategy while he built up his popularity through his radio addresses and newspaper columns. His skills as a communicator, mixing simplicity and smooth, casual delivery, had started to win him more followers. He was at his best now, giving counter-explanations to the way the world worked and the way Carter's policies didn't in his mellow voice.[67]

On June 28 Reagan was putting the finishing touches on his latest radio address about John Wayne and planning his appearance in front of Virginia Republicans on July 1, when he and Connally would face off. Reagan came across as more conservative, but what really got the crowd going was his populist bravado: "Let us reveal to the people that we are not a stodgy, fraternal organization beholden to big business and the country club set. We're the party of main street, the small town, the farmer, the city neighborhood where the working people live. Our strength comes from the shopkeeper, the craftsman, the farmer, the cop on the beat, the fireman, the blue-collar and the white-collar worker." He could have probably added to his list: the trucker. Reagan

closed by saying that in 1980, Republicans should aim—here he bor-
rowed a quote from Tom Paine—"to begin the world over again." It
was the perfect distillation of Reagan's dreamlike populism. Even better, it stole from the optimism that had marked the radical and revolu-
tionary tradition in America's past, from the language of Tom Paine.
Reagan sounded not just like a true conservative but like a politician
who could speak in the American vernacular.[68]

12.

Ham Jordan oversaw White House operations while his boss was gone.
He would talk to the president while Carter was on Air Force One and
write up memos for his return. Jordan was growing alarmed at how
bad things were going on the home front while Carter was away. He'd
write the president about the angry gas lines he saw on the television almost every day, with people shouting "What in the hell is Carter doing
in Japan and Korea when all the problems are here at home?" and he
even hinted that Carter should fire some cabinet members in order to
exert some authority. Jordan's only good fortune was that his car was
booted for too many traffic tickets so he didn't have to venture out and
get gas.[69]

Others among the president's men also worried. Rafshoon freaked
out about OPEC, of course, and must have been in a lather about
people screaming in gas lines. Hendrik Hertzberg, who had gone to
Korea in order to meet the president and talk about whatever speech
he planned to write on his return, recorded in his diary: "Back home
everything is going down the drain." He wondered how the president
could have "left on this trip without doing something, anything . . .
about the gas lines." Jody Powell, who had remained in D.C., watched
his fuel gauge hit empty and then coasted his car into a long gas line.
The only thing he could hope at this moment was that gas lines in the

nation's capital might force Congress to get behind the president's call to action. Stuart Eizenstat waited in a long gas line too and while he did, his mind drifted to a memo he was writing with fellow staff members. The memo started, appropriately enough, by labeling late June "the worst of times."[70]

Eizenstat had spent most of the month of June dealing with angry truckers. So long gas lines must have seemed a minor nuisance. Still, the thought crossed his mind: Why isn't the president here to witness this? The best way to convey what his boss was missing was to describe the crisis at home. He recounted the anger of "the truckers," the "gas lines growing," the "sporadic violence," and the "angry" complaints about the president's distance from the problems that Jordan heard every night on the television. Eizenstat recounted how Mayor Edward Koch of New York City "had not witnessed anything comparable to the current emotion in American political life since Vietnam." Eizenstat wasn't entirely comfortable with the "Vietnam analogy," but he used it. (Later in July, the *National Review* pulled no punches, arguing "Gasoline is President Carter's Vietnam.") It all seemed to add up to the apocalypse that Caddell had forecast.[71]

Like Caddell, Eizenstat coupled his "worst of times" description to "a time of opportunity." Here's your chance, he cajoled the president, to rivet your audience. Certainly, at the least, the president could reintroduce the rationing plan he had tried to get last month; this time it would likely sail through to victory. But there was more: Take on OPEC forcefully and get the nation prepared to think of itself unified as if the energy crisis was a war to be fought. Eizenstat outlined the need for "a National Energy Mobilization Board" that could steer national policy toward energy alternatives and regulate fuel consumption simultaneously. It would be modeled on federal organizations that had pulled America through World War II. "With strong steps" like this, Eizenstat assured the president, "we can mobilize the nation around a real crisis and with a real enemy—OPEC."[72]

The memo leaked to the press and became the talk of the town, at least inside the Beltway. For Carter, it meant that Caddell wasn't the only one thinking in terms of a crisis. Eizenstat was usually a well-mannered policy wonk, methodical and hardworking, not prone to outbursts. But now he was sounding an awful lot like Pat Caddell, the person Carter expected to provide memos full of hand-wringing melo-dramatics and risky ventures.

If Carter thought he could take Eizenstat's memo and come up with a speech, he had another thing coming. The day after Eizenstat wrote his, a memo from Gordon Stewart and other speechwriters hit the desks of Jerry Rafshoon and Hendrik Hertzberg. The aggravated speechwrit-ers cited "gas lines" and the "independent truckers strike" as evidence "that the social fabric is crumbling." But they warned: "We strongly ad-vise against another televised energy speech." People were too aggra-vated to listen. This wasn't exactly a writers' strike, but it came close. (Hertzberg agreed with the sentiment expressed in the memo: He didn't want to write another energy speech any more than the others did.) If a speech was written in this context, there would still be a lot of battles be-fore it was completed. The White House itself was looking more and more like a heated-up war zone, with fights brewing and personalities ready to have it out with one another.[73]

In other words, all the president's men seemed to be losing it. It was time for the president to return and get things straightened out. If he could.

13.

The day Gordon Stewart and other speechwriters balked at another speech, Jimmy Carter flew to South Korea, where he planned to plea for one of the causes closest to his heart: more human rights within countries that received American support. When reporters asked if he would return home to give a speech, the president said no. He was on his way to review the honor guard at Camp Casey in Korea. The next day, he flew from Korea to Honolulu, Hawaii, arriving early in the morning to wave to cheering supporters and be wreathed with Hawaiian leis. He then flew to the White House.

Carter's head must have percolated with questions. Where would the anger bubbling up in the nation go? Wasn't government now perceived to be part of the problem? How now to enter the situation and propose a governmental solution to the crisis? And how to break the mind-set that the oil crisis was just a hoax? Anger in the gas lines and among independent truckers could cut in all sorts of different ways.

But there was one person who was certain that this was breakthrough time. Pat Caddell was waiting in D.C. as the president flew back. He was ready to corner the president and announce: *Now is the time to go to the American public and tell them the truth about the state of the nation. Tell them to look at themselves in the mirror and wonder what they've become.* Carter was about to conclude the same.

4

"ONE OF MY BEST"

JULY 1979

This is not a message of happiness or reassurance, but it is the truth and it is a warning.

—JIMMY CARTER, JULY 15, 1979[1]

1.

Tension hung in the thick July air as Carter's helicopter touched down at the White House. What next in a nation of gas lines and riots and still no gas? Hinged to this anxiety was relief. *Finally*, at least, Carter was back home. No more foreign escapades. Learning of his impending return from Hawaii, the *New York Times* applauded the president. He had "been out of synch with events here, pretending in Vienna that Russian missiles are the nation's greatest worry and, in Tokyo, that lukewarm pledges of allied cooperation will meet the problems of oil and stagflation. Home is where the action needs to be."[2]

Home is where exhaustion set in too. Carter returned to the White House jet-lagged, stepping off a plane and moving, after a little sleep, into morning meetings with defense experts about the impending fall of Nicaragua's dictator, Anastasio Somoza, and then meeting about the energy crisis with a select group of experts. Eizenstat used this chance to talk up his idea of an energy mobilization board. Carter seemed interested but drowsy. He eyed the pile of memos in his in-box. One set out the full damage done by the truckers' strike. Jack Watson, who helped negotiate peace with the truckers along with Eizenstat, provided this account: "Some 200 incidents of shooting, 121 incidents of property damage, and 35 incidents of personal injury were reported by Justice during the period June 9-28." It was sinking in for the president. The energy crisis had torn holes in the country's civic fabric.[3]

The fact that most Americans thought he was doing an awful job confronting (or not) the situation sank in when he read recent polls about his presidency. Ham Jordan had told Carter about those where-the-hell-is-Carter cries emanating from gas lines that he watched on newscasts; now those voices translated into numbers. On July 3, one newspaper reported that Carter had the "lowest score ever accorded any president in modern political history," *even* Richard Nixon. *Nixon:* That, after all, was the presidency that helped Carter frame himself as a good-guy-outsider and that still haunted the larger project of rebuilding political trust. (The first movie Carter ever saw in the White House was *All the President's Men*, which reminded him of the awesome power and capacity for abuse that resided in the presidency.) Now Carter could read reports about how he stood "at 73 percent disapproval, two points lower than Richard Nixon in the darkest days of Watergate."[4]

Morning meetings on July 2 dragged Carter through discussions of oil import reductions, synthetic fuels, and the politics of decontrol—all wonkisms that must have barely sliced through his exhaustion. Then came an hour-long meeting in which his staff tried to persuade him to give what would be his fifth energy speech, the last being the April 5 speech that so few Americans had watched. Rafshoon and Jordan told Carter that the people needed to hear from their president at this perilous moment, that the angry gas lines were more than enough to justify another speech. Eizenstat, who always had a cooler head than Rafshoon or Jordan, concurred, making the consensus seem almost airtight. When Eizenstat was asked if he could put together an energy plan in a few days for the speech, he said, "Can do, Mr. President." The meeting concluded with the decision that Carter would give a speech about energy on Thursday, July 5.[5]

Carter left the meeting with a sense of ambivalence and exhaustion. Rafshoon was too excited to get a good read on the president's mood. He wanted a speech and had gotten at least verbal approval. So he puffed himself up, got on the phone, and called the television network pool to have them set aside an hour on the evening of July 5: "The President will address the nation next Thursday." The address would be about "energy, of course," Rafshoon explained.[6]

Rick Hertzberg had a better read on Carter during the meeting. He had dissented from Rafshoon, Jordan, and Eizenstat. "The country does not want or need another energy speech," he had told his colleagues recently. "It wants and needs energy actions." But it wasn't his job to make an executive decision. His job was to write. The command had come, so he contacted Gordon Stewart to give him the bad news. Stewart himself had already protested another speech. As he started to write it with Hertzberg, Stewart felt his heart sink. "I was just feeling worse and worse about it," he explained. "I knew it was not going to fly."[7]

Carter had his own regrets about his early return to the White House and his canceled vacation and all of those meetings he had pushed himself through. Why not leave for Camp David? he thought. That might renew his own energy. Then again, it would create an image problem: *The president went fishing while the nation continued to tear itself apart, bereft of leadership.* He would leave that to Rafshoon or Powell to explain. And so the next day, July 3, he flew to Camp David, where he fished and waited for the drafted speech to arrive.[8]

2.

"What do you mean he's canceled the speech? It's been announced," Eizenstat asked Ham Jordan on the phone. Well, he's the boss, Jordan sulked. Eizenstat knew the speech Hertzberg was working on was uninspired, but he still thought the president should give it. The country was falling apart, after all. Jordan concurred with Eizenstat and then told him to get up to Camp David the next day. They had to figure out what to do. Usually July 4, Independence Day, would be a day of rest for the staff. Not this year; this year, it would be a day for worrying and trying to figure out just what the president was up to.[9]

As usual, the burden fell to Jordan, the president's right-hand man, to rally the staff. This time, though, he did something different; he called Pat Caddell, who wasn't present at the meeting when the speech was canceled. Carter requested that the young pollster be pulled in at this moment, which likely worried Jordan. In any case, Jordan's message to Caddell followed the ones to the others: *Get to the White House tomorrow. You'll meet Eizenstat, Mondale, Rafshoon, and Powell and then helicopter to Camp David.* Figuring this was an emergency meeting, Caddell brought clothes for one night; he stayed longer than a week.[10]

Meanwhile, Jody Powell was trying to figure out ways to avoid the press. The president had told him that there was no need to explain why he canceled the speech, but Powell knew the feeding frenzy that would set in. By now, rumors about the president installing rubber wallpaper were circulating, the dollar was falling, and questions about the president's health were spreading. Before leaving for Camp David, Powell told the press the president was "assessing major domestic policy issues" that "include but go beyond the question of energy." Not even Powell knew what that meant. But it was the best he could manage.[11]

So the stage was set for all the president's men to assemble for one of the longest and most gruesome meetings in the history of the Carter administration. On July 5, from three forty P.M. until almost midnight, Eizenstat, Powell, Jordan, Rafshoon, Caddell, and Mondale duked it out in the Laurel Lodge, with Rosalynn shuffling in and out. The gloves came off. Eizenstat screamed that Caddell's ideas were "bullshit." Mondale fought off a nervous breakdown, arguing that if Caddell's ideas were put into a speech that the president might be thought crazy at worst and out of touch at best. Telling Americans of a psychic crisis—the kind that Caddell seemed obsessed with—made Carter sound like he was blaming them for the energy crisis. All the president had to do, so Mondale and Eizenstat argued, was trot out a new set of energy policies that were firmer and grounded in the sense of emergency that had taken hold. Powell and Jordan acted as mediators as this argument shaped up, trying to prevent things from getting out of control. But no matter what they did, it felt like the Carter presidency had melted down. Eizenstat called it the most "acrimonious" meeting he'd ever seen in his time in the administration.[12]

Caddell tried to seize the moment, speaking with the assuredness he'd gained over the last several months. This was his chance and he knew it. He argued that the energy situation had changed the nature of the crisis he had diagnosed back when he wrote his long memo in April. As people were stuck in gas lines and watching the truckers' strike turn violent, there was chance for what he consistently called a "breakthrough." People were ready to *listen*, to understand the severity of the broader crisis of confidence that plagued the country. The president could use a war analogy and get Americans to bond together the way they did during war. "OPEC has attacked the rest of the world, holding it ransom," he explained. Ironically, Eizenstat, whose recently leaked memo sounded like what Caddell was suggesting here, muttered something about how it wasn't so simple. Earlier that day, one of his colleagues had pointed out that "no matter how much we think OPEC" nations need our goods, "we need their oil more." Trade wars were out of the question. Eizenstat liked the war analogy up to a point; his idea of an energy mobilization board was indebted to it after all. But he worried that thinking in terms of a war could be taken too far. Besides, he went back to the point that Mondale had tried to make earlier, that what the president really needed to do was just announce a coherent energy policy. He had already provided something like that for the speech that had just been canceled.[13]

As Carter listened to this acrimonious debate, even taking his vice president for a walk at one moment in order to prevent a nervous breakdown, he made up his mind. Once again, his steely side showed. He was not going to give another energy speech of the sort he had canceled the day before. Rosalynn had already convinced him that sort of speech would doom his presidency, would force Americans to tune him out and to see him as a laughingstock, as a weak leader incapable of anything but meaningless speeches in a country that had fallen to its knees. And it was dawning on Carter that he couldn't talk about the energy crisis unless people believed there *was* a crisis, that it wasn't just the oil companies jerking them around. *That* required them to *listen* to him as president, which meant he had to address the problems in public trust that Caddell had diagnosed, those reasons they had tuned him out in the first place.

The president had brought Caddell's memo and stats with him to Camp David. He pored over them again and thought about what to do while his staff screamed at one another. As the midnight hour approached, he proposed an idea hatched with Rosalynn earlier that day—to hold a domestic summit with ordinary citizens and leaders who could discuss the state of America, including those problems discovered by his young pollster. Carter, after all, thought of himself as a listening president, as someone who loved to learn from others about what was happening. He wanted to pop the perpetual bubble in which the presidency resided. Caddell, of course, loved the idea. The president, he believed, had lost touch with ordinary citizens, especially during his foreign forays. The others likely felt a summit provided time to temper Caddell's arguments. At least the idea ended a meeting that had gone on far too long.[14]

3.

The summit began with a group of America's governors on the evening of July 6. Carter had been scheduled to give a speech at their annual meeting in Louisville, Kentucky, just as he was set to kick off his summit. Instead of canceling the appearance outright, which would have added to the nation's panic, he invited eight governors to Camp David and then dispatched his wife and Vice President Mondale to substitute for him in Louisville during the time he was scheduled to speak. Carter met the governors dressed casually and set a tone of confidence, but he also started sharing some of Caddell's findings with them.[15]

Carter did well in small groups. He looked in command while listening intently. He had broken out yellow pads of paper and started to scratch out notes. White House photographers took the opportunity to release pictures of Carter looking sane and healthy. But after Carter talked about Caddell's findings, some of the governors grew confused. One worried the president showed too much "self-deprecation," and another reported the meeting to be "a bit bizarre." Talk about the problems of the me decade—the sort that Caddell had diagnosed in his long April memo—wasn't what they expected.[16]

The next day Carter met with a wider array of people. Invitations were made hastily, creating mystery about who was there and why. Gathering for an evening meeting and a dinner of shrimp cocktail and steak came J. Lane Kirkland, secretary treasurer of the AFL-CIO; Robert Keefe, a businessman who had advised the president on numerous occasions; Barbara Newell, president of Wellesley College; and Sol Linowitz, an ambassador who had helped Carter negotiate the Panama Canal treaty. Two people from the late May dinner were there too: Jesse Jackson and John Gardner. White House organizers simply labeled the group "prominent citizens."

The strangest choice was Clark Clifford, a man who symbolized the American establishment that always made members of Carter's Georgia mafia feel like unqualified outsiders. Clifford was seventy-two years old, with a big mantle of white hair. He was tall, towering over others. More impressive was his résumé. He had risen through the ranks of Washington's circles of power, starting as President Harry Truman's counsel and then becoming secretary of defense under Lyndon Johnson after Robert McNamara left. These experiences made him one of the "wise men" who expected to be sought out for advice. Approached first by Carter's people to gain legal assistance for Bert Lance, Clifford happily entered the president's inner circles on regular occasion.[17]

Carter explained to those gathered that their meeting was off the record and that they should be honest. He scribbled in his diary, "It's not easy for me to accept criticism and to reassess my ways of doing things." If the participants noted his nervousness, they didn't show it. They let him have it. "They told me that I seemed bogged down in the details of administration, and that the public was disillusioned in having to face intractable problems like energy shortages and growing inflation after their expectations had been so elevated at the time of my election." That was a zinger—the idea that being a squeaky-clean outsider didn't translate well into actual governance, a brutal truth about Carter's presidency. They piled on more, arguing that his own secretary of energy, James Schlesinger, did him harm and was an arrogant man who brought few political benefits. At moments like these, Carter's jaw tensed up, but he took it all in, making notes. Jordan and Powell had drifted in and out during the meeting (they were the only ones Carter allowed), but then the president asked them to leave and close the door behind them. When they did, the participants ripped into them as well, arguing that they were both competent and loyal but seemed overworked and stressed.[18]

Carter asked what he should do. Jackson suggested, as he had at the late May dinner at the White House, that the president do a run around the mass media and communicate Caddell's themes directly to the public somehow. Other participants concurred that political apathy and a loss of faith in public institutions should become part of whatever speech he might sometime give. A few days after leaving Camp David, Clifford gave an interview to journalists and told them that the president worried about "malaise," a term that started to buzz and circulate inside the Beltway and throughout the press.[19]

Carter ensured some levity to counteract the intense discussions at Camp David. He tuned in the Wimbledon tennis tournament any chance he got and played with Amy or went for a swim. The next morning, he jogged with Jesse Jackson and then took a bike ride. Clark Clifford couldn't figure out the way handbrakes worked, lost control of his bike, and burned a hole in his trousers. "The last time I rode a bicycle, you reversed the pedals to stop. This time I reversed the pedals and it went faster," he recounted. The establishmentarian looked more human to the nervous Georgia mafia as he sat on his backside next to a fallen bicycle.[20]

Meanwhile Vice President Mondale whipped up support in Louisville, Kentucky, among the governors. "The country that developed synthetic rubber overnight during World War II, the country that put a man on the moon, must now create an Apollo project to produce alternative fuels." Mondale was still hoping the president might ignore his young pollster's emphasis on a nationwide psychic crisis. He believed the best way to push forward was, as he told the governors, to develop a coherent energy policy bolstered by assurance and confidence. Carter was in partial agreement with that sentiment, except he was starting to believe—having heard the bad news from those he invited to Camp David—that it required talking openly and honestly about the problems Caddell had diagnosed. Only then could confidence be made real. Carter's humility and realism demanded this. And so the president was becoming committed to giving a speech that would force Americans to face up to the civic crisis his young pollster had documented. Only then could he speak of renewing the confidence that Mondale spoke about.[21]

4.

Carter disliked *People* magazine, but copies of it could still be found lying around Camp David, perhaps brought by bored staff members to pass the time. Launched just five years before, it had become the "greatest publishing success of the 1970s." The magazine modeled itself on the "personalities" sections found in the back pages of magazines like *Time* and *Newsweek* (with their short profiles of movie stars or rock musicians). Most readers thought the magazine a rip-off of Andy Warhol's *Interview* and its treatment of celebrities, voyeurism, and gossip. *People* enjoyed peeling the curtain away from the private lives of celebrities, making it the perfect magazine for the me decade. The magazine also conflated politicians with celebrities, seeing very little difference between the two. It had slapped Jerry Brown and Linda Ronstadt on its cover in late April without suggesting much difference between California's governor and the rock star. Now the issue that hit newsstands the first week of July had the beaming, broad-smiling face of Carter's enemy, Ted Kennedy, who looked almost like a movie star on the magazine's cover.[22]

People's readers enjoyed stories about celebrities' personal problems. Kennedy provided perfect material. The scoop inside was about the "drinking problem" of his wife, Joan, and the "couple's separation." Joan admitted she might not even support her husband's potential run for the presidency. The story also documented Kennedy's exercise regimen—the man, at the time, was enormous, bloated on food and alcohol. Trimming down was placed within the context of the senator's "coquettish noncandidacy."[23]

It was getting harder to ignore the man; his face and celebrity seemed to be everywhere. So too were the mounting whispers about his candidacy. The first day of Carter's summit, a mass mailing went out to fifty thousand people to raise money for the Draft Kennedy movement. It was signed by William "Wimpy" Winpisinger, president of the International Association of Machinists and Aerospace Workers. Despite his nickname, Wimpy was a tough guy who littered his speech with swear words and a jabbing finger. "The problem with this country is not the people," he told a journalist, "It's the leadership." Wimpy thought Carter was a weakling.[24]

Wimpy had reason for hope in his call for Kennedy to run. On July 8 the Darden Research Corporation released a survey that showed Ted Kennedy running close to Carter in the South and even beating him in, of all places, Georgia. Just a few days after that, Jerry Wurf, president of the American Federation of State, County, and Municipal Employees (AFSCME), made a public statement that suggested labor unions were starting to bolt Carter. Wurf had supported Carter in 1976 but had grown disaffected. Though invited to Camp David for the summit, he secretly supported Kennedy, having grown alienated from the president's centrism and fiscal austerity. Wurf told reporters soon after leaving Camp David that his union was giving serious consideration to endorsing a Republican Party candidate for president—a first-ever that made clear how the once "Siamese" relationship between organized labor and the Democratic Party had grown fragile under Carter's leadership.[25]

For sure, Carter still thought he could whip Kennedy's ass. But the senator's rising popularity in the South and among labor leaders must have given the president pause. It likely boosted Kennedy's interest in a run. In the meantime, the liberal senator would wait to see what came out of the weird things happening at Camp David.

5.

The room in the Laurel Lodge where all of the domestic summit meetings took place had wooden walls with maps on them. Overhead lights provided a soft amber glow and shone down on a long thin table that seated numerous people. Chairs were placed on the perimeter of the room, along with small tables for coffee urns and food. Carter, of course, would sit at the head of the table, able to make eye contact with all participants. Often Rosalynn would sit next to him holding his hand and whispering into his ear, and staff members would come in and sit on the perimeter if Carter hadn't warned them away. The room provided a homey atmosphere.[26]

On July 9, members of Congress packed into the room to discuss energy policy. There was Tip O'Neill, Speaker of the House, lighting up a stogy and patting Carter on the back, assuring him that his rationing plan would make it through the House if he pushed again. Senator Robert Byrd, the majority leader from West Virginia who remained critical of Carter's policies, plied the president with the promise of coal to solve the energy crisis.[27]

That started what Carter probably expected: a meeting in which each senator or representative put forth a predictable list of demands. Senator Ted Stevens of Alaska (one of two Republicans present despite nasty rumors that none were invited) told Carter he should drill for oil in his state's wilderness areas. Senator J. Bennett Johnston from Louisiana, a conservative Democrat, suggested the president relax environmental standards to allow for more synthetic fuel development. Toby Moffett, the liberal congressman from Connecticut who had overheard Carter talk about whipping Kennedy's ass two months ago, pressed for tougher regulation of the oil industry. The first and only consensus that formed in the room was that the Department of Energy and James Schlesinger had no legitimacy. The other consensus was Carter's alone: Congress would still be a royal pain in the ass for any unified energy policy.[28]

Things turned worse the next day, July 10, during a morning meeting with economists, labor representatives, and businessmen. Lawrence Klein, an expert in the technical field of econometrics who had given Carter advice in the past, launched into a defense of decontrolling oil prices. The lanky liberal eminence John Kenneth Galbraith immediately countered with the idea of rationing. Bickering followed. The meeting got bogged down with technical issues, even though Carter tried to steer it toward things like, in the words of one participant, "people not believing their leaders, people thinking everything is a result of a conspiracy." The wonks kept circling back to technical and economic issues. Carter deemed the meeting "a waste of time." He was moving away from his inner technocrat to his inner moralist. The problem of America, he concluded, just couldn't be diagnosed purely in economic or policy-wonk terms.[29]

Carter found salvation that evening when he met with the "God Squad," a group of religious leaders and one academic sociologist. Anne Wexler, the president's special assistant known for her organizational acumen, pulled the meeting together at the last moment. She called one participant, Robert Bellah, the day before the meeting at ten thirty A.M. her time, seven thirty A.M. his time (he taught at the University of California and lived in Berkeley) and asked if he could be in Washington, D.C., the following day. Curiosity as much as excitement compelled Bellah, and he found himself the next evening on a helicopter with a wide assortment of religious leaders heading for Camp David.*

Carter greeted them with a sense of relief, believing this would be better than the last meeting. He welcomed them in "Christian fellowship." Then as they sat down, Carter said he felt "lonely" and worried about his isolation from the country. The group exuded support, convincing the president that the problems the country faced were not his alone. After making some preliminary comments about the spiritual crisis, Carter sat back and listened as these religious thinkers started to write key elements of the speech that he was now preparing in his mind and on paper.

Marc Tanenbaum saw Carter as a Moses going into the wilderness to find his first principles, and he quickly offered a "vision of America" the president could bring with him off the mountain. Tanenbaum opened by saying how symbolic it was to be at Camp David, in the same room where the president had hammered out Middle Eastern peace. Draw on those qualities of leadership now, he counseled. He then set the historical context: "We have passed from an era of superabundance to an era of growing scarcity of resources." Tanenbaum railed against "unrestrained consumerism" and "mindless self-indulgence." The energy crisis forced a critical reexamination of our nation's values. "How do we achieve personal happiness that does not depend on the endless accumulation of goods? It will come down, ultimately, to moral will. It will come down to who we are, what we stand for, and our will to

---

* The list included: Reverend Otis Moss Jr., a Baptist pastor in Cleveland; David Preus, president, American Lutheran Church; Claire Randall, general secretary, National Council of Churches; Jimmy Allen, former president, Southern Baptist Convention; Reverend Patrick Flores, Roman Catholic bishop in El Paso, Texas; Cardinal Terence Cooke, New York; Theodore Hesburgh, president, Notre Dame University; Archbishop Iakovos, Greek Orthodox archdiocese of North and South America; and Marc Tanenbaum, national director, Interreligious Affairs, American Jewish Committee.

change." This posed a special challenge to Americans who thought of themselves as the "chosen people" blessed by God's abundance. Carter started coming alive at this moment, and as he looked around the room, he noticed other participants nodding affirmatively.[30]

Robert Bellah was nodding too. He pushed his large scholarly glasses onto his nose, looked at notes he jotted down on his plane ride, and then started giving his own advice. He suggested the president frame Tanenbaum's remarks within the historical tradition of "the covenant." In his fifties with a comfortable academic career, Bellah was a democratic socialist and still a committed idealist. A Marxist in his youth, he now transferred his faith into "civil religion," what he called the "religious dimension found in the life of every people through which it interprets its historical experience in the light of transcendent reality." The American language of covenant, he was quick to point out, descended from the Puritans who developed the City on the Hill ideal. "In the covenant model," Bellah once explained, "people participate in each others' lives because they are mutually committed to values that transcend self-interest." Bellah contrasted this with the language of "contract." Reviving the language of covenant could renew a "civic consciousness" and challenge the narcissism Tanenbaum derided.[31]

Bellah then doubled back on himself. The ideal of the "chosen people" could just as easily turn nasty, prompting Americans to embark on imperial ambitions overseas. "We must remember that the best and the worst in a society are often closely related." Bellah warned Carter that he shouldn't "just give a speech that said OPEC was at fault." Carter assured him: "It would be rather self-righteous to blame it all on OPEC. Americans don't like it when a foreign country can interfere in our life, but we've been interfering in OPEC countries' and most other countries' lives rather heavily for a long time." Bellah was shocked by the statement. He could never imagine Nixon or Ford saying something like that.[32]

Finally, Carter started to panic. The president had decided now that he must give a speech to the nation. But all the counsel provided by the God Squad added up to an intense indictment of the American way of life, of consumerism, greed, selfishness, and materialism. So he turned to Bellah and asked: "How much can the American people take?" "Scold" and "grouch"—words Mondale used in his warnings about Caddell's ideas—still rang in the president's head. Bellah reassured the president: *Don't worry about politics. It's time that the American people heard some difficult truths.* Become a "teaching president," an idea remarkably similar to James MacGregor Burns's concept of "transformational leader." A good speech could be precisely the time in which he could become such a leader.[33]

Carter was thrilled by the meeting. It offered him the language he was searching for—especially the covenant and jeremiad (ideas Caddell had already suggested but that the God Squad had shown had deep roots in America's past). Carter closed the meeting by asking Tanenbaum to give the last prayer. The participants held hands, knowing they had just witnessed a unique episode in the history of presidential advising. Religion had entered the public square, not in the way Jesse Helms or Jerry Falwell wanted, but in a way that might help Americans get through the energy crisis with a sense of higher national purpose. Instead of religion squaring itself with self-interest and the free market—key elements in Jerry Falwell's and Jesse Helms's worldview—religion here took a distinctly Niebuhrian turn, prompting questions about the limits of selfishness. So on the evening of July 10, Carter must have slept soundly, knowing that he would make a speech informed by religious ideas dear to his heart—about sin and selfishness and about those national values, like the idea of a covenant, that could push the country out of the crisis it presently faced.

One person remained silent throughout the meeting with the God Squad. Hendrik Hertzberg had just traveled to Camp David and was thrilled by what he heard in the room. Clearly he was drawn to Bellah's democratic socialist leanings, but, more important, he was relieved that none of the conversation added up to just another energy speech. He had no regrets when the president had shredded the speech that he and Gordon Stewart had written up in haste just six days ago. What he heard in the room—the language of covenant and the criticism of consumerism—seemed ideas he could incorporate into a much-improved speech, in fact, a completely new speech. The next day Hertzberg got to work. Gordon Stewart soon joined him.

6.

There had been Three Mile Island in late March and the DC-10 crash in May. Now NASA's Skylab was catapulting toward earth. It was to hit on July 11. "The largest craft ever put into earth's orbit," Skylab weighed 77.5 tons and was "the size of a three room house." When entering the atmosphere, it would travel at 260 miles per hour and be 2,192 degrees hot. Launched into space six years ago as a work station for astronauts, the government couldn't shoot it down or direct its course.[34]

National buzz surrounded Skylab's descent. Clubs formed throughout America to take bets on where Skylab would land. Members printed T-shirts, hats, and signs that read: LAND HERE! There were bumper stickers that blurted: "THE SKYLAB IS FALLING! THE SKYLAB IS FALLING!" And in Washington, D.C. Chicken Little Associates organized to monitor Skylab's crash location.[35]

In the end, Americans didn't need to worry. Skylab hit on July 11 as expected, but it did so far away from America, exploding in a big blaze over the Indian Ocean, with debris shooting over the Australian desert.

Carter got on the phone and apologized to the Australian prime minister; fortunately, Aborigines in the outback had reported no injuries.[36]

But Skylab still worried Americans. Its story held its own miniature crisis of confidence by fitting a broader narrative: Technology no longer seemed something promising a better future but rather a monster, a Frankenstein gone berserk. Science had created forces that stung their creators, that whiplashed and punished more than they benefited.

The story also highlighted growing distrust in government. When warnings about Skylab came out in 1976, NASA denied them, but two years later reversed itself. Especially depressing was how Skylab's fall closely coincided with the tenth anniversary of America's first moon landing. President Nixon had called that event "the greatest" event "since the creation of the world." The hero at its center, astronaut Neil Armstrong, had gone on to become a professor at the University of Cincinnati. A less illustrious turn in his career occurred in 1979 when he became an advertising spokesperson for Chrysler, which lost money hand over fist during the last years of the 1970s while trying consistently cheesy commercial campaigns to recover. Every time Armstrong was interviewed, though, he criticized his country for being stingy with the space program's budget. It seemed further testimony to Americans' fall from those grand old days when President Kennedy promised that the country's race to space ensured its national greatness and that he would provide public resources to fulfill that dream.[37]

Perhaps the best way to understand Skylab's meaning in the context of July 1979 was a cartoon printed in *U.S. News & World Report*. It showed a husband and wife waiting in a long gas line, exhausted but exhilarated as they approached the pumps. The husband says wide-eyed, "Seven hours, honey—after 7 hours in line we're just one car away! Nothing can stop us now!" And right above them was Skylab about to fall on their car.[38]

7.

Bill Clinton was then a thirty-two-year-old governor of Arkansas, having served the state as attorney general. Ham Jordan saw him as a rising star among the Democrats, bringing new energy to a party that had fallen on hard times. So he invited him to Camp David. When Clinton sat in the Laurel Lodge conference room on July 11, he listened to the president decry the nation's spiritual state and then told Carter to be more relaxed when he gave his next speech. The boy governor also suggested the president find a bridge between executive action and citizen participation, between a top-down and bottom-up approach. "I strongly urged," Clinton explained, to show how the "federal government" could help develop "alternative sources of energy" and promote "conservation." But at the same time, "this is not a problem which government alone can solve. Every individual citizen in this country has a role to play." Invite ordinary citizens into the public realm, for sure, the governor implored, but expect something back from them. Clinton hammered the message home: "What people are looking for is someone who will" endorse a "war of independence" in which "everybody has some role and some mission to play."[39]

The other citizens gathered around the table on July 11—labor union spokespeople, businessmen, civil rights activists, a senator, and another governor—agreed with Clinton. Benjamin Hooks of the National Association for the Advancement of Colored People (NAACP) told Carter to "come out fighting" and exert his leadership, like a leader during war. Vernon Jordan from the National Urban League pushed Carter to "preach the right sermon." He hoped Carter would link the theme of spiritual decline to the energy crisis. By the end of the meeting, Carter had written down numerous quotes he wanted to use in his forthcoming speech.[40]

The voice of citizens entering the public forum—the idea of not just an educating president or a transformative president but a *listening* president—was starting to take hold. This wouldn't be pandering or allowing citizens off the hook. This had to be a national conversation, a back and forth between leader and citizen.

Caddell was in love with this idea. He had been pressing the president to go out and talk to regular citizens in order to remain in touch. Much earlier, he suggested the president do town hall meetings or maybe even one-on-one meetings in the White House. When Daniel Bell suggested the president write personal letters and when Bill Moyers talked about having meetings with citizens in the White House during their May dinner with Carter, the idea reasserted itself. Now Caddell was well positioned to turn this sort of idea into reality. He got some assistants to find ordinary citizens who might be interested in meeting with the president (or at least with representatives from the White House) to talk about what ailed America. The research was done off the cuff; families were interviewed quickly and memos drafted about their background, political affiliation, and general demographics. Caddell sorted through them to plan the impending visit.

On the evening of July 11, Carter, Rosalynn, Caddell, and some other White House staff took a flight from Camp David to the closest thing resembling America's heartland—Carnegie, a suburb just outside the city of Pittsburgh (close to where parts of *The Deer Hunter* were filmed). There Carter met William Fisher, a twenty-nine-year-old machinist for the Power Piping Company who was married with an infant daughter. Fisher was joined on his back porch by steelworkers, a carpenter, and a county employee. Expecting representatives from the White House (including Caddell), they panicked when learning the president himself would be present. They weren't even sure they'd have enough food for everyone. Secret Service men circled their home, as the Fisher family and their friends tried to figure out what to say. As they sat in lawn chairs and listened to Carter, they decided to come clean. Fisher argued that the country was in a "downhill spiral" and was shocked to find Carter shaking his head, saying *yes*.[41]

8.

The next day, a twenty-four-year-old disc jockey for WLUP-FM ("The Loop") in Chicago made history. Steve Dahl had quit one radio station after it abandoned AOR (album-oriented rock) for disco. He immediately formed the Disco Destruction Army at WLUP, wearing fatigues and a military helmet during public appearances. The whole military look had a whiff of fascism to Dahl's critics. When he encouraged listeners to smash disco records, the idea of book burnings rushed to some people's minds.[42]

Whatever Dahl's motivations, he found an unlikely ally in Bill Veeck, president of the Chicago White Sox, whose baseball team had fallen on hard times. Veeck wasn't drawing crowds to watch ball games at Comiskey Park the way he wanted. So he sought promotional gimmicks. "Disco Demolition Night" sounded like a good idea. If fans brought a disco record to the park, they'd get in for next-to-nothing. The "demolition"—blowing up a big vault of the records fans brought to the stadium—would happen between games of a doubleheader between the White Sox and the Detroit Tigers the evening of July 12.

The Tigers beat the White Sox in the first game, and their pitchers descended on the field to practice for the second just as Steve Dahl drove out in a Jeep and trademark military garb. The crowds chanted "Disco Sucks!" and threw beer cans down on Dahl. They lit up joints and torched John Travolta dolls laced with firecrackers. Dahl whipped up the crowd and told them to direct their attention toward the back of the field where the vault of records stood. *Kaboom!* The whole thing went up in flames.[43]

And then what should have been expected to happen happened: Hundreds of kids streamed onto the field. A few climbed the foul pole to dangerous heights, others tore up chunks of sod on the field. Dahl escaped to the press box and watched the whole thing unravel. The crowds turned over batting cages and lit the field on fire as "Back to your seats" chants came over the sound system. Veeck sang "Take Me Out to the Ball Game," in a pathetic attempt to quell the mob. But neither his nor Dahl's pleas worked. The only thing that did was releasing the cops on the crowds. In the end, the riot forced the White Sox to forfeit the second game.[44]

Some people pondered what the rampage meant. It was certainly the country's first full-fledged riot against disco. The music industry, like the oil industry, appeared out of touch. Just two months after Blondie's "Heart of Glass" blasted to the top of the charts and led industry leaders to think that the disco genre assured profits, record sales actually started to plummet. The chants of "Disco Sucks!" at Comiskey Park had initiated a cultural revolution of sorts.[45]

Gay and civil rights activists worried, though, that this was a revolt against anything upsetting heterosexual whiteness, the stoner equivalent of the Moral Majority. There was some truth to the charge. But in a place like Chicago, economic resentment mattered as much. The first six months of 1979 saw the proliferation of discotheques throughout the city; most set up shop on North Rush Street—a trendy and wealthy neighborhood (eventually labeled "yuppie" in the 1980s). The kids who cheered Dahl were the long-haired working-class guys who had problems affording the paraphernalia—gold chains and polyester suits—necessary for discotheques. Their resentment took the form of angry populism the evening of July 12. They almost seemed allied to the angry truckers and Levittown rioters.[46]

Maybe the kids descended on the baseball field because they hated disco and because of the music's association with the me decade. Then again, maybe it wasn't necessary to analyze the event at all.

Consider it by its first appearances: On the field were kids stoned out of their minds, going on a rampage, looking a lot like the kids who had set fire to Levittown less than a month earlier. It seemed like another example of a nation turned unruly, perhaps for the sheer sake of being unruly.

9.

Friday the thirteenth. An appropriate day for Carter to meet with journalists. Writers and broadcasters were brought by helicopters to Camp David, unsure why. Jody Powell told them the meeting was off the record. They could listen but not report.

Most went in search of Jimmy Carter's state of mind, finding it troubled and troubling. Hugh Sidey of *Time* saw Carter as a "yellow-pad President," entranced by conversations with citizens but unable to lead. Carl T. Rowan, opinion writer for the *Chicago Sun-Times*, described the president as being "brutally honest about himself" but rather "tired." The famous anchorman for CBS News, Walter Cronkite, found the president a "deeply troubled man."[47]

David Broder came to a different conclusion, seeing more confidence and vindication in the president's mind-set. Broder's memory traveled back through the years to Carter's April 1977 speech when the president announced his National Energy Policy (NEP) and called for a "moral equivalent of war" against the energy crisis (now derisively referred to as the MEOW speech). That was an underrated speech, Broder thought, and perhaps he could do it again but with more gusto this time. Broder's hopefulness was echoed in the thoughts of the journalist H. Brandt Ayers, a columnist for the *Anniston (Alabama) Star*, who believed Carter was figuring out how to speak to a country that had lost "its innocence."[48]

Jack Germond, a political journalist from the *Washington Star* who enjoyed covering the rough and tumble of politics, was the most honest. He admitted that he couldn't figure out *what* was happening. He grew more confused when Rosalynn intervened in the discussion and recounted a meeting she and Jimmy had earlier that morning. The president and first lady had just returned from the home of the Porterfields in Martinsburg, West Virginia, their second visit to heartland America. Numerous citizens, recruited in the same way the Fishers in Carnegie, Pennsylvania, were, joined a give-and-take meeting in Martinsburg. Rosalynn explained to Germond and the others that citizens worried about inflation but seemed hopeful about the country uniting to overcome the energy crisis. Germond thought: Did the president really need to meet with citizens to figure out they worried about inflation and the energy crisis?[49]

As the journalists scratched their heads, Carter's speechwriters were close by pounding typewriters. The president had now demanded a speech different from the one aborted for July 5. The new date had been chosen: July 15, a Sunday. That day, the president would descend from his mountain retreat and address the nation about a "crisis of confidence." Time was now pressing in on his writers.

Rafshoon had corralled both Hertzberg and Stewart into a cabin where he'd pick up drafts and then shuffle to the Aspen Lodge to get the president's feedback. Rafshoon still wanted to tone down Caddell's more "apocalyptic" and "negative" tone, but Carter held firm. They agreed that quotes from people at Camp David should be included. But the speechwriters had to massage those, and so did Carter as he worked on revisions. For instance, Jesse Jackson had said during the meeting on July 7: "Our vital organs are stretched over the fence, and our neighbors in OPEC have the knife." That sounded gross and extreme and so was changed to: "Our neck is stretched over the fence, and the people in OPEC have the knife." Carter also insisted the speech be moral rather than sociological, taking his cue from the God Squad. One draft had decried "leisure, mobility, and

consumption." Carter changed that to "self-indulgence and consumption," which sounded less historically analytical and more morally castigating. The speech was starting to take shape.[50]

Finally, Hamilton Jordan gathered the speechwriters together with
Caddell and Eizenstat. "How's it going?" Jordan asked with his
southern twang. The speechwriters handed what they had to Eizenstat. He skimmed it and grew alarmed. He knew full well he had lost
the battle with Caddell. But there was next to nothing about energy
policy here, he argued. The writers and staff started to bicker. Gordon Stewart fixed Eizenstat in his sights, and said: "*OK, give it to us.*"
Suddenly all of the thinking Eizenstat had done since his June 28
memo came pouring out of his head, and Stewart scribbled away.
Eizenstat gave them six points—the typical bullet-point language of
a wonk—that served as Carter's energy policy in the speech and from
that point on.[51]

Stewart and Hertzberg pondered these six points, which ranged
from limiting exports to creating the energy mobilization board Eizenstat had recently proposed. How could these points be grafted onto
Caddell's language of civic crisis? Too often in the past, the president
would just cut and paste different ideas together, creating disjointed
speeches. So Stewart and Hertzberg worked up a transition where the
president could explain that if the country tried to confront the energy
crisis, it could come together to solve the broader civic crisis. It still
seemed like two speeches, but they appeared at least tentatively hinged.

This editing job also allowed for an optimistic twist to a gloomy
speech. Mondale had warned against the "grouch" factor up to the
day of the speech, and even Caddell believed "opportunity" must be
twinned with "crisis." The president's own theology served him well
here. He had read Niebuhr and wanted to speak about sin and humility. But there needed to be some uplift that stemmed from Norman Vincent Peale, a contemporary of Reinhold Niebuhr who had
famously developed the idea of "positive thinking" in Christian

theology. God's blessings must provide signs of health, Peale had counseled in his bestselling books written during the 1950s (as did Carter's own sister, Ruth Carter Stapleton, when she claimed in a 1979 book that accepting Jesus cured her "lower back pains"). Only with indicators of redemption could believers be motivated enough to change their behavior. American Christianity could serve as uplift—promising salvation for those who opened their hearts to Christ—as much as a confession of sin and critical self-examination. Carter hoped his civil religion could do the same by combining Niebuhr with Peale, Caddell with Mondale, and thus crisis with opportunity.[52]

The final draft of the speech included just a bit of Rafshoon's optimism as well, which sounded mostly hortatory in this context. Consider the line: "Whenever you have a chance, say something good about our country." That sounded out of sync with the rest of the speech, like a moment of boosterism amidst a list of the nation's sinful faults. Rafshoon, of course, had wanted more, but it would have to suffice. The president had sided, for the most part, with Caddell, insisting this was no time for cheer.[53]

Rafshoon talked with not just the speechwriters but a young and savvy aide who worked for him. Greg Schneiders, who had owned a Washington, D.C., bar before joining Carter's team, was managing things back at the White House while Rafshoon was at Camp David. Schneiders wrote his boss, "People listen to Presidential speeches the way they listen to rock music." They usually get the "tone, the beat, the rhythm" but little content. Make sure you work with the president on how he looks and sounds, Schneiders counseled. How well my protégé learns, Rafshoon must have thought. This time, Rafshoon *would* work with the president on delivery, no matter if Carter wanted to or not. It was too damn important. They had spent over a week on this thing—one of the weirder weeks in the history of the Carter administration—and he wouldn't let Carter's poor delivery skills blow it.[54]

10.

July 14 had been spent in a most peculiar way for Carter. Much of it took place in a room usually reserved for church services at Camp David. Jerry Rafshoon had turned the space into a rehearsal studio, a stand-in for the Oval Office. With cameras pointed at him, Carter read the speech, and then Rafshoon reviewed the tapes, pointing out flubs. Rafshoon kept telling him: *Speak with your hands. Talk louder. Don't flash your grin all the time.*[55]

Gordon Stewart was still at Camp David that day too, putting finishing touches on speeches that would follow the next day's. He walked into the president's rehearsal and started to think about all of the techniques learned in his drama classes in graduate school that he had applied on Broadway. Stewart was alarmed at how Carter still mumbled and told him so. "I'm sorry, I didn't hear that," the speechwriter said. Carter looked up flustered, then continued with more volume. Stewart still worried that Carter's delivery was too flat. He didn't get into the moment or think about those listening to what he was saying. In one last effort to make his point, Stewart told Carter he was getting bored and was going to leave the room. Carter got angry. The president became louder, more animated, using his hands to speak. At that moment, Stewart blurted out, "Now you've got it."[56]

Carter hated being coached this way, just as he hated listening to criticisms of his presidency. But too much rode on this speech. One of his advisers had been quoted in the *New York Times* as saying, "If you don't have something to say in the first five minutes and you don't grab public attention then, you won't have it for the rest of your Presidency." The political stakes were high—the speech was a tarot card about the president's future. The *Wall Street Journal* had declared, "Some view the outcome of the 1980 presidential election as hinging on Mr. Carter's handling of the energy issue." And it wasn't just conservatives who believed that. Democratic National Committee chairman John White commented on Carter's speech and said, "It's the most dramatic thing he's ever done. He's really pushed all his chips into the middle of the table."[57]

Around six P.M. on July 14, after having done as much rehearsing as he could, Carter hopped on a copter back to the White House. Usually when he flew in from Camp David to the White House, an army of reporters and photographers gathered on the lawn to shout questions or snap pictures. But when the president's helicopter touched down this evening, no press was in sight. Powell had barred the media. An aura of mystery shrouded the president's return, just as when the president had disappeared to Camp David ten days earlier.

11.

At ten P.M. EST, on Sunday, July 15, some television viewers watched *The Gambler*, a 1974 movie about an English professor addicted to betting tables. CBS broadcast *Moses the Lawgiver*, in which Burt Lancaster played the prophet who came down from Mount Sinai with the Ten Commandments. Then came Carter, the gambler and prophet who descended the Catoctin Mountains with his own commandments.[58]

On ABC, an announcement flashed on the screen: *The Gambler* would return later. Then these words: "The President Speaks: Energy and the Nation" emblazoned on a shot of the White House lit with dim floodlights. Frank Reynolds of ABC told viewers they would watch "the most eagerly awaited speech of the Carter presidency." It was also the biggest audience Carter ever wrangled.

The president wore a dark blue suit and gray-and-blue tie. He sat at his desk in the Oval Office with his hands folded. He smiled nervously. And then he said, "This is a special night for me. Three years ago I accepted the nomination of my party to run for president of the United States. I promised you a president who is not isolated from the people, who feels your pain." The camera moved in. Carter started to pick up his hands from the desk in order to talk.

The president recounted how he had canceled his July 5 speech. "I began to ask myself," he said, "the same question that I now know has been troubling many of you. Why have we not been able to get together as a nation to resolve our serious energy problem?" With those words, he made a fist. He mentioned "gasoline lines" and the "deeper" problems plaguing America. Then he softened: "And I realize more than ever that as president I need your help." He talked about his ten days at Camp David, reading, from a set of notecards, the quotes he had written down, pausing between each quote, smiling or biting his lip. Some of the quotes were quite alarming, especially the first: "Mr. President, you are not leading this nation—you're just managing the government."

Then after putting down the cards, his voice got louder as he moved into his jeremiad. "All the legislation in the world can't fix what's wrong with America," he declared. The "threat" to America— and here Carter swept his hands around and looked almost confused for a moment—"is nearly invisible." This was a "crisis of *confidence*," and the fist came down again, accentuating the word "confidence," as he would over and over throughout the speech. The crisis included "self-indulgence and consumption" and an accompanying decline in civic participation ("two thirds of our people do not even vote"). He let out this profound thought: "Human identity is no longer defined by what one does, but by what one owns." The president now was condemning the American way of life established in the wake of World War II. He worried that private self-satisfaction created a "disrespect for government." He argued that Americans were "losing faith" in the idea of "progress," a gloomy prognosis that drew from Caddell's numbers. The people, Carter intoned, had been heard from, their concerns registered, but the president would not allow them to shirk his moral inventory.

Before he sounded like he was blaming Americans for the crisis, he glanced backward at history—at the "murders of John Kennedy and Robert Kennedy and Martin Luther King," "the agony of Vietnam," and "the shock of Watergate." There was "inflation" and the country's "growing dependence on foreign oil." These "wounds are still very deep." This was not purely a psychological crisis but a historical crisis rooted in very real events.

The loss of faith in public institutions created a "gap between our citizens and our government." Evoking the language of good government reformers—both the progressives of the early twentieth century and those who joined Common Cause during the 1970s—he damned "a Congress twisted and pulled in every direction by hundreds of well-financed and powerful special interests." Government's inaction mirrored the "fragmentation and self-interest" that took hold of the country's citizens.

"What can we do?" Carter asked. His voice lilted up, almost playing a musical scale with each word in the question, as he looked at the camera.

There was a forked road, he insisted. There was first the possibility the theologian Niebuhr had warned about: "Down that road lies a mistaken idea of freedom, the right to grasp for ourselves some advantage over others." But there was another possibility, to face the energy crisis realistically. "Energy will be the immediate test of our ability to unite this nation." He then launched into Stuart Eizenstat's bullet points: Limit our reliance upon foreign oil by setting "import quotas"; invest in "massive funds" to "develop America's own alternative sources of fuel"; create "an energy security corporation" and "energy mobilization board"; tax the gas companies to fund these proposals; and create a "bold conservation program" that will involve "every average American in our energy battle." All of this would be done while ensuring that the poorest citizens didn't suffer from rising fuel prices.

Carter suggested that this war against the energy crisis would not "be easy," for there was not a "quick way out of our nation's problems." And then Carter motioned with his hands, reaching out to the camera and then back to himself. "We will act together," he said. "It is time for us to join hands in America." At that point, he clasped his hands together, as if symbolizing what had taken place at Camp David and in the private homes in Pennsylvania and West Virginia. "Thank you and good night."

The whole thing was over in a little more than thirty-two minutes. The cameras faded and then Frank Reynolds came on. He looked slightly stunned as he called the speech "remarkable." It was, in the newscaster's words, "almost a sermon."

12.

Immediately after Carter exited the Oval Office, the White House phone lines lit up. White House operators couldn't handle the number of calls pouring in. Thousands of Americans telephoned, 84 percent of them supporting the speech. Over the next few weeks, the postal service found it hard to manage the mail coming into the White House. There were more letters than those received when Richard Nixon announced the invasion of Cambodia or when Gerald Ford pardoned Nixon. Except in this case, the letters were positive: 85 percent of them oozed with praise for the president's speech.[59]

The response suggested a counterintuitive reaction to the speech. The American people didn't think the president blamed them for their problems; instead, many embraced his jeremiad. More than might have been expected believed the country's way of life—consumerism and impulsive self-interest—held self-destructive tendencies. They wanted a leader who inventoried the nation's spirit and asked serious questions about its past and future. This was the speech's magic and why it resonated.

Robert Bellah's advice had worked: The president had spoken honestly and had reminded Americans of their national "covenant." A recent and fairly obscure little book entitled *The American Jeremiad* had shown how Americans, since the time of the Puritans, consistently talked about decline and resurrection, effectively hardwiring that kind of rhetoric into the American subconscious. The author, a Canadian scholar named Sacvan Bercovitch, traced the jeremiad, as did Bellah, back to the Puritans. Bercovitch didn't see those settlers as dour or pinched in their sensibilities. In fact, though the jeremiad used chastising language, it had an optimistic undertone. A reviewer of Bercovitch's book in the *New York Review of Books*, just four days after Carter's speech, had pointed out that "the distinguishing characteristic of the jeremiad . . . was not its condemnation of backsliding . . . but its prophetic assurance of a bright future." Carter had hoped—and was proven right, it seemed—that the jeremiad tradition might still work in the summer of 1979, even if framed more from the perspective of civil religion than Puritanism.[60]

The letters to the White House confirmed this. Thomas Winslow wrote from Malden, Massachusetts, the night he heard the speech: "You are the first politician that [*sic*] has said the words that I have been thinking for years. Last month I purchased a moped to drive to work with. I plan to use it as much as possible, and by doing so I have cut my gas consumption by 75 percent." Judith Avery in Brookings, Oregon, wrote, "The American people are so spoiled, so wasteful." The day after the speech Mrs. William Schriever of Orient, New York, typed a note: "To me it is unconscionable that we Americans let our love of luxurie [*sic*] consume us as we consume oil." One woman from Texas handwrote the president: "Jimmy, you are a dear

Christian man. You are like a Moses trying to lead us to freedom. Every time you turn your back we turn to Pagan idols (Gas, money, and material things)." And so on.[61]

As these letters poured in, journalists across the country tried to get the full scoop on the speech. Those at *Newsweek* labeled it Carter's "best," but even they were surprised when they examined the poll numbers. The president's approval "zoomed 11 points over night" after the speech. That was the biggest bump he ever received and ever would after giving a speech. How could a castigating president wind up bumping his numbers? It all seemed so strange.[62]

Carter followed up with two appearances on July 16, in Kansas City and Detroit. He spoke more specifically on the energy policies he had outlined and received warm responses at both events. He also stepped back and recognized the radical nature of what he had just done: "Last night I sounded a warning in harsh terms, terms not often used by a president speaking to the people of our country." He reiterated his intention to unify the nation. "On the battlefield of energy," he explained, "this democracy which we love is going to make its stand." The speech now required mobilization at the grass roots. His audiences at both appearances, it bears noting, gave him standing ovations.[63]

Unsurprisingly, the first to join Carter on the battlefield were religious leaders who advised him at Camp David. Marc Tanenbaum called a meeting with his fellow God Squad members and issued a public statement: "The energy crisis facing our nation points to a greater moral crisis—the apparent inability of Americans to unite behind worthy goals." They pleaded a "common good" against the "materialism" dominant in American life and explained how their faith required a war on energy dependence and selfish individualism. Tanenbaum simultaneously planned a conference on the interesting topic of "the theology of waste."[64]

When he heard about the letters and phone calls, the president's follow-up speeches, and the bump in the polls, Hendrik Hertzberg grew proud. He had been there when the God Squad had presented the language of covenant to the president. He had balked at the original speech and hoped to contribute to a more honest speech that confronted the difficulties Americans faced during the summer of 1979. He wanted the president to speak about what brought Americans together in unity, rather than what turned them apart. He knew that Carter could speak the American vernacular and touch ordinary citizens if he tried. He also knew the president could have laid low, waited for the even-odd sales systems to work their magic, and allowed the gas crisis to pass. He could have rested once his staff quelled the truckers' strike. Instead, he gambled and took the risk of talking honestly about Americans' problems. Hertzberg believed the speech symbolized "in the most unorthodox and extraordinary way, the president of the United States speaking truth."[65]

13.

Problems nonetheless emerged quickly, as they would be expected to for a president whose numbers had sunk so low in the polls before they bumped after the speech. There were clear cracks in the wall of Carter's breakthrough. The first was ironic. The energy crisis had lessened as Carter holed up at Camp David. Most of the nation's gas lines waned as the even-odd sales policies started to work. By July 11, the *New York Times* reported that gas lines were "dwindling." Thus, the "battlefield" Carter alluded to in Kansas City—the sense of gripping emergency that the gas lines had prompted—was sinking under his feet. The screaming and violence on the gas lines riveted attention on the president, but would citizens listen now? Of course, the ultimate gas crisis—America's dependency on foreign oil—was just as strong as ever, but the urgency had waned in a country with short attention spans, one where violence, anger, and fights fixated attention more than anything.[66]

There was another problem. Certainly many citizens who watched the president on television liked what they saw. The phone calls and letters testified to that. But the media had a distinct spin that interrupted the direct communication between president and citizen. For instance, after Frank Reynolds came on ABC and called the speech "remarkable," Sam Donaldson bounded on the screen to call Carter's speech an "extraordinary performance." Such praise, if that was what it was, hinted at the problem that Rafshoon's presence in the White House had already suggested: the problem of authenticity, the difficulty in distinguishing between real leadership and image and between truth-telling and a performance.

This problem of authenticity was highly ironic, for Carter confronted the problem directly in his speech. Caddell, in his original April memo, had pointed out that a new set of "technicians" who crafted politicians' appearances had further denigrated politics (Caddell included himself here), replacing "character" with image. Carter himself had recognized that there was "growing disrespect for government" and an understandable "gap between our citizens and our government" during his speech. But it didn't register for him how the media posited itself between citizens and government and spun messages through its lens of cynicism and jadedness.[67]

Soon after the speech, Hugh Sidey wrote a piece that *Time* headlined, TRYING TO SHOW HIS TOUGHNESS. Carter, it was suggested, wasn't talking about an issue nor tackling complex questions; he was putting on a show, the "performance" Donaldson had alluded to earlier. The journalist Jack Germond, who was confused by his July 13 meeting between journalists and the president, explained the speech this way: Carter wanted to forget he was president and turn himself back into a political candidate using the formula that won him office in 1976. The *New Republic* expanded this cynical line of reasoning. The president's disappearance, domestic summit, and speech were, for these liberal editors, so much "Rafshoonery," a hoax to build drama. "Even at his most serious," the magazine's editors would conclude later, Carter "is concerned only with the appearance of things." Carter hadn't thought hard enough about the fact that though he could cut through the cynicism for a moment in his speech, the news media would be reporting it immediately through its filter. And citizens were affected by the reporting, no matter what Carter hoped. Jesse Jackson's dream of doing a run around the mass media was never a possibility.[68]

This dynamic became amazingly circular: The fixation with "appearance" and spin was due in large part to the media's reception of the speech. Soon after the "crisis of confidence" speech was given, "malaise," a word Carter never used within it, became its keyword. Clark Clifford's interview with journalists soon after meeting with the president on July 7 initiated the idea that the speech would be about "malaise." On July 15, before the speech occurred, the *Washington Post* announced that "the President has made malaise a household word." On the heels of the speech, the media turned itself into an echo chamber in which "malaise" bounced around. Martin Schram, at the *Washington Post*, used "malaise" twice in a piece about the speech. Jack Germond agreed that the president was "persuaded that there is a national malaise." The next day David Broder announced that the president would continue to address "what he sees as a malaise in the country."[69]

On and on it went. The day after the speech, the *Los Angeles Times* explained that Carter had outlined "the moral malaise into which he said the country had descended," while the *Washington Star* used the term "malaise" twice, placing the word in quotation marks, implying the term was the president's. Rowland Evans and Robert Novak wrote about how Carter "opened group discussions" at Camp David "by warning of a 'malaise' in the land."[70]

Perhaps malaise sounded more psychological, thus suggesting an almost permanent state of mind difficult to escape, therefore more like the way people felt about their prospects in 1979 than the words Carter actually used during the speech. Or perhaps malaise represented the feelings the press had for Carter. The president's questioning whether or not a consumer and materialistic mentality could pull Americans through a major energy crisis—this inquiry was replaced with the idea that the president had pondered a psychic state of malaise that gripped the American people and dragged them down into a state of ungovernability.

Carter should have foreseen this treatment of his speech. He had consistently worried about the media (as he did during his dinner with intellectuals and social critics in late May). But what really should have disturbed him now was the reaction of those who had favored him, including H. Brandt Ayers. This journalist from Alabama had been at the July 13 meeting and had supported the president. Returning to Anniston, Alabama, Ayers listened to the speech and liked it. But then he heard from ordinary citizens in Anniston who were "still a little vague about the essential meaning of the mission" Carter set out. What exactly were they to *do* now given the charge?[71]

One unwitting adviser to the speech shared these worries. Daniel Bell had been at the late May dinner with the president, along with Christopher Lasch and other intellectuals. He had watched the speech and remembered a strange feeling he had had at the May dinner conversations at the White House. Bell thought the speech was honest and forthright. But he kept recalling a thought that crossed his mind as he listened to the president ruminate back in late May at dinner and then speak on July 15: "I do not think one can yoke a theme that is primarily moral and cultural to a 'cause' or 'crusade' that is so complex as energy.

Many persons, while appreciating the seriousness of the President's effort, in the end found themselves confused as to what was being asked." There was a growing sense that the speech floundered on the crisis it broached. The speech hadn't made clear what the next steps were and thus allowed others—including the media—to fill in with interpretations that went in different directions from where the speech and the president hoped to go.[72]

Ayers and Bell had argued cogently that the speech provided a vision citizens wanted to get behind but also confused them. The speech entered a world not of its own creation, with the media bantering about it even before it took place. It opened a possibility that others were ready to fill in. As was always the case, the president was the first but not the last to speak. His own words—and even words that he didn't use, like "malaise"—echoed back to him and haunted him. As they did, the president did something else that did more harm than words ever could. He opened a door to walk through and also slammed it shut.

5

THE SPEECH BECOMES
A "TURNING POINT"

JULY 1979–JANUARY 1981

I remember the exact moment I knew Ronald Reagan could beat Jimmy Carter. The date was July 15, 1979.

—RICHARD WIRTHLIN, RONALD REAGAN'S POLLSTER[1]

1.

On July 17, just two days after his speech, Jimmy Carter took a good situation and messed it up. He had ridden the waves of glory promised by the speech—the favorable letters and phone calls that flooded the White House and the standing ovations given him at speeches on July 16. But that lasted only for a moment before he threw a wrench into the works. During a series of bizarre meetings and one-on-one sessions that started on July 17 and then quickly leaked to the press, Carter followed the advice of Ham Jordan and asked for the resignation of his entire cabinet. Jordan planned the firings, including writing up questionnaires that cabinet members filled out about their level of loyalty to the president. By the end of the week, Carter had fired five cabinet chiefs, Michael Blumenthal (Treasury), Joseph Califano (Health, Education and Welfare), Griffin Bell (attorney general at Justice), Brock Adams (Transportation), and the cabinet member who deserved the booting the most, James Schlesinger, the secretary of energy about whom Carter had heard complaint after complaint during the summit. The move was bold and shocking. Journalists called it a "purge," the sort expected from the Kremlin.[2]

"Armageddon happened today," one presidential adviser told the *New York Times*. Once again, much like when he canceled his speech on July 4, Carter created a national buzz and crisis that quickly got out of hand. The dollar dropped again. Carter's critics, including senators, speculated openly about the president's mental health, and international rumors spread that the U.S. government had collapsed. The country moved back to the state of mind—chaotic and cynical—it had on July 5 when faced with an inexplicable and unexplained speech cancellation. *Time* summed up the situation perfectly: "The President basked in the applause" after his July 15 speech "for a day and then, on Tuesday morning, he set in motion his astounding purge, undoing much of the good he had done himself."[3]

Carter knew he blew it. "I handled the Cabinet changes very poorly," he recounted in his memoirs. That was demure. The announcement sent shock waves throughout the country and the world. By asking for across-the-board resignations, Carter created an appearance of meltdown. He also sent conflicting messages. He had said a "crisis of confidence" existed in America's psyche but then suggested the crisis resided squarely within his own administration. Carter had embraced criticism at the summit but then demanded absolute loyalty from his cabinet; he had counseled openness but then governed with authoritarianism and stiffness. So it felt like the "crisis of confidence" bounced off walls from the White House and landed squarely on its own doorstep. Two authors wrote a psychobiography of Jimmy Carter in 1979 and called the president "a contemporary Sisyphus." The term fit. The president seemed to have rolled a gigantic rock up a hill only to watch it roll down on top of him, crushing his vision of unifying the country around fighting the energy war.[4]

Ham Jordan, who after the dust settled became Carter's first *official* chief of staff, had argued for the firings. He did so before anyone else knew about them. What he heard from participants at the summit simply confirmed his suspicion about cabinet disloyalty. Carter had postponed any decision on this matter but then agreed, even though he still felt apprehensive. Once talk of disloyalty (there had been a single line about the issue in the speech) became a purge, things immediately changed. What Jordan and Carter didn't foresee was how the firings could backfire and derail the momentum set in place on July 15. Americans might have been able to take a tough speech about the state of their country and the energy crisis, but they couldn't take a complete shakedown of the government at the same time.[5]

American citizens wanted action on the energy front, a follow-through on the war against energy dependence outlined on July 15 as a way to reunify the country around its better principles. They might have been unclear, as H. Brandt Ayers had worried, about what exactly was expected of them, but those who wrote the White House seemed poised for action, already turning down their thermostats and buying mopeds or walking to work. But now Americans experienced whiplash, no longer hearing about the energy policy or the civic crisis but about cabinet disloyalty and government implosion. Throughout Carter's administration, citizens complained that the president was unfocused, spread out over a number of issues. (James Fallows had famously written: "I came to think that Carter believes fifty things, but no one thing."). The "crisis of confidence" speech had successfully seared Americans' attention, but the cabinet firings scattered it once again and thus returned it to apathy, anger, and confusion.

2.

All the president's men scrambled to figure out what to do as the high ground briefly won by the speech passed into chaos.

Jerry Rafshoon had simple advice: *Spin it and make it work for you.* Like Jordan, he had hoped for firings some time ago, especially because they could improve the president's style by enhancing his toughness. So the backlash didn't worry Rafshoon. The president just needed to tell people: "I can lead this effort [to regain confidence] much more effectively with a united team behind me." The problem was, the speech never outlined the cabinet purge as a solution to its broader themes. To spin the speech this way now would be hard, especially as the press turned its "bullshit detector" on high.[6]

Jody Powell, who had held some fears about Pat Caddell's advice even if he didn't articulate them, saw the speech now as the right thing to have done. "It was on the money and it was something that needed to be said," he concluded. But the cabinet firings were poorly timed; they should have been postponed at least. Nonetheless, even though he felt this way, Powell as usual remained silent; his job was to explain the situation to the press, not coach the president or take sides. He knew one thing for sure: His job had just gotten a whole lot harder. But on July 17, he didn't know the half of it.[7]

Stuart Eizenstat, who opposed the speech at first, now admitted it "went over spectacularly well." The next day, he was eager to push for the policies the speech rolled out. But then the cabinet shake-up ruined "our good headlines," harming any ability to win legislation. Recognizing summer for its sluggish legislative activity, Eizenstat expected Congress to stall. He knew the president had lost credibility as a leader, transactional, transformational, or otherwise, and he realized that the bad relations established with Congress earlier had now been provided justification. The cabinet firings sent the message that the president didn't work well with others.[8]

The speechwriters were even more depressed; no words could erase Carter's actions. A number of days ago, when he was pounding away on his typewriter at Camp David, Hendrik Hertzberg hadn't known about the upcoming purge. When he learned about it along with everyone else on July 17, he felt the president had lost the moral high ground the speech had won him. Gordon Stewart agreed, worrying the firings would draw attention away from the speech's broad themes and rivet it on inside-the-Beltway gossip. People would gab about "who's-he-going-to-fire-next" rather than about the energy crisis or civic decline. Any effort to mobilize the grass roots to fight the energy war—the essential next step Stewart believed Carter needed to take—would be sidelined by the news of the purge. The president had blown his "opportunity."[9]

More than anyone else, Pat Caddell freaked out at the backlash against the firings. Maybe they were necessary, he thought, but all of the work he had put into the speech now seemed dashed. He pleaded with the president on July 19 "to move out of this personnel pit and back to the broad high ground of themes begun on Sunday and Monday." Caddell patted himself on the back and worried simultaneously: "There is an immediate need to recapture the momentum of positive substantive direction so skillfully begun earlier in the week and . . . blunted by the necessary personnel changes." Caddell suggested a string of town meetings and media chat sessions. That sounded like constructive advice, but the subtext must have been: All my efforts for nothing. Well, watch your poll numbers fall again.[10]

And, the numbers did fall. By late July, "71% of those interviewed agreed" with the statement that the president "may well not have the basic competence to do the job." If Caddell had grown depressed on July 19, he had good reason. The president had blown it. Now it was time to watch the consequences play themselves out.[11]

3.

Since news of the purge erupted two days after the crisis of confidence speech, it became difficult to disentangle the two events. The speech now received a second birth, reentering the torpidity created by the firings. Of course, journalists had already chiseled Carter's words into a speech about "malaise." Now it would be reworked again, becoming, in the words of the *Los Angeles Times*, a "turning point for this Administration and perhaps for the nation." Editors at the *New Republic* bundled the speech and firings together into an obituary printed the first week of August: "The past two weeks will be remembered as the period when President Jimmy Carter packed it in, put the finishing touches on a failed presidency." Perhaps most stinging of all was Francis X. Clines's observation in the *New York Times*. He now called it the "cross of malaise speech," a wicked play on words. He was alluding to William Jennings Bryan's famous "cross of gold" speech given about eighty years earlier, when the Democratic Party candidate for president attacked the money standard and then wound up losing the election. The other meaning was worse: Carter had created his own cross that he would now carry to his crucifixion.[12]

The speech, not as a text or a set of actual words but as an imagined event, provided a script for Carter's end. The script's lines generated fuel for the fires burning in the minds of those who hoped to depose the president. The logic of this script helped write speeches like those given in a Greek tragedy in which the audience foresees the central character's inevitable fall but cannot prevent it.

A few in the Carter administration read the handwriting on the wall. Perhaps many of the president's men thought to themselves that things were over now, but they, of course, could not say so. But consider the words of one who left the White House in September—deputy assistant to the president for communications Greg Schneiders, the young man who pleaded for Rafshoon to coach the president on delivery of the crisis of confidence speech. Just five days before the speech, Schneiders wrote his boss another panicked note, "Look carefully at each self-deprecating remark and each negative comment about America." Schneiders warned that the president would "hear them thrown back ad nauseam during a campaign. 'Jimmy Carter thinks America has lost its spirit. Well, I say he's wrong!' "[13]

Just two months after this warning, Schneiders left the White House. He had grown frustrated with the cavernous bureaucracy—the incessant "meetings" and "paper flow"—just as James Fallows had. But before leaving, he had warned of assassins waiting in the wings who would use the president's speech as ammunition. (Unlike Fallows he didn't go public with this.) The lines Schneiders had offered in his panicked memo fit like bullets into the metaphorical guns held by Carter's political assassins.[14]

4.

Jerry Brown criticized the speech before it happened. Carter has "been building up the drama of Camp David," Brown complained to reporters at an event organized by Jesse Jackson. The whole thing looked like a show—the "performance" Sam Donaldson talked about. Journalists pounded the young governor with the question: Are you saying this because you're running for president? "I'm not running for anything," Brown insisted. In the next breath, he admitted: "It's no secret, I'm interested in the presidency." This was typical Brown: confusion rather than clarity but also dark wishes for the president so his own long shot run for the presidency might have a chance.[15]

Carter's number one opponent in the Democratic Party, Ted Kennedy, was galvanized by the speech—July 15 became his turning point too. After switching off his television that evening, Kennedy phoned friends to complain about the speech. He thought Carter had "violated the spirit of America." Portending his future verbosity and tendency to lose track of his thoughts, he told one friend, "The essence of political leadership is basically challenge and response. Constantly, that's sort of the central element in terms of my makeup, and I think then you are getting response to the challenging again. In this country, I think it is an essential aspect of the soul of this society, and one of the things that's made it sort of great. And it seems to me that this is sort of what the Democrats have been about." This indecipherable statement meant two things: that Kennedy had decided to run against Carter for the presidency due to what he perceived as failed leadership and that his decision had not made him any more articulate. Indeed, his inarticulateness would be his own cross to bear as time proceeded.[16]

Kennedy had been readying himself for the primary, as *People* had pointed out, by shaping up. Some worried that once in the race Ted Kennedy would be shot, his idealism gunned down like that of his older brothers. The promise of Camelot still engaged the memories of Americans, but so too did the dark tragedies within Kennedy's dynasty. He was still the "last brother" who lived with the "imprisonment" of his family name.[17]

Four months passed between July 15 and Kennedy's official declaration of his candidacy. He told the president privately on September 20 of his intention to run, and a month later, he saw Carter at the dedication of the John F. Kennedy Library (Carter gave a moving speech). Throughout this time, Kennedy remained fixated on Carter's crisis of confidence speech as the rationale for his candidacy. In front of crowds gathered at Boston's Faneuil Hall on November 6 to hear his announcement, Kennedy bellowed, "Now, the people are blamed for every national ill, scolded as greedy, wasteful, and mired in malaise." The senator then went on to reject Carter's pessimism for "the native energy of the people" and "the golden promise that is America." He even had his overly coached wife, Joan, come out and say she supported his candidacy, though many believed she grimaced as she spoke.[18]

The problem was that the times were not Kennedy's. His liberalism—with its faith in government's role to solve problems like energy or health care—didn't fit the mood of the nation in 1979. When the liberal journalist Richard Reeves touted Kennedy's candidacy earlier in March, he had written that the senator was "the only politician on the scene capable of tapping America's most traditional trait, optimism." These words showed off the blind spot of liberals more generally, this idea that Kennedy was the *only* optimistic candidate around. In fact, Kennedy's vision of America's "golden promise" belonged to others whose optimism about the times and their prospects were more legitimate.[19]

5.

The real winners in Carter's Sisphyean act, America's conservatives, saw three things in the July 15 speech: more government, more taxes, and thus more evil. *Human Events*, a conservative magazine that had published throughout the post–World War II years, complained that the speech was full of "fist-pounding and dramatic gestures" but remained devoid of "private enterprise solutions" to the energy crisis. The *Wall Street Journal* warned in more ominous tones: "There'll be a new army of government inspectors scouring the country," plus big bureaucracy and taxes. "In short, Mr. Carter has reacted to the public's low opinion of his administration by 'getting tough' and proposing a further suspension of private freedoms." Another writer at the *Wall Street Journal* zinged the president personally: "You roam America in your Boeing 707 and helicopter seeking insight into the nation's soul."

The image was perfect: Carter the elitist hovering above and seeing others' faults but never his own.[20]

Countering the themes of his speech allowed America's conservatives to sharpen their message. The problem wasn't the people. The problem was the government. And somehow the two entities, the people and the government, were separated. Get the government out of the picture, and the energy crisis would be fixed. Private industry—even the maligned oil monopolies that Americans saw only in conspiratorial terms—could do better than government. That was the right's remarkable gamble with history.

Anger, as the editorials following Carter's speech testify, energized the right. For the last year, activists had engaged numerous causes, but anger at taxes mobilized the foot soldiers more than anything. Proposition 13, an initiative that lowered California's property taxes, became law on June 6, 1978, after a groundswell of citizen activism. (Governor Jerry Brown had derided the proposition and then supported it after seeing its popularity.) Its success gave rise to a flurry of antitax activism across the country in 1978 and 1979. In November 1978, sixteen states organized antitax initiatives for the ballot; twelve passed. By July 6, 1979, *National Review* celebrated Proposition 13 as a major breakthrough and victory in the conservative war for America, a sign of the country's grassroots rejection of liberalism that had worked successfully as reform. (The doomsday predictions that liberals had made about the state government self-destructing due to a lack of funds hadn't come true.) Howard Jarvis, who led the successful revolt for Proposition 13 in California and moved onto the national scene soon afterward, entitled his 1979 memoir and polemic *I'm Mad as Hell*.[21]

Though drawing upon citizen anger, the tax revolt envisioned a happy ending once government shrunk. This was conservatism's promise, a combination of guttural self-interest mixed with a utopian vision of the future. It was a vision that Carter could never offer and the sort Reinhold Niebuhr had warned against. The right dreamed of a world in which the self lived without limits placed upon its ambitions and where these ambitions worked in harmony. Carter rejected this dream, in part because he believed self-love and sinfulness were too closely allied, and in part because he read Caddell's polls and ruminations about the me decade and its pathologies. But what the president couldn't foresee was that the most effective champions of self-love were not the narcissists depicted in Woody Allen's films or the voyeurs who gathered around Andy Warhol at Studio 54. They were the new right activists knocking on doors to limit taxes and thereby limit government. Caddell had reported about Proposition 13 in his April memo (it would have been hard not to), but he downplayed its significance, especially the "panic reaction" it had elicited among liberals. What Caddell and Carter didn't realize was that antitax activists mattered more than long-term pessimists or nonvoting narcissists in pushing the country in a different direction from where the two of them wanted to take it.[22]

6.

Carter's speech opened a Pandora's Box that released the American right's vision of redemptive patriotism and helped make the movement's anger more palatable to a wide audience. Case in point: *The Conservative Decade*, a little book conceived in 1979 and published in 1980. Ronald Reagan wrote the book's foreword, ripping into Carter's malaise speech in his first sentence. In the book, author James C. Roberts, a young conservative, developed biographical portraits and interviews with activists, intellectuals, and politicians. The book showed that an incredible conservative infrastructure was in place by this time. Kevin Phillips, the new right's wunderkind strategist, shared this secret about the right's goal: The American people "want to be number one again." The book closed with an explanation of the worldview that galvanized the right. "God has bestowed upon" America, Roberts wrote, "both a special grace and a special responsibility" and a "mission in the world." Moving from Carter's speech to redemptive nationalism became a coherent narrative arc on which conservatives built their strategy to win over the country.[23]

The worldview that informed the book's optimism burgeoned during Carter's presidency, especially under the guidance of those neoconservatives who had argued for bolder military action in the Middle East and who had celebrated films like *The Deer Hunter*. Their central task, after all, was to develop a counterhistory to the one that Carter offered in his speech, explaining, for instance, why the "Vietnam syndrome" should no longer stall America's ambitions overseas. No symbol worked better than the boat people who worried Joan Baez out of the peace movement. As the *American Spectator* pointed out, the boat people "have run in one direction only—away from Communist rule." The enemy's viciousness could now be seen in full light, providing vindication for the right, hammered home with counterfactual accounts of the past.[24]

As reverberations from Carter's speech and the cabinet firings spread, the August issue of *Commentary* magazine went to press. Here a reader could find an innocuous review of a book about Cambodia and America, under the byline Charles Horner (who was, not surprisingly, an aide to Carter's chief foreign policy foe, the hawkish Scoop Jackson). The review was a meditation on the meaning of the Vietnam War, and it successfully pulled together, in three short pages, four years of neoconservative thinking since the fall of South Vietnam in 1975.

Horner argued that "Vietnam is no longer to be argued about," because everybody in American political life "now chooses to remember himself in opposition to the war." (The statement was apt in describing Carter, who came to his opposition to the war late but held firm to it now, as he showed during his speech at the Vietnam Veterans' Week gathering.) A consensus about the war's legacy had emerged and now papered over the events taking hold in Southeast Asia. Horner believed two key symbols of the post-Vietnam era troubled this antiwar consensus: the "refugees of Indochina" and America's veterans. On the faces of refugees was etched the suffering of "totalitarianism," the plight of living with torture and reeducation camps in the newly unified Vietnam that Joan Baez had condemned. The cause of the war—to battle the spread of Vietnamese communism—now seemed just, even if its tactics and methods were botched. The boat people, in other words, were proof that America had been right all along about what would happen under communist rule. Horner then trumpeted the "courage, honor, and humanity of our soldiers." Yes, he wrote, "if they had prevailed, maybe, just maybe, what has happened in Indochina these past four years might not have happened." Horner rewrote the Vietnam legacy with the language of the counterfactual, the "maybe, just maybe" reframing past events.[25]

Horner's short review built upon the thinking of more prominent neoconservatives like Guenter Lewy, Carl Gersham, and Norman Podhoretz, the editor of *Commentary*. Their counternarrative went like this: America's actions weren't as bad as reported during the war (especially the bombings of North Vietnam). Every boat person notches up our moral calculus. Only the remnants of the protest classes, the overeducated who didn't fight in the first place or Hollywood traitors like Jane Fonda (an actress neoconservatives loved to hate), continued to doubt America's role in the world. And so the time for détente (SALT II) was over; anything that limited American power needed to be shucked and the assuredness that America had during the early cold war renewed. These arguments spilled out from the pages of *Commentary* into magazines such as *National Review*, *Human Events*, and the *American Spectator*.[26]

But rewriting Vietnam's history was not the end of it. The same issue of *Commentary* with Horner's ruminations on Vietnam included an article with the shocking title, "Watergate: Toward a Revisionist View," by James Neuchterlein. Here was the second front launched by the neoconservatives against the historical conclusions Carter had drawn in his speech. To overcome the legacy of Watergate would take some heavy lifting. There was no new evidence that Nixon hadn't known about the Watergate break-ins or hadn't been complicit with a cover-up. But true confidence—not the paltry form Carter spoke of with its humility and sense of shame—demanded a return to something more closely resembling the imperial presidency.

Neuchterlein, a young American who taught history in Canada, opened his essay discussing the "mood of stupefied exhaustion" that closed debate about Watergate's legacy. He pointed to cracks in the standard narrative of moral decline that most political critics squeezed out of the event. First, he employed relativism: All presidents grab power, Neuchterlein suggested, providing Nixon with a "precedent." "We have the Nixon tapes," he went on; perhaps we are fortunate *not* to have "the Roosevelt, Kennedy, or Johnson ones." The counterfactual imagination worked its wonder here again (what *would* those tapes include, he left his reader wondering). Neuchterlein also spread the blame from Nixon to the president's critics, including Judge John Sirica, who overstepped his role in prosecuting the Watergate trials, making "gratuitous pronouncements on the character and fate of Richard Nixon." And then Neuchterlein stumbled across the Watergate equivalent of the boat people, the victim who allowed a moral case to be made: It was none other than President Jimmy Carter himself. Examine his failure "to get much of anything at all that he wants from Congress," this young conservative wrote. The abuse of power under Nixon need not worry Americans; the lack of it under Carter should. It was a quick move from fearing the imperial president to bemoaning the anti-imperial president.[27]

Neoconservatives provided the empiricist and rationalist argument for America to stop "wallowing" in the past, as Neuchterlein

put it. Vietnam and Watergate needn't hold Americans back, and neoconservatives had the details and historical counterfactuals to prove it,
or at least to argue it. But American conservatism's tale of national redemption demanded more than scholars and intellectuals; it needed a
voice that could resonate outside the cramped corner of conservative
magazines. It found that in a bizarre and unspoken alliance of pre-
dominantly Jewish neoconservatives with Christian fundamentalists,
urban sophisticates writing scholarly essays who could march hand in
hand with rural fundamentalists convinced of the inerrancy of the
New Testament.

7.

Jerry Falwell's stumping at "I Love America" rallies and the thinking
that went behind the formation of the Moral Majority got cobbled into
a book with the evangelistic title *America Can Be Saved!* It was published
by Sword of the Lord Publishers just as the Moral Majority got off the
ground, offering a potent counter-jeremiad to Carter's as well as a fer-
vid counterpart to neoconservatives' reimagining of the American
past. Falwell's beginning was crystalline: "America is a Christian nation. Our founding fathers had that in mind when they carved this
nation out of the wilderness." The decline of the country and its concomitant salvation were therefore much easier to diagnose for Falwell
than they were for Carter: "I believe the creeping decadence of our society can be attributed to this defection from God and His Word." He
explained, "Our Republic is in grave danger, but I believe there is
hope. America can be saved. Revival is the key." Here was the rationale
for the "I Love America" rallies, the Moral Majority, and the new
right's general war against secular humanism.

Falwell's worries coalesced with Carter's in some ways. Both hated
the coarseness and decadence of pop culture. But Falwell focused most

of his venom on enemies he shared with the new right and on issues that had galvanized the founding of the Moral Majority: abortion, the ERA, secular textbooks, gay rights, and pornography (he was still annoyed that Carter had granted *Playboy* an interview in 1976). More significantly, Falwell linked his story of domestic redemption to the country's fall from grace in the eyes of the world. "We shamefully lost in Vietnam," he admitted. The emphasis here fell on shame.

The country's recovery, both domestically and internationally, didn't require Carter's humility, Falwell explained. Instead, it required Americans to rethink themselves as God's chosen people. "God loves America," Falwell assured. "If the world is to have revival, I believe it must begin here." He asserted that "America is the last logical launching pad for world evangelization." Employing a strange turn of phrase, Falwell claimed that "God has a hedge built around this nation." If the country rediscovered its Christian roots, America would be certain of redemption. His "vision" provided "faith" with "promises." America was still a City on the Hill blessed by God, no matter what President Carter might think.[28]

Robert Maddox, the man brought to the White House three months earlier to write speeches but who quickly found himself spending more of his time monitoring Falwell, was pressing Carter to confront this televangelist. Maddox was convinced that Falwell's rhetoric was pealing off Southern Baptist support that the president took for granted. But in the summer of 1979, at least, Falwell still eluded Carter's radar.

So when the president spoke in Kansas City and Detroit on July 16 about a "battlefield" on which to fight the energy crisis and received standing ovations, he forgot that the battle of ideas had not yet been won. Many people were not persuaded. Carter's vision of the country faced a new kind of old patriotism, one much simpler than the president's, even though it had been built from the same shards of history provided by the 1970s. Carter's speech on July 15 had forced his enemies to search their own battery of ideas. The president's vision of America, with its humility and recognition of the sores produced by Vietnam and Watergate, could never offer what Falwell's vision of Christian redemption could.

While Maddox went back to building his thickening file on Falwell, the televangelist lifted his pen to write another book entitled *Listen America!* It would be published in 1980 on a trade press that ensured it a wider audience than the smaller, religious publisher that issued *America Can Be Saved!* Falwell cited the Vietnamese boat people in the introduction of the book and then proceeded through much of the same terrain he covered in his earlier work, especially the decade of contemporary American culture. As he approached the end of the book, though, he looked forward to the 1980s and called it a "decade of destiny." Part of that destiny would be his own. Around the same time that Falwell started thinking about the 1980s, his fellow Moral Majority founder Richard Viguerie gave an interview to *U.S. News & World Report*, in which he predicted that "nearly 10 million conservative Christians will desert Baptist Carter for a conservative Republican in 1980." Although a tad optimistic, it seemed to explain just why Falwell was starting to call the 1980s a "decade of destiny."[29]

8.

The front-runners in the Republican Party race for the presidential nomination were already speaking their own language about American renewal. John Connally consistently embraced "reviving America's strength." Tall, tan, and looking a little like John Wayne, he personified toughness. When he watched Carter's speech on July 15, he got so angry that he immediately plotted a counterspeech. He shadowed the president and wound up speaking to Republican Party county officials at the same convention Carter spoke to in Kansas

City on July 16. Connally blamed "the president's own inaction" and lack of "leadership" for the country's problems. He got in this political dig: "The Democrat-controlled Congress has not done anything except make it harder to mine and burn coal, harder to drill for oil, harder to build nuclear power plants." He melded a faith in freedom from government to his faith in a renewed America. And he reached out to evangelical Christians to seek their support and absorb their language, meeting with them at his ranch in Texas a few days after giving his July 16 speech.[30]

The reaction that mattered most, though, was that of the Republican front-runner. Ronald Reagan had already come to Connally's policy conclusion about energy, just in bolder terms. "If the government will get the hell out of the way," he had explained in May, "the oil industry could produce more oil and compete freely in the marketplace." A few days before Carter's crisis of confidence speech, Reagan belted out the same line to whooping applause at the Petroleum Landmen's convention. A perfect audience for an easy message.[31]

Such antigovernment sentiment highlighted Reagan's optimism. He shared the anger of the new right, for sure, but emphasized the movement's more optimistic tones. The words Carter spoke on July 15 convinced Reagan, as it did Kennedy, that the president was "losing faith" in the American people. In the case of Reagan, though, the difference went deeper, conjuring a clash of national theologies. The journalist Garry Wills argued that Carter's "theology" included the "fallibility of America" (a fallibility that Kennedy believed was made clear in Vietnam). For Reagan, fallibility only meant defeatism. There was no place in his world for sin or self-inquisition. Vietnam was not a mistake. America remained a City on a Hill, a term Reagan used consistently in his speeches as he ran for president. That term didn't mean God might test its citizens; it meant God loved Americans as they were.[32]

Four days before Kennedy announced his candidacy, Reagan announced his own. Like Kennedy, Reagan placed "malaise" at the center of his justification for running: "For the first time in our memory many Americans are asking: does history still have a place for America, for her people, for her great ideals? There are some who answer 'no': that our energy is spent, our days of greatness at an end, that a great national malaise is upon us." Those people who said "no"—and that clearly included Carter—told "our children not to dream as we once dreamed," Reagan explained. "I find no national malaise," he insisted. "I find nothing wrong with the American people."

Reagan plied Kennedy's logic against Carter up to a point. But when it came to the question of government, his message zipped in a different direction. Redemption looped back to Reagan's (and the new right's) distinction between government and citizens. "I am confident that we can get government off our backs, out of our pockets." And if so, Reagan implied, the country could unleash its greatness once again. Making clear his own national theology in its boldest terms, he closed by using the language Carter and Robert Bellah had chafed at—the language of the chosen people. "Let us resolve tonight," Reagan ended, "that we did protect and pass on lovingly that shining city on a hill."[33]

9.

Reagan's memory often failed him. He forgot details. There was much more to his attack on the "malaise" speech than his belief that Carter had lost "faith" in the American people or his own sunshiny disposition on life. Reagan differed from Carter in numerous ways, except one: Both men had a pollster whispering into their ears who offered strategy grounded in statistics.

Reagan's pollster was Richard (Dick) Wirthlin. A devout Mormon with a large family, he had a more optimistic disposition toward life than Patrick Caddell. But besides that, the two shared a great deal.

Wirthlin had polled throughout the 1970s, serving as the president of Decision Making Information (DMI), an organization that provided independence from those he advised (including Reagan in 1976). DMI was also a place Wirthlin could experiment with new techniques, the way Caddell had with deepening (rather than yes-no) questions he asked in focus groups. For instance, Wirthlin developed the Political Information System (PINS), "a massive computerized chessboard" that tested out "rhetorical 'moves'" a candidate might make. He honed in on "power phrases" that elicited positive responses from listeners, calling this his "PulseLine technologies."[34]

Wirthlin also shared Caddell's discovery of "a sense of malaise among many people in America." But it never prompted Wirthlin to carry out historical or sociological investigations like Caddell's. Instead, Reagan's pollster drew the simplest conclusion requiring little social scientific examination: "We could counter" malaise "by speaking rather hopefully about an America that can deal with its problems if challenged and if led by leaders who were strong." This became the campaign strategy Wirthlin offered his boss for 1980, mapped out in what journalists called the black book. He tested the supposition out in focus groups and then explained, "Leadership is the ability to enlarge men's vision about the future and give them expectations of a less uncertain and more gratifying future. The Carter Administration has failed to fulfill this expectation of a less uncertain and more gratifying future." Quite simply, Carter's crisis of confidence speech could win Reagan the presidency.[35]

Everything Wirthlin saw in the polls confirmed his sense of victory. By June 1979, a straw poll showed Reagan leading Carter, 51 to 43 percent, almost the reverse from late 1978 when Carter outpolled Reagan 55 to 38 percent. Best of all, by July, Reagan ran ahead of Carter in the South. Wirthlin knew the significance of this; after all, Carter was the first president elected from the Deep South since the Civil War. If he was losing the South, he was losing, period.[36]

10.

August 1979 seemed a month in which the news reports confirmed the dreams of Carter's critics. The script that Wirthlin gleefully drew up and that Schneiders had gloomily foreseen played out as the plot's momentum built. Anyone watching saw things rolling toward their inevitable conclusion.

By the middle of the month, Carter's energy initiatives stalled in Congress. Stuart Eizenstat worried that as gas lines tapered during the rest of the summer, the sense of urgency about the energy crisis would collapse, and he was right. The feeling of unity and purpose of mid-July had evaporated. The summer nurtured slowness in legislation, as members of Congress became more intent on taking vacations than on solving the energy crisis. *Time* concluded that energy legislation came to a "halt" during August. The anti-imperial president seemed stymied once again.[37]

Then came really bizarre news: Hamilton Jordan's life suddenly intersected with the downfall of disco and generated precisely the sort of gossip that some in the White House worried about after the cabinet firings. Studio 54, the dance club that helped move disco into the mainstream and where Andy Warhol's minions gathered nightly to indulge in drugs and voyeurism, had fallen on bad times. The club's manager, Steve Rubell, had become victim of his own club's high-flying decadence. The chickens had come home to roost, but not before ensnaring the Carter administration.

IRS agents had raided Studio 54 back on December 14, 1978, but the indictments that followed didn't come until late June 1979. Agents had seized evidence of cash skimmed from the club's registers, faulty accounting, and loads of quaaludes and some cocaine. The indictments confirmed both tax evasion and drug possession.

Steve Rubell hired Roy Cohn, who had been the legal assistant to Senator Joseph McCarthy during the 1950s, to serve as his defense attorney (some believed the two men to be lovers). Cohn pushed Rubell to come up with something big for his defense. And Rubell came up big: He claimed Hamilton Jordan came to Studio 54 back in April 1978, descended to the caves below the club, flirted with women, and most important of all snorted cocaine. Rubell claimed he had witnesses. The story hit television news on August 25, 1979.[38]

Rubell's charges played into the perception of Jordan as a man of lewd behavior. Those stories about his lurid comments to an Egyptian diplomat's wife and his spitting at a woman in a bar were already in the media. Therefore, Rubell's allegation seemed more truthful than it should have. After all, *now* Jordan was the president's chief of staff and a lightning rod for criticism. The story that hit newsstands and televisions in late August offered the details for the sort of chatter that Gordon Stewart had feared would take hold after the cabinet firings: sex, drugs, and, if not rock 'n' roll, then at least disco.

Some speculated that a special prosecutor would have to take up the case. That position had been created in the wake of Watergate—an independent office that could not be blocked by executive action (the way Nixon had fired Archibald Cox, the investigator originally assigned by the attorney general to scrutinize allegations about Watergate). So it looked like the Carter administration might become victim of a reform instigated in the wake of Watergate and Nixon's abuse of power once again, as it had with Bert Lance earlier. The line of logic stemming from this—the once squeaky clean president handing the reins of power to a grotesque lawbreaker—couldn't have come at a worse time for Carter. This was not where Carter had hoped to be a month after his speech, in the midst of what those who had called a previous scandal Lancegate could now, if they wished, call Jordangate.[39]

The brunt of defending Ham Jordan against the media onslaught fell on Jody Powell's shoulders. He was used to defending Jordan, but that didn't stop his blood from boiling. When the story about Jordan spitting Amaretto hit the papers, Powell had gotten on the phone with the report's author, Rudy Maxa, and screamed, "You make your living ruining other people's reputation. How can you sleep at night?" The stress hit Powell again this time. He grew exasperated when sounding off to journalists about the Studio 54 story: "Any time someone makes a charge against Hamilton, the FBI's got to investigate it; then it gets headlines and Hamilton's career is ruined." Not to mention that it made Powell's job harder.[40]

It seemed things couldn't get worse for the White House and Powell, but they did. Just five days after Rubell's accusation hit national news, the *Washington Post* rang out with a page-one headline: "Rabbit Attacks President." *What the hell*, some at the White House must have thought. But not Powell. He knew what this was about. It was that story Carter had told him after returning from his vacation in mid-April, the one about the president whacking at a rabbit with his canoe paddle. Powell hadn't believed it at the time and quickly forgot it, but now the story had leaked into a different and more dangerous atmosphere.

The *Washington Post*'s article recounted that Carter's staff didn't believe his story about what happened on that pond, so the president ordered enlarged photographs to prove that the thing swimming toward him really was a rabbit. Next to this story the newspaper printed a cartoon portraying a befuddled president sitting in a canoe. Below him a huge rabbit with teeth bared swam upward. The word PAWS was emblazoned above the scene, a play on the blockbuster film *Jaws* about a deadly white shark.[41]

What seemed like little more than comic relief held enormous ramifications. Rumors took off that Jerry Falwell believed the rabbit a tool of Satan. Others made hay about how the president couldn't get his own staff to believe him. But what this little event really suggested was something larger: The president was now stereotyped as a weakling, incapable of handling a crisis, let alone a small animal.

The president who once spoke openly of whipping Kennedy's ass now looked like a loser and a sissy. The swimming rabbit and frightened president became an image that would stick forever and speak volumes.

Throughout August, reporters scoured the heartland to find out what citizens thought of their president now that the speech had been given and the cabinet firings completed. The president's decline in the polls that Caddell had correctly predicted was confirmed in anecdotes reported back by journalists. A *New York Times* story quoted a woman from Missouri who compared the president to Charlie Brown, the sad kid who could never kick the football that Lucy kept pulling away from him. *Time* printed a letter from one citizen who complained that "it isn't a case of the emperor having no clothes" but that "there is no emperor." These comments were made even before the killer rabbit incident resurfaced.[42]

The script had been perfected throughout the month of August, and it was working: weak president, overwhelming crisis, and American decline that demanded a stronger—and different—leader. It was just about a perfect story line.

11.

The rest of the story is, as the cliché goes, history. Different strands wrapped around to their ultimate conclusion. First, Iran reentered the picture with a vengeance. After Carter allowed the shah into America in October to manage his health problems, Iranian students seized the U.S. Embassy in Tehran, taking hostages on November 4, 1979 (Reagan's announcement of his candidacy had fallen the day before, Kennedy's three days after). And although Americans stood behind their president in a time of emergency, they grew weary when news of release never came. A botched rescue attempt in April 1980 accentuated the growing sense that the world's strongest superpower was being bullied by a third world country run by an elderly fanatical cleric. Chants of "Death to America" on the streets of Tehran and burning American flags showed up on the news regularly.

Then came Afghanistan in December 1979. When the Soviet Union protected its puppet regime by suppressing an uprising of radical Islamists, Carter pulled back from SALT II's ratification, an initiative that had taken almost as much of his time as the energy crisis had during the spring and summer of 1979. Neoconservatives watched their dreams come true: The president who had moved in the direction of détente now swerved back to the recognizable hostility of the cold war. Anger at the world situation increased. The graffiti found on the halls of America's high schools—"Russia Iran Disco Suck"—symbolized the mood of late 1979. As in June 1979, malaise turned into rage.[43]

Carter's biggest domestic enemy, inflation, continued apace, growing to almost 20 percent. No one could buy ordinary goods without hurting, and no one could buy a house as interest rates rose. There was little question that Americans were living in a very deep recession.

Congress continued a policy of inaction on the energy front. By March 1980, the watered-down windfall profits tax passed Congress to little fanfare, barely recognizable to those who had conceived it. As the year of 1979 waned, the Republicans plotted to kill off the energy mobilization board. They did so in 1980, "noting Reagan's opposition to it," as the scholar Garland Haas explains.[44]

The anger of the Christian new right mounted and finally drew the attention of Jimmy Carter. Robert Maddox officially changed his position to "religious liaison" in the summer of 1979. His file on Jerry Falwell had grown. He worked with Anne Wexler, who had organized the God Squad summit event, in order to arrange a meeting between Falwell and the president. It took place in January 1980 and went badly. Falwell claimed Carter had endorsed gay marriage (against all evidence) and then spread the rumor in numerous speeches. Maddox's olive-branch meeting backfired. The "decade of destiny" that Falwell predicted was now a battle plan with lines drawn.[45]

The Democratic Party primary heated up and added to the general narrative of a presidency besieged. Fortunately for Carter, Jerry Brown never got his campaign to kick into high gear. Kennedy *did*, though, campaigning as the antimalaise Democrat. But when asked to explain what he stood *for*, Kennedy broke into monologues of incoherence. He did an interview with television journalist Roger Mudd that exhibited his inarticulateness to a national audience and then he made gaffes about the Iranian situation after the hostage crisis erupted. He lost to Carter in Iowa during January 1980 in their first contest. Kennedy persevered and won some later primary victories, forcing Carter to fight his left flank while the right grew in power. Just as important, Kennedy's primary attack provided more ammunition for Reagan's attack during the general election. To a large extent, both Kennedy and Reagan campaigned against Carter as antimalaise candidates.

While Kennedy sank, so did John Connally. Throughout the second part of 1979, Connally focused his energy on the Middle East, making bizarre attacks on Israel—a political no-no—and was pegged as an anti-Semite. There was a brief boost in the candidacy of George H. W. Bush after Connally's fall, but nothing could prevent Reagan from barreling ahead toward the nomination and the presidency, the way most activists in the party had predicted.[46]

November 1980 brought the climax to the story, the final scene in the play that Dick Wirthlin had helped write. Carter lost big time in terms of both the popular and the electoral vote. The election was a slaughter, much like Lyndon Johnson's victory over Barry Goldwater in 1964 and Franklin Roosevelt's over Herbert Hoover in 1932. Political scientists were quick to label it a "critical election," meaning one that had long-term consequences, as it appeared the country was moving in a conservative direction. In other words, a "turning point" toward a new "decade of destiny."

12.

On January 20, 1981, a small crowd milled about on the terrace of the Capitol before Chief Justice Warren Burger got things under way. The sky was clear, the weather brisk. Burger administered the presidential oath of office to Ronald Reagan, his hand placed firmly on the Bible. The audience cheered as ceremonial guns blasted. At that moment, Ronald Reagan walked over and shook Jimmy Carter's hand. The president looked uncomfortable and exhausted. He had arrived barely in time for the ceremony, busy with last-minute negotiations on the hostage crisis that still hadn't prompted their release. Reagan beamed as he turned back and went to the podium. The new president was about to give the final lines in the play he and Wirthlin had conceptualized.

The speech Reagan gave grounded itself in his reaction against the malaise speech and his own public philosophy. Reagan explained, "It is time for us to realize that we are too great a nation to limit ourselves to small dreams. We are not, as some would have us believe, doomed to an inevitable decline." Carter must have winced at those lines. Reagan then explained how his dreams need not require collective endeavors. In one of his most famous lines, he said that "government" wasn't the solution but the "problem." The greatness of America didn't rely upon citizens banding together but on "individual genius." Where Carter feared selfishness and fragmentation, Reagan saw sunshine.

But then Reagan seemed to go back on his own words and talked of "sacrifice." He used, as was his wont, an anecdote. It was about an

American soldier named Martin Treptow who died during World War I. Reagan claimed that the man's body lay in Arlington Cemetery, a place not too far from where he spoke. (Treptow, in fact, was buried in Wisconsin, a complication Reagan ignored even against the wishes of his speechwriter.) Reagan quoted lines from Treptow's diary: "America must win this war. Therefore, I will work, I will save, I will sacrifice, I will endure, I will fight cheerfully and do my utmost, as if the issue of the whole struggle depended on me alone." The new president cautioned against concluding, the way some might, that he dreamed of the same sort of sacrifice at the present moment, say, the sort of sacrifice Carter believed was necessary to fight the energy war. "The crisis we are facing today," Reagan concluded, "does not require of us the kind of sacrifice that Martin Treptow and so many thousands of others were called upon to make."[47]

There was no better expression of Reagan's political philosophy than this: the right to dream "heroic dreams" without sacrifice. It wasn't clear from the speech if those dreams would require much of *anything* from the citizens he addressed. Reagan assembled what the journalist Joan Didion called "a dreamwork" that expelled anything from it that "might trouble the dreamer." Floating on those dreams, Americans had coasted around a turning point.[48]

13.

The pain on Carter's face as he walked back to his seat after shaking Reagan's hand was real. The loss to Reagan threw Carter into depression. Rosalynn took the loss even harder, as she watched Nancy Reagan come into the White House to measure for drapes and plan an interior decorating overhaul. Reagan's dreams constituted Carter's nightmares.

But history is full of ironies. And so is this story. As much as the path toward defeat was written in the malaise speech—not its actual words but how it nurtured Reagan's dreamwork—Carter's redemption was written in it as well. As he packed up his office, Carter might not have imagined a happy ending to this turning point. But eventually he would.

EPILOGUE

IN DREAMS THERE BEGIN
NO RESPONSIBILITIES

America is a vast conspiracy to make you happy.

—JOHN UPDIKE, 1979[1]

There is an odd passage in Jimmy Carter's autobiography, *Why Not the Best.* Written in 1976, the book is usually treated as a political campaign tract. But at one point, Carter makes a strange confession for someone running for president. He remembers his return to Plains, Georgia, after serving in the navy, the move that pained his wife, Rosalynn. He came back to a "tiny town, a church, a farm, an uncertain income." But he found happiness: "I had only one life to live, and I wanted to live it as a civilian, with a potentially fuller opportunity for varied public service." The passage highlights a tension that consistently marked Carter's biography and that the crisis of confidence speech evoked again.[2]

Carter thirsted for political power throughout his life, but he also held profound ambivalence about the world of politics and an abiding love for the world of citizens. In 1975 Carter gave a speech entitled "I Intend to Win" in which he expressed hesitation rare in a candidate: "I don't have to be President." During his crisis of confidence speech, he complained that government seemed a distant island from ordinary citizens. After Reagan was sworn in, Carter gave a farewell address in which he embraced the role of "citizen," the only "title in our democracy superior to that of President." It's easy to dismiss the statement as cover for sour grapes, but that would be unfair.[3]

The statement highlights, in fact, the happy ending of the malaise speech's aftermath. If Carter worried about the civic bonds fraying in the world of citizens, what better place for him to go to heal those bonds? As advisers far and near as Daniel Bell and Patrick Caddell argued, the speech broached a question whether political solutions existed for cultural problems, whether government could improve the status of civil society. H. Brandt Ayers raised the same question when he reported that citizens told him they were confused about what they could do to engage Carter's charge.

Some critics who listened to the July 15 speech wondered what happened to the president's 1976 campaign slogan, "a government as good as its people." The populist president who saw virtue in the people now saw problems of selfishness and conspiratorial distrust. But Carter also admitted his own weaknesses, asking for the country's help. When he examined Caddell's polls and turned his speed-reading skills to critics of American culture, Carter ditched the pieties of populism, but he didn't flip-flop and blame citizens for their problems. The speech suggested a solution to the problem: *improve* the people by improving himself in direct relation to them. As the president inquired about the state of the people, the people came to their own conclusion about him. It's wrong to remember these conclusions as purely negative. When polled, citizens criticized Carter's leadership skills but never his moral character. The speech hinted at a new possibility of Carter's rebirth if he reentered the world of citizens; the November 1980 election forced the decision.

Carter outperformed all expectations after leaving the presidency for the world of citizens. He became a megacitizen. For a few years, he sank into depression, finding solace in his woodworking shop or watching movies with Rosalynn. But when he came out of that, his postpresidency became as well known if not better known than his presidency. If there were questions about what a citizen could do to improve the civic bonds in this country, Carter answered them through a life of active engagement. He built houses on the Lower East Side of Manhattan and in rural communities with Habitat for Humanity. He created the Carter Center in Atlanta, which supported nonviolent conflict resolution and grassroots solutions to poverty. He traveled abroad to work on Middle East peace initiatives and to monitor political elections for fairness.

Carter's desire to live as a citizen, to embrace civic responsibility without holding office, became a source of amazing inventiveness. The crisis of confidence speech had revealed a dirty little secret that "all the legislation in the world can't fix what's wrong with America." Carter knew that many problems he had outlined could be solved locally not nationally, that is, on an equal playing field where he didn't wield political power. Perhaps at an unconscious level, the crisis of confidence speech promised Carter redemption in the world of the "civilian" with "its fuller opportunity for varied public service" once again.

Of course, it's unfair to suggest the speech and the events in its aftermath foreordained the president's return to the world of citizens. Carter did everything he could to retain office, battling first Kennedy then Reagan. Stranger things have happened, and perhaps Carter could have persevered and won in 1980. But counterfactuals rarely illuminate history, and the president seemed doomed to defeat soon after the cabinet firings and his sinking poll numbers in late July 1979. As the *New Republic* saw it, Carter had "packed it in" and resigned himself to a "failed presidency." Others made clear that a turning point, a passing of an era, had been reached.

This narrative comes easy: the end of a loser decade presided over by a loser president. In the words of historian Bruce Schulman, Carter became a "relic of the despised, disparaged Seventies" just like "yellow smiley faces, disco records, and leisure suits." The 1970s became a decade critics loved to flog even before it had ended. In 1979, for instance, *New West* magazine declared the 1970s a decade of "cultural recession," "gas lines," and "stoned school buses," a time of the "sordid," "half-assed," "mediocre." Riffing on the name of a car about to go off the market because it blew up after rear-end collisions, *New West* called the 1970s "a Pinto of a decade." The editors concluded: "If ever a decade deserved to close out of town, this is the one."[4]

The end of Carter's presidency *was* a turning point and it aligned, almost perfectly, with the end of the 1970s. Carter's demise seemed part of a larger cultural shift. Consider Studio 54 again. When Steve Rubell made his last-minute accusation that Ham Jordan had snorted coke there, two of the club's central doyens, Bianca Jagger and Margaret Trudeau, were leaving the scene. Trudeau returned to her family after her husband's recent loss to conservatives in Canada; Jagger returned to her family in Nicaragua after the dictator Somoza fell, in order to perform humanitarian work with the Red Cross. It was as if the glitterati grew bored with decadence and accepted the responsibility only found in obligation to others. Steve Rubell was shipped off to jail, his charges against Jordan refuted. And then on February 4, 1980, Studio 54 held its final party, appropriately entitled "The End of Modern Day Gomorrah."[5]

The story of disco's collapse creates another happy ending. It goes like this: A decade during which Americans lost their minds in a haze of drugs, bad music, and bad taste evaporated. Decadence and narcissism fluttered away. Americans threw away their polyester, long-collared shirts, and humongous platform shoes. So too those silly fads like new-age extravaganzas or mood rings. Looking back, we roll our eyes. It had to be the drugs—pot, coke, and quaaludes—that destroyed people's better judgment. Goodbye to all that, the country seemed to say, returning only out of ironic nostalgia, a sad admittance of what we once stupidly were.

This narrative comes easiest to conservative critics. They interpret the late 1970s as a holding pattern—what one journalist called a "time of pause"—before a return to national greatness in Reagan's presidency. Here is conservative pundit David Frum:

> The 1970s were America's low tide. Not since the Depression had the country been so wracked by woe. *Never*—not even during the Depression—had American pride and self-confidence plunged deeper. But the decade was also, paradoxically, in some ways America's finest hour. America was afflicted in the 1970s by a systemic crisis analogous to the one that struck Imperial Rome in the middle of the third century A.D. . . . But unlike the Romans, Americans staggered only briefly before the crisis. They took the blow. For a short time they behaved foolishly . . . Then they recouped . . . Out of the failure and trauma of the 1970s they emerged stronger, richer, and—if it is not overdramatic to say so—greater than ever.[6]

It *is* overdramatic. Maybe even melodramatic as it reads like a movie script: Bad times and bad leader fall to the good ending provided by a great leader. For sure, this story congeals around Studio 54's collapse symbolizing the end of the me decade. One of the earliest (and still one of the best) books about the 1970s had the indicative title *It Seemed Like Nothing Happened*. The decade had no greatness to it, just crummy leaders who feared killer rabits and narcissistic citizens who got stoned. But there was another element in the 1970s that bears remembering. It goes to the heart of Carter's speech and its historical resonances.

Recall here two films Carter watched during the spring and summer of 1979: *Manhattan* and *Apocalypse Now*. For sure, Woody Allen could seem a whiny narcissist, and his film *Manhattan* received praise beyond merit. But Allen tried, in part, to portray the fragility of relationships and the challenge of living morally in an immoral world. He laughed at his own weaknesses. When asked about the film's character, who seemed the quintessential antihero, Allen said about himself: "The real question in life is how one copes in" a crisis. "I worry that I tend to moralize as opposed to being moral." This sort of humility and recognition of moral frailty were as much a part of the 1970s as cocaine-snorting narcissism.

Or take the film story that dominated the summer of 1979 and tested itself out at the White House. *Apocalypse Now* can be understood as part of 1970s excess—a narcissistic director with a movie spinning out of control and actors stoned out of their minds. But it was also a film that tried to confront the difficult legacy of Vietnam. It demanded Americans examine what they did to themselves in the jungles of Vietnam ("the horror") and what they became. Pompous perhaps, but the film insisted we could not ignore scars from the past, refusing the construction of counterfactual dreamworlds.

Or consider the intellectual infrastructure that built Carter's speech. The 1970s was certainly an age of narcissism, but it was also an age of narcissism's critics. It was a time when a historian wrote a difficult book about America's prospects that turned into a bestseller. A book whose author, when pressed at the White House, couldn't provide quick-fix political solutions. It was a time when religious leaders didn't just whip up the faithful's emotions but pushed Americans to examine their complicity in a culture of selfishness and materialism, the way the God Squad had during and after the domestic summit.

Consider the loser president himself: Like conservatives, he hated the narcissism and decadence of the decade. He thought the media trivialized issues (he complained openly about *People* magazine during the domestic summit). He worried that the American way of life had become identified too strongly with consumerism. "Human identity is no longer defined by what one does, but by what one owns," he said during the speech. Carter wanted to pull Americans out of this mire of materialism and civic decline.

But Carter didn't believe the country could pull itself out by ignoring the past. The speech provided a history that troubled any easy celebration of America, as it remembered Vietnam, Watergate, and the violence and assassinations of the 1960s. Carter essentially said: We really did elect a man to office in 1972 who lied and abused power. We really did choose a war that was destructive and pulled the country apart. We really have killed some of our best, most promising leaders. We really have become a nation of "fragmentation and self-interest." Yes, we can rebuild confidence, but not the sort built on dreams or wishing away history. Carter demanded recognition of frailties in his "theology of fallibility." This too: The country could move forward only by confronting the energy crisis and its troubling message that America had grown too dependent on foreign oil in a world beyond its control. Carter's speech set out the challenge of *post-traumatic confidence* or *confidence tempered by realism*.

Finally, the speech tells us something about Jimmy Carter's legacy. Its words were some of the best that Carter offered the nation. James Fallows quit his job as speechwriter because he denied that Carter had any political vision; his tough assessment of Carter in the *Atlantic Monthly* helped codify a view of the president's weakness—that he lacked unifying ideas—that sticks to this day. Reading the crisis of confidence speech complicates this interpretation.

Carter reimagined the nation in his speech, a reimagination common to all good political speeches from the past. Though he rejected pietistic populism (the championing of the American people as pure and virtuous), he allowed the people into his speech by including the quotes gathered at Camp David and his trips to Pennsylvania and West Virginia. He argued that citizens and the federal government must work together—bottom-up and top-down approaches energizing one another—in order to tackle the energy crisis (an idea that came partially from Bill Clinton and that the young governor expanded upon when he became president). Carter embraced the covenant tradition in the American past, an idea he took from Robert Bellah and Marc Tanenbaum, and used it to push Americans to think of "common purpose," to transcend individual fragmentation and self-interest. The nation would move ahead with a sense of humility, recognizing scars from the past while meeting the challenge of the energy crisis with a sense of realism and united purpose.

It's hard to remember these elements in the speech or the coherence of its vision. That's partially Carter's own fault. In just a few days after giving the speech, Carter killed its possibilities. Soon it became what it was for Kennedy and Reagan: a big blame game in which Carter threw down the gauntlet before the American people—the "cross of malaise speech."

Historians continue to gloss it that way to this day. "By sermonizing," Sean Wilentz writes in *The Age of Reagan*, "Carter appeared to be abdicating his role as leader and blaming the people themselves for their own afflictions." Kennedy's and Reagan's political attacks on the speech substitute for an examination of the speech itself in this interpretation. Carter's words and thinking vanish from this account, an account heard consistently in history textbooks. The speech becomes an act in which a president artfully dodged responsibility and excoriated citizens.[7]

This interpretation is both too cynical and an overestimation of Carter's political acumen at the same time. Carter wasn't crafty enough to map out such a grand dodge of political responsibility. Besides, this interpretation ignores the path Carter took after his presidency—

engaging as a citizen to build civic trust from the bottom up—that historians have to their advantage in looking back on the speech. Carter did not *blame* the people for their ills, but he did expect something from them. Just as he expected something from himself and from the nation's spirit that previous presidents like Abraham Lincoln and Franklin Roosevelt invoked.

The speech shouldn't be understood as a blame game but as a moment when a president took time to explore the different traditions that informed the American past, the traditions of self-interest and the language of covenant. Carter was no intellectual, but it is remarkable to consider what he read going into the speech. And in May 1979, he opened the doors of the White House to intellectuals in a way not seen since Kennedy was in the White House. Pat Caddell might appear "a guru still in his 20s" who offered Carter "half-baked ideas," as Garry Wills remembered him. Such an interpretation confirms contemporary suspicions about pollsters. But Caddell's thinking was much richer and morally complex than the tripe current pollsters offer about Soccer Moms or Office Park Dads. Here was a young man reading some difficult academic work about narcissism and the "cultural contradictions of capitalism" as well as John Maynard Keynes and Alexis de Tocqueville. The speech's depth and sophistication reflect the seriousness of its intellectual inquiry into the nation's values.[8]

Examining its immediate aftermath—the favorable responses flooding the White House and an 11 percent jump in the polls—the speech seemed to offer sophistication and an examination of values that *worked*. Carter became, in the words of one citizen who wrote the White House, "the first politician" who "has said the words that I have been thinking for years." That tells us something about Carter's view of leadership. He hoped to say things that could disturb and challenge citizens. "This is not a message of happiness or reassurance, but it is the truth and it is a warning," Carter reminded his listeners during the speech. He didn't intend to make people happy. He wanted instead to press them to think about their complicity in a political culture of self-interest and a way of life no longer sustainable, with the hopes of pushing them beyond where they were.

In the end, Carter could not compete with the "transformational" leadership offered by Ronald Reagan. The speech served as a turning point away from Carter's humility and toward Reagan's dreams, from Carter's Niebuhr to Reagan's Ralph Waldo Emerson (the nineteenth-century transcendentalist who dreamed of the possibilities of romantic individualism). Carter offered "confidence" every time he brought his fist down during the speech, but it was a confidence tinged with humility about the sins of the country's past and the tragedies that lingered in the nation's unconscious. Reagan offered confidence based upon his own optimism and the "dreams" he upheld. These required no self-inquiry on the part of ordinary citizens. "I find no national malaise," Reagan insisted. "I find nothing wrong with the American people." To paraphrase the writer Delmore Schwartz: In Reagan's dreams there began no responsibilities.

The year 1979 seems not just a turning point, but to many it seems a very distant point in the past. It was a unique year, full of chaos and hard times. The "American berserk," as the novelist Philip Roth called it, reared its ugly head in violent gas lines, trucker strikes, and conspiracies that took hold of angry minds. It is hard to recall such a moment.

But we should recall it now as a time of contingency, when a turn was taken that wasn't carved in stone. This story is intended to show how critics twisted Carter's words against him and how Carter himself destroyed the possibility that his speech offered. History cannot tell us a great deal about the future, but it can remind us of where we went in the past and why we didn't necessarily have to go there.

This book also assumes that Carter's speech still resonates to this day. Consider the speech's major insights in light of the present. We are still a nation dependent on foreign sources of oil and lacking a national energy policy that searches for alternatives. So Carter's suggestion that

America had to generate a sense of national purpose and a "common good" to fight the energy crisis doesn't sound all that distant. We are still a nation infatuated with private self-interest, whose civic culture seems torn apart, a nation that still "bowls alone," as one political scientist recently described it. We are still a culture that prizes consumerism and materialism, whose pop culture seems vapid and distracting at best. Foreign wars still warn us against thinking of America's greatness in simplistic terms, as if it can be easily projected throughout the world without blowback. So in the end, this book ends with a question about 1979 as a turning point. Are we so certain that the turn taken was the right one? To remember Jimmy Carter's speech today allows us to ask that question with the sort of moral import it deserves.

APPENDIX

THE SPEECH
"A CRISIS OF CONFIDENCE"

JULY 15, 1979

Good evening.

This is a special night for me. Exactly three years ago, on July 15, 1976, I accepted the nomination of my party to run for president of the United States. I promised you a president who is not isolated from the people, who feels your pain, and who shares your dreams, and who draws his strength and his wisdom from you.

During the past three years I've spoken to you on many occasions about national concerns, the energy crisis, reorganizing the government, our nation's economy, and issues of war and especially peace. But over those years the subjects of the speeches, the talks, and the press conferences have become increasingly narrow, focused more and more on what the isolated world of Washington thinks is important. Gradually, you've heard more and more about what the government thinks or what the government should be doing and less and less about our nation's hopes, our dreams, and our vision of the future.

Ten days ago I had planned to speak to you again about a very important subject—energy. For the fifth time I would have described the urgency of the problem and laid out a series of legislative recommendations to the Congress. But as I was preparing to speak, I began to ask myself the same question that I now know has been troubling many of you. Why have we not been able to get together as a nation to resolve our serious energy problem?

It's clear that the true problems of our nation are much deeper— deeper than gasoline lines or energy shortages, deeper even than inflation or recession. And I realize more than ever that as president I need your help. So, I decided to reach out and listen to the voices of America.

I invited to Camp David people from almost every segment of our society—business and labor, teachers and preachers, governors, mayors, and private citizens. And then I left Camp David to listen to other Americans, men and women like you. It has been an extraordinary ten days, and I want to share with you what I've heard.

First of all, I got a lot of personal advice. Let me quote a few of the typical comments that I wrote down.

This from a southern governor: "Mr. President, you are not leading this nation—you're just managing the government."

"You don't see the people enough any more."

"Some of your cabinet members don't seem loyal. There is not enough discipline among your disciples."

"Don't talk to us about politics or the mechanics of government, but about an understanding of our common good."

"Mr. President, we're in trouble. Talk to us about blood and sweat and tears."

"If you lead, Mr. President, we will follow."

Many people talked about themselves and about the condition of our nation. This from a young woman in Pennsylvania: "I feel so far from government. I feel like ordinary people are excluded from political power."

And this from a young Chicano: "Some of us have suffered from recession all our lives."

"Some people have wasted energy, but others haven't had anything to waste."

And this from a religious leader: "No material shortage can touch the important things like God's love for us or our love for one another."

And I like this one particularly from a black woman who happens to be the mayor of a small Mississippi town: "The big shots are not the only ones who are important. Remember, you can't sell anything on Wall Street unless someone digs it up somewhere else first."

This kind of summarized a lot of other statements: "Mr. President, we are confronted with a moral and a spiritual crisis."

Several of our discussions were on energy, and I have a notebook full of comments and advice. I'll read just a few.

"We can't go on consuming forty percent more energy than we produce. When we import oil we are also importing inflation plus unemployment."

"We've got to use what we have. The Middle East has only five percent of the world's energy, but the United States has twenty-four percent."

And this is one of the most vivid statements: "Our neck is stretched over the fence and OPEC has a knife."

"There will be other cartels and other shortages. American wisdom and courage right now can set a path to follow in the future."

This was a good one: "Be bold, Mr. President. We may make mistakes, but we are ready to experiment."

And this one from a labor leader got to the heart of it: "The real issue is freedom. We must deal with the energy problem on a war footing."

And the last that I'll read: "When we enter the moral equivalent of war, Mr. President, don't issue us BB guns."

These ten days confirmed my belief in the decency and the

strength and the wisdom of the American people, but it also bore out some of my long-standing concerns about our nation's underlying problems.

I know, of course, being president, that government actions and legislation can be very important. That's why I've worked hard to put my campaign promises into law—and I have to admit, with just mixed success. But after listening to the American people I have been reminded again that all the legislation in the world can't fix what's wrong with America. So, I want to speak to you first tonight about a subject even more serious than energy or inflation. I want to talk to you right now about a fundamental threat to American democracy.

I do not mean our political and civil liberties. They will endure. And I do not refer to the outward strength of America, a nation that is at peace tonight everywhere in the world, with unmatched economic power and military might.

The threat is nearly invisible in ordinary ways. It is a crisis of confidence. It is a crisis that strikes at the very heart and soul and spirit of our national will. We can see this crisis in the growing doubt about the meaning of our own lives and in the loss of a unity of purpose for our nation.

The erosion of our confidence in the future is threatening to destroy the social and the political fabric of America.

The confidence that we have always had as a people is not simply some romantic dream or a proverb in a dusty book that we read just on the Fourth of July. It is the idea which founded our nation and has guided our development as a people. Confidence in the future has supported everything else—public institutions and private enterprise, our own families, and the very Constitution of the United States. Confidence has defined our course and has served as a link between generations. We've always believed in something called progress. We've always had a faith that the days of our children would be better than our own.

Our people are losing that faith, not only in government itself but in the ability as citizens to serve as the ultimate rulers and shapers of our democracy. As a people we know our past and we are proud of it. Our progress has been part of the living history of America, even the world. We always believed that we were part of a great movement of humanity itself called democracy, involved in the search for freedom, and that belief has always strengthened us in our purpose. But just as we are losing our confidence in the future, we are also beginning to close the door on our past.

In a nation that was proud of hard work, strong families, close-knit communities, and our faith in God, too many of us now tend to worship self-indulgence and consumption. Human identity is no longer defined by what one does, but by what one owns. But we've discovered that owning things and consuming things does not satisfy our longing for meaning. We've learned that piling up material goods cannot fill the emptiness of lives which have no confidence or purpose.

The symptoms of this crisis of the American spirit are all around us. For the first time in the history of our country a majority of our people believe that the next five years will be worse than the past five years. Two-thirds of our people do not even vote. The productivity of American workers is actually dropping, and the willingness of Americans to save for the future has fallen below that of all other people in the Western world.

As you know, there is a growing disrespect for government and for churches and for schools, the news media, and other institutions. This is not a message of happiness or reassurance, but it is the truth and it is a warning.

These changes did not happen overnight. They've come upon us gradually over the last generation, years that were filled with shocks and tragedy.

We were sure that ours was a nation of the ballot, not the bullet, until the murders of John Kennedy and Robert Kennedy and Martin

Luther King, Jr. We were taught that our armies were always invincible and our causes were always just, only to suffer the agony of Vietnam. We respected the presidency as a place of honor until the shock of Watergate.

We remember when the phrase "sound as a dollar" was an expression of absolute dependability, until ten years of inflation began to shrink our dollar and our savings. We believed that our nation's resources were limitless until 1973, when we had to face a growing dependence on foreign oil.

These wounds are still very deep. They have never been healed.

Looking for a way out of this crisis, our people have turned to the federal government and found it isolated from the mainstream of our nation's life. Washington, D.C., has become an island. The gap between our citizens and our government has never been so wide. The people are looking for honest answers, not easy answers; clear leadership, not false claims and evasiveness and politics as usual.

What you see too often in Washington and elsewhere around the country is a system of government that seems incapable of action. You see a Congress twisted and pulled in every direction by hundreds of well-financed and powerful special interests. You see every extreme position defended to the last vote, almost to the last breath by one unyielding group or another. You often see a balanced and a fair approach that demands sacrifice, a little sacrifice from everyone, abandoned like an orphan without support and without friends.

Often you see paralysis and stagnation and drift. You don't like it, and neither do I. What can we do?

First of all, we must face the truth, and then we can change our course. We simply must have faith in each other, faith in our ability to govern ourselves, and faith in the future of this nation. Restoring that faith and that confidence to America is now the most important task we face. It is a true challenge of this generation of Americans.

One of the visitors to Camp David last week put it this way:

"We've got to stop crying and start sweating, stop talking and start walking, stop cursing and start praying. The strength we need will not come from the White House, but from every house in America."

We know the strength of America. We are strong. We can regain our unity. We can regain our confidence. We are the heirs of generations who survived threats much more powerful and awesome than those that challenge us now. Our fathers and mothers were strong men and women who shaped a new society during the Great Depression, who fought world wars, and who carved out a new charter of peace for the world.

We ourselves are the same Americans who just ten years ago put a man on the Moon. We are the generation that dedicated our society to the pursuit of human rights and equality. And we are the generation that will win the war on the energy problem and in that process rebuild the unity and confidence of America.

We are at a turning point in our history. There are two paths to choose. One is a path I've warned about tonight, the path that leads to fragmentation and self-interest. Down that road lies a mistaken idea of freedom, the right to grasp for ourselves some advantage over others. That path would be one of constant conflict between narrow interests ending in chaos and immobility. It is a certain route to failure.

All the traditions of our past, all the lessons of our heritage, all the promises of our future point to another path, the path of common purpose and the restoration of American values. That path leads to true freedom for our nation and ourselves. We can take the first steps down that path as we begin to solve our energy problem.

Energy will be the immediate test of our ability to unite this nation, and it can also be the standard around which we rally. On the battlefield of energy we can win for our nation a new confidence, and we can seize control again of our common destiny.

In little more than two decades we've gone from a position of energy independence to one in which almost half the oil we use comes from foreign countries, at prices that are going through the roof. Our excessive dependence on OPEC has already taken a tremendous toll on our economy and our people. This is the direct cause of the long lines which have made millions of you spend aggravating hours waiting for gasoline. It's a cause of the increased inflation and unemployment that we now face. This intolerable dependence on foreign oil threatens our economic independence and the very security of our nation.

The energy crisis is real. It is worldwide. It is a clear and present danger to our nation. These are facts and we simply must face them.

What I have to say to you now about energy is simple and vitally important.

Point one: I am tonight setting a clear goal for the energy policy of the United States. Beginning this moment, this nation will never use more foreign oil than we did in 1977—never. From now on, every new addition to our demand for energy will be met from our own production and our own conservation. The generation-long growth in our dependence on foreign oil will be stopped dead in its tracks right now and then reversed as we move through the 1980s, for I am tonight setting the further goal of cutting our dependence on foreign oil by one-half by the end of the next decade—a saving of over four and a half million barrels of imported oil per day.

Point two: To ensure that we meet these targets, I will use my presidential authority to set import quotas. I'm announcing tonight that for 1979 and 1980, I will forbid the entry into this country of one drop of foreign oil more than these goals allow. These quotas will ensure a reduction in imports even below the ambitious levels we set at the recent Tokyo summit.

Point three: To give us energy security, I am asking for the most massive peacetime commitment of funds and resources in our nation's history to develop America's own alternative sources of fuel—from coal, from oil shale, from plant products for gasohol, from unconventional gas, from the sun.

I propose the creation of an energy security corporation to lead this effort to replace two and a half million barrels of imported oil per day by 1990. The corporation will issue up to five billion dollars in energy bonds, and I especially want them to be in small denominations so that average Americans can invest directly in America's energy security.

Just as a similar synthetic rubber corporation helped us win World War II, so will we mobilize American determination and ability to win the energy war. Moreover, I will soon submit legislation to Congress calling for the creation of this nation's first solar bank, which will help us achieve the crucial goal of twenty percent of our energy coming from solar power by the year 2000.

These efforts will cost money, a lot of money, and that is why Congress must enact the windfall profits tax without delay. It will be money well spent. Unlike the billions of dollars that we ship to foreign countries to pay for foreign oil, these funds will be paid by Americans to Americans. These funds will go to fight, not to increase, inflation and unemployment.

Point four: I'm asking Congress to mandate, to require as a matter of law, that our nation's utility companies cut their massive use of oil by fifty percent within the next decade and switch to other fuels, especially coal, our most abundant energy source.

Point five: To make absolutely certain that nothing stands in the way of achieving these goals, I will urge Congress to create an energy mobilization board which, like the War Production Board in World War II, will have the responsibility and authority to cut through the red tape, the delays, and the endless roadblocks to completing key energy projects.

We will protect our environment. But when this nation critically needs a refinery or a pipeline, we will build it.

Point six: I'm proposing a bold conservation program to involve every state, county, and city and every average American in our energy battle. This effort will permit you to build conservation into your homes and your lives at a cost you can afford.

I ask Congress to give me authority for mandatory conservation and for standby gasoline rationing. To further conserve energy, I'm proposing tonight an extra ten billion dollars over the next decade to strengthen our public transportation systems. And I'm asking you for your good and for your nation's security to take no unnecessary trips, to use carpools or public transportation whenever you can, to park your car one extra day per week, to obey the speed limit, and to set your thermostats to save fuel. Every act of energy conservation like this is more than just common sense—I tell you it is an act of patriotism.

Our nation must be fair to the poorest among us, so we will increase aid to needy Americans to cope with rising energy prices. We often think of conservation only in terms of sacrifice. In fact, it is the most painless and immediate way of rebuilding our nation's strength. Every gallon of oil each one of us saves is a new form of production. It gives us more freedom, more confidence, that much more control over our own lives.

So, the solution of our energy crisis can also help us to conquer the crisis of the spirit in our country. It can rekindle our sense of unity, our confidence in the future, and give our nation and all of us individually a new sense of purpose.

You know we can do it. We have the natural resources. We have more oil in our shale alone than several Saudi Arabias. We have more coal than any nation on Earth. We have the world's highest level of technology. We have the most skilled workforce, with innovative genius, and I firmly believe that we have the national will to win this war.

I do not promise you that this struggle for freedom will be easy. I do not promise a quick way out of our nation's problems, when the truth is that the only way out is an all-out effort. What I do promise you is that I will lead our fight, and I will enforce fairness in our struggle, and I will ensure honesty. And above all, I will act.

We can manage the short-term shortages more effectively and we will, but there are no short-term solutions to our long-range problems. There is simply no way to avoid sacrifice.

Twelve hours from now I will speak again in Kansas City, to expand and to explain further our energy program. Just as the search for solutions to our energy shortages has now led us to a new awareness of our nation's deeper problems, so our willingness to work for those solutions in energy can strengthen us to attack those deeper problems.

I will continue to travel this country, to hear the people of America. You can help me to develop a national agenda for the 1980s. I will listen and I will act. We will act together. These were the promises I made three years ago, and I intend to keep them.

Little by little we can and we must rebuild our confidence. We can spend until we empty our treasuries, and we may summon all the wonders of science. But we can succeed only if we tap our greatest resources—America's people, America's values, and America's confidence.

I have seen the strength of America in the inexhaustible resources of our people. In the days to come, let us renew that strength in the struggle for an energy-secure nation.

In closing, let me say this: I will do my best, but I will not do it alone. Let your voice be heard. Whenever you have a chance, say something good about our country. With God's help and for the sake of our nation, it is time for us to join hands in America. Let us commit ourselves together to a rebirth of the American spirit. Working together with our common faith we cannot fail.

Thank you and good night.

ACKNOWLEDGMENTS

I am indebted to scholars who have explored this area already. I wouldn't have known where to start without the insightful work of Daniel Horowitz, Leo Ribuffo, and Robert Schlesinger.

Thanks to the staff at the Jimmy Carter Library who made it an ideal place to work. Especially kind thanks to Bert Mason.

I interviewed several people for this book, and I want to thank them for their time. These include Gordon Stewart, Hendrik Hertzberg, Jody Powell, Haynes Johnson, Robert Bellah, Charles Peters, Anne Wexler, Greg Schneiders, and Wynton Hall (about Dick Wirthlin). From this list, Gordon Stewart merits special thanks—not just for his interview but for his amazing knowledge and his kind hospitality.

Three people played a key role in seeing this book to publication. Heather Schroder is my agent and pressed to make this a better project than it would have been otherwise. Pat Connor Study donated money to Ohio University to endow a professorship under her name, and that endowment provided necessary research funds. Kathy Belden has served as a marvelous editor and a great person to work with. She encouraged me to deepen my insights and my analysis without dropping my intention of writing a narrative history.

George Cotkin read the manuscript with diligence, providing his superior insights about American culture. I cannot thank him enough. So too did Daniel Horowitz, a great mind who knows this area extraordinarily well. Also thanks to Eric Alterman, who not only knows American history and politics but has a marvelous capacity to spot bad writing on my part.

Closer to home, I thank Kevin Uhalde and Jackie Maxwell for lending me their library office to work out of while I finished this book. The folks at Interlibrary Loan in Ohio University's Alden Library diligently worked to get me some peculiar stuff from other libraries.

My wife, Vicky, did her usual: She worked hard on a political campaign (and helped win it this time!) while home schooling our supercool kid, Jay. My family has stood beside me in ways that make me happier each day.

NOTES

INTRODUCTION: "WHAT THE HECK ARE YOU UP TO, MR. PRESIDENT?"

1. *Time,* July 9, 1979, 61; *Washington Post,* July 5, 1979, C1.
2. *Washington Post,* July 5, 1979, 8; *Washington Star,* July 5, 1979, A-2.
3. *Washington Post,* July 5, 1979, C4; *Newsweek,* July 9, 1979, 25.
4. *Los Angeles Times,* July 4, 1979, II, 7; *New York Post,* July 2, 1979, 30.
5. Hamilton Jordan to President Carter, July 3, 1979, memo in Jimmy Carter Library, Chief of Staff Jordan: Press—President through WH Staff Coordination, Box 37, File: Speech, President's 7/10/79; Gordon Stewart Exit Interview, Jimmy Carter Library (taped interview, not yet transcribed).
6. Garry Wills, *Lead Time* (Garden City: Doubleday, 1983), 251.
7. "Energy Speech—Proposed Energy Speech 7/5/79," in Rafshoon: Energy-Speech, Box 46, Folder "Energy Speech President Carter's Addresses," Jimmy Carter Library; Rosalynn Carter, *First Lady from Plains* (New York: Fawcett, 1984), 286.
8. *New York Times,* July 22, 1979, 1; *Chicago Tribune,* July 15, 1979, 12; *Time,* July 16, 1979, 9.
9. White House News Summary, July 5, 1979 (a notebook with these summaries in chronological order is in the Jimmy Carter Library); *Wall Street Journal,* July 6, 1979, 3.
10. Gerald Rafshoon Exit Interview, Sept. 12, 1979, 8, posted at the Jimmy Carter Library Web site.
11. Mondale quoted in Steven Gillon, *The Democrats' Dilemma: Walter Mondale and the Liberal Legacy* (New York: Columbia, 1992), 262; Leo Ribuffo, " 'Malaise' Revisited: Jimmy Carter and the Crisis of Confidence," in *The*

Liberal Persuasion, ed. John Patrick Diggins (Princeton: Princeton University Press, 1997), 170.

12.   *Washington Star*, July 16, 1979, 10; Hugh Sidey, "A Man Searching for Consensus," *Time*, July 23, 1979 (online archive); David Broder, "After 30 Months, Self-Criticism, Sense of Purpose," *Washington Post*, July 16, 1979, A1; *Time*, July 23, 1979, 20; Hertzberg Interview, Miller Center Interviews: Box 1, 67, Jimmy Carter Library.

13.   *Washington Star*, July 16, 1979, A-7.

1. DIAGNOSING A NATION'S HEART OF GLASS

1.   *Andy Warhol Diaries*, ed. Pat Hackett (New York: Warner, 1989), 204.

2.   Andrew Hacker quoted in Bruce Schulman, *The Seventies* (New York: DaCapo, 2001), 49.

3.   David Frum, *How We Got Here: The 70's* (New York: Basic Books, 2000), 284; Haynes Johnson, *In the Absence of Power: Governing America* (New York: Viking, 1980), 24.

4.   *Progressive*, May 1979, 4; Mark Stephens, *Three Mile Island* (New York: Random House, 1980); *Variety*, March 28, 1979, 9.

5.   *Washington Post*, April 2, 1979, 1; *New York Times*, April 2, 1979, 6; *Nation*, May 19, 1979, 559; *Washington Post*, June 6, 1979, 1. See also the fascinating account provided by feminist writer Kate Millett, *Going to Iran* (New York: Coward, McCann, and Geoghegan, 1982).

6.   *New York Times*, April 5, 1979, A22; *Business Week*, April 9, 1979, 96.

7.   Jackson quoted in *Business Week*, April 9, 1979, 104; *Commentary*, March 1979, 55; Garry Dorrien, *The Neoconservative Mind: Politics, Culture, and the War of Ideology* (Philadelphia: Temple University Press, 1993), 169–72; the best statement of neoconservative foreign policy is still Norman Podhoretz, *The Present Danger* (New York: Simon & Schuster, 1980), written during 1979 as Podhoretz watched some of the events described here.

8.   *National Journal*, March 17, 1979, 425; see also Theodore Draper, "Ghosts of Vietnam," *Dissent*, Winter 1979, 30–32.

9.   NEP quoted in Russell D. Motter, "Seeking Limits: The Passage of the National Energy Act as a Microcosm of the Carter Presidency," in *The Presidency and Domestic Policies of Jimmy Carter*, ed. Herbert Rosenbaum and Alexej Ugrinsky (Westport: Greenwood Press, 1994), 577; see also John Barrow, "An Age of Limits: Jimmy Carter and the Quest for a National Energy

Policy," in *The Carter Presidency: Policy Choices in the Post-New Deal Era*, ed. Gary Fink and Hugh Davis Graham (Lawrence: University Press of Kansas, 1998).

10. Carter's April 1977 speech quoted in Bruce Schulman, *The Seventies*, 127; *Seven Days*, June 5, 1979, 7.

11. Daniel Yergin, *The Prize: The Epic Quest for Oil, Money, and Power* (New York: Free Press, 1992), 617; *National Journal*, June 23, 1979, 1029; *Time*, May 7, 1979, 74; see also the series on the "Great Gas Crunch" in *Los Angeles Times*, June 24, 1979, 1, 12–16, and *Los Angeles Times*, May 20, 1979, 1, 3; see also *National Journal*, June 23, 1979, 1028–31.

12. Jimmy Carter, "Energy," in the *Public Papers of the Presidents of the United States: Jimmy Carter, 1979 (in two books), Book I–January 1 to June 22, 1979* (Washington, D.C.: United States Government Printing Office, 1980), 609–14 (hereafter cited as *PP*).

13. *PP*, 613.

14. Betty Glad, *Jimmy Carter, In Search of the Great White House* (New York: Norton, 1980), 444.

15. Carter quoted in "Playboy Interview: Pat Caddell," *Playboy*, February 1980, 78, 66; on Cambridge Survey Research, see Michael Wheeler, *Lies, Damned Lies, and Statistics: The Manipulation of Public Opinion in America* (New York: Dell, 1976), 75.

16. The term "long-term pessimists" is taken from a memo he wrote to the president about the "State of America," January 17, 1979, in Jimmy Carter Library: Rafshoon Collection, Box 32, File State of Union, 1979: Caddell; see especially Caddell's "Of Crisis and Opportunity," April 23, 1979, Jimmy Carter Library, Staff Offices Press Powell: Memoranda: President Carter Box 40, Folder: Memoranda: President Carter, 1/10/79–4/23/79. For more on Caddell's biography and background, see Joe Klein, *Politics Lost* (New York: Doubleday, 2006), ch. 1; Sidney Blumenthal, *The Permanent Campaign: Inside the World of Elite Political Operatives* (Boston: Beacon Press, 1980), ch. 2; "Playboy Interview: Pat Caddell"; Wheeler, *Lies, Damned Lies, and Statistics*, 75–81; and Stephen Chapman, "The Public Opinion Hustle," *New Republic*, November 25, 1978, 12–14.

17. *Maclean's*, July 30, 1979, 29; on conflict between Caddell and Jordan, see Joe Klein, *Politics Lost*, 46. For more background on Jordan, see Jimmy Carter, *Keeping Faith: Memoirs of a President* (Fayetteville: University of Arkansas Press, 1995), 43–44; *Politics Today*, Summer 1979, 43–44; and Nicholas Lemann, "Jordan, Georgia, and the Establishment," *Washington Monthly*, April 1978, 37–47. Also important is Jordan's own memoir of the last year of

Carter's presidency (which unfortunately doesn't cover the material covered here), *Crisis* (New York: Putnam, 1982), and his *No Such Thing as a Bad Day* (Atlanta: Longstreet, 2000), which details his life.

18. All details from Rosalynn Carter, *First Lady from Plains* (New York: Fawcett, 1984).

19. "Playboy Interview: Pat Caddell," 78.

20. *Harper's*, August 1978, 18.

21. *Los Angeles Times*, April 10, 1979, 3, and May 27, 1979, 5.

22. Carter quoted in Anthony Barnett and John Pilger, *Aftermath: The Struggle of Cambodia and Vietnam* (Manchester: Manchester University Press, 1982), 25.

23. Rosalynn Carter on using films to relax, *First Lady from Plains*, 141; see the lead essay in Michael Paul Rogin, *Ronald Reagan, The Movie* (Berkeley: University of California Press, 1987).

24. Ronald Reagan radio address, in *Reagan's Path to Victory*, ed. Kiron Skinner, Annelise Anderson, and Martin Anderson (New York: Free Press, 2004), 453–54.

25. *Commentary*, April 1979, 81; *New York Times*, April 22, 1979, D35; *Commentary*, April 1979, 81.

26. *Human Events*, May 5, 1979, 9 (originally in *Los Angeles Times*); Barbara Zheutlin and David Talbot, *Creative Differences* (Boston: South End Press, 1978), 132–34; Tom Hayden, *Reunion* (New York: Random House, 1988), 456; Pauline Kael, *For Keeps* (New York: Dutton, 1994), 768, 770.

27. *Washington Post*, April 10, 1979, B9; *Los Angeles Times*, May 7, 1979, 1 (Late Final Edition); *Commentary*, June 1979, 68.

28. *Los Angeles Times*, June 12, 1979, 22.

29. *Los Angeles Times*, April 10, 1979, 3. See also Garry Wills, *John Wayne's America* (New York: Simon & Schuster, 1997).

30. Powell quoted in John Dumbrell, *The Carter Presidency: A Re-Evaluation* (Manchester: Manchester University Press, 1995), 46.

31. *PP*, 655; Carter on prayer and "religious connotations" of presidency: *A Government as Good as Its People* (New York: Signet, 1977), 94.

32. Jesse Helms, *When Free Men Shall Stand* (Grand Rapids, Mich.: Zondervan, 1976), 108; William A. Link, *Righteous Warrior: Jesse Helms and the Rise of Modern Conservatism* (New York: St. Martin's Press, 2008), 175, 176.

33. Jody Powell, *The Other Side of the Story* (New York: William Morrow, 1984), 104; *Washington Post*, August 30, 1979, 1; *Washington Post*, April 21, 1979, 3.

34.   Caddell to Carter, April 4, 1978, Jimmy Carter Library, Jody Powell Subject Files, Box 30: Folder: Memorandum from Pat Caddell.

35.   Caddell to President, January 17, 1979, Jimmy Carter Library, Chief of Staff Jordan: Press, Box CF/0/A: #743, Box 1 of 3; Thomas Hine, *The Great Funk: Falling Apart and Coming Together (on a Shag Rug) in the Seventies* (New York: Farrar, Straus and Giroux, 2007).

36.   Barbara Tuchman, *A Distant Mirror: The Calamitous 14th Century* (New York: Knopf, 1978). "Doomsday chic" comes from Paul Boyer, *When Time Shall Be No More* (Cambridge, Mass.: Harvard University Press, 1992).

37.   William Shirer, *The Collapse of the Third Republic* (New York: Simon & Schuster, 1969), for the comparison between Blum and Stevenson, see 288–89; Caddell, "Of Crisis and Opportunity," 59.

38.   "Of Crisis and Opportunity," 26.

39.   Jerry Rubin, *Growing (Up) at Thirty-Seven* (New York: Evans, 1976), 20, 19.

40.   Robert Greenfield, *The Spiritual Supermarket* (New York: Saturday Review Press, 1975), 38–39; Tom Hayden, *Reunion*, 464. See also the insightful and funny book by Stephen Kent, *From Slogans to Mantras: Social Protest and Religious Conversion in the Late Vietnam Era* (Syracuse: Syracuse University Press, 2001).

41.   *American Spectator*, May 1979, 24, 26.

42.   Tom Wolfe, *The Purple Decades* (New York: Farrar, Straus and Giroux, 1982), 277.

43.   Michael Rossman, *New Age Blues* (New York: Dutton, 1979), 122; Beth Bailey and David Farber, eds., *America in the Seventies* (Lawrence: University of Kansas Press, 2004), 6; see the original issue of *Self*, January 1979, 6; *The Complete Book of Running* (New York: Random House, 1977), 17–26. On this theme more generally, see Peter Marin, "The New Narcissism," *Harper's*, October 1975, 45–56.

44.   Tom Wolfe, *The Purple Decades*, 284, and *In Our Time* (New York: Farrar, Straus and Giroux, 1980), 5; *New York Times*, March 30, 1979, A22; Nicholas Lemann, "How the Seventies Changed America," in *A History of Our Time*, ed. William Chafe, Harvard Sitkoff, and Beth Bailey (New York: Oxford University Press, 2003), 361; Peter Carroll, *It Seemed Like Nothing Happened* (New Brunswick: Rutgers University Press, 1990), 280; *New West*, February 26, 1979, 42; *New York*, June 4, 1979, 51.

45.   *New York Times*, April 1, 1979, 54; *Time*, October 5, 1981, 92; John

Updike, *Too Far to Go: The Maples Stories* (New York: Fawcett, 1979), 9–10; *Vogue*, March 1979, 44.

46.   *Time*, August 6, 1979, 14.

47.   Carter quoted in Haynes Johnson, *In the Absence of Power*, 149–50.

48.   The quotes come from Lester Bangs, *Blondie* (New York: Simon & Schuster, 1980), which is unfortunately not paginated.

49.   *The Philosophy of Andy Warhol* (New York: Harcourt Brace Jovanovich, 1975), 43.

50.   *Rolling Stone: The Seventies*, ed. Ashley Kahn, Holly George-Warren, Shawn Dahl (Boston: Little, Brown, 1998), 228; Albert Goldman, *Disco* (New York: Hawthorn Books, 1978), 6; Vreeland quoted in Christopher Andersen, *Jagger Unauthorized* (New York: Delacorte, 1993), 315. The best source on Studio 54 is Anthony Haden-Guest, *The Last Party: Studio 54, Disco, and the Culture of the Night* (New York: William Morrow, 1997).

51.   Albert Goldman, "The Delirium of Disco," *Life*, November 1978, 43; "The Disco Style: Love Thyself," *Esquire*, June 20, 1978, 77, 78.

52.   *Harper's*, July 1979, 75; Christopher Lasch, *The Culture of Narcissism* (New York: Warner Books, 1979), 17.

53.   *The Culture of Narcissism*, 288, 322, 29.

54.   *Commentary*, April 1979, 82; *Harper's*, July 1979, 75; *Newsweek*, January 22, 1979, 75.

55.   Christopher Lasch, *The Culture of Narcissism*, 170; Shirley Sugerman, *Sin and Madness: Studies in Narcissism* (Philadelphia: Westminster, 1976), 16.

56.   Lasch to Genovese, September 28, 1976, Christopher Lasch Papers, University of Rochester, Rush Rhees Library.

57.   *National Journal*, May 28, 1977, 813, 816–17.

58.   "Of Crisis and Opportunity," 72, 69.

59.   James MacGregor Burns, *Leadership* (New York: Harper & Row, 1978), 4, 449–50.

60.   *Time*, May 7, 1979, 18–19.

61.   *PP*, 711, 700, 710.

62.   William Goodman and James Price, *Jerry Falwell: An Unauthorized Profile* (Lynchburg, Va.: Paris and Associates, 1981), 38.

63.   Frances FitzGerald, *Cities on a Hill* (New York: Simon & Schuster, 1986), 169; Jerry Falwell, *Falwell: An Autobiography* (Lynchburg, Va.: Liberty House, 1997), 311–12.

64.   Dinesh D'Souza, *Falwell: Before the Millennium* (Chicago: Regnery,

1984), 103–4; *Washington Post*, April 28, 1979, B2; Jerry Strober and Ruth Tomczak, *Jerry Falwell: Aflame for God* (Nashville: Thomas Nelson, 1979), 67–71; Falwell, *Listen America* (Garden City, N.Y.: Doubleday, 1980), 4–6; *Falwell: An Autobiography*, 382–83.

65.   *Washington Post*, April 28, 1979, B1, B2.

66.   Robert Maddox Exit Interview, Jimmy Carter Library (Audio); Robert Maddox, *Preacher at the White House* (Nashville: Broadman Press, 1984).

67.   Peter Bourne, *Jimmy Carter*, 365; Kenneth Thompson, ed., *The Carter Presidency* (Lanham, Md.: University Press of America, 1990), 211.

68.   Peter Bourne, *Jimmy Carter*, 186; on the paper that he wrote about Wallace, see Howard Norton and Bob Slosser, *The Miracle of Jimmy Carter* (Plainfield, N.J.: Logos, 1976), 60.

69.   Interview with Jody Powell, April 25, 2008.

70.   Carter to Caddell, July 16, 1979, Jimmy Carter Library, Staff Offices: Office of Staff Secretary Handwriting File, Box 139, 7/16/79 (2) File.

2. MAKING FRIENDS AND ENEMIES IN A TIME OF CRISIS

1.   Jimmy Carter in the *Public Papers of the Presidents of the United States: Jimmy Carter, 1979 (in two books), Book I—January 1 to June 22, 1979* (Washington, D.C.: United States Government Printing Office, 1980), 972 (hereafter cited as *PP*).

2.   *Washington Post*, May 1, 1979, 18.

3.   Kenneth Morris, *Jimmy Carter: American Moralist* (Athens: University of Georgia Press, 1996), 180.

4.   *Esquire*, March 13, 1979, 26; Memorandum to the President, n.d., Jimmy Carter Library, Rafshoon Collection: Box 28, Folder "Memoranda from JR: June, July, August, 1979"; Ohio newspaper cartoon quoted in *New Republic*, September 1978, 10. For more on Rafshoon, see *Newsweek*, January 29, 1979, 22–23; *Time*, May 29, 1978, 46; *National Journal*, April 14, 1979, 588–93.

5.   *Newsweek*, May 7, 1979, 23.

6.   *PP*, 758.

7.   Reinhold Niebuhr, *Christian Realism and Political Problems* (New York: Scribner's, 1953), 122, 30; Niebuhr, *The Irony of American History* (New

York: Scribner's, 1952), 133. For more on Niebuhr's influence on Carter, see William Lee Miller, *Yankee from Georgia: The Emergence of Jimmy Carter* (New York: Times Books, 1978), and Frank Ruechel, "Politics and Morality Revisited: Jimmy Carter and Reinhold Niebuhr," *Atlanta History* 37 (1994): 19–31.

8.   Jimmy Carter, "Law Day," in *A Government as Good as Its People* (New York: Pocket Books, 1977), 33, 36; Hunter Thompson, *The Great Shark Hunt* (New York: Rolling Stone Press, 1979), 485.

9.   *PP*, 790, 791.

10.   *People*, May 28, 1979, 31.

11.   James Fallows, "The Passionless Presidency," *Atlantic Monthly*, May 1979, 34, 38, 43.

12.   *Washington Post*, April 25, 1979, D1, D3; Fallows, "Passionless President," 35. For details on Fallows's biography, I relied on his printed Exit Interview in the Jimmy Carter Library.

13.   Jim Fallows Exit Interview, Jimmy Carter Library, 18.

14.   *National Journal*, April 14, 1979, 611.

15.   Hendrik Hertzberg, *Politics: Observations and Arguments, 1966–2004* (New York: Penguin, 2004), xviii, 33.

16.   *Human Events*, April 28, 1979, 343; Hendrik Hertzberg Exit Interview, Jimmy Carter Library; *Newsweek*, April 30, 1979, 31.

17.   *National Journal*, May 5, 1979, 752.

18.   Joan Didion, *The White Album* (New York: Simon & Schuster, 1979), 83.

19.   *Time*, May 7, 1979, 70; *Los Angeles Times*, May 22, 1979, 3, May 4, 1979, 1, May 13, 1979, 21.

20.   *New Yorker*, May 28, 1979, 28; *Washington Post*, May 13, 1979, 1; *Los Angeles Times*, May 26, 1979, Part II, 1.

21.   I rely here upon Robert Pack, *Jerry Brown, The Philosopher Prince* (New York: Stein & Day, 1978); Orville Schell, *Brown* (New York: Random House, 1978); Roger Rapoport, *California Dreaming: The Political Odyssey of Pat and Jerry Brown* (Berkeley: Nolo, 1982), 250–56; *New West*, June 18, 1979, 47–59; *Newsweek*, April 23, 1979, 24–29; *Harper's*, July 1979, 13–20.

22.   Robert Pack, *Jerry Brown*, 218; *New Yorker*, March 19, 1979, 136–43; *Newsweek*, April 23, 1979, 29.

23.   Melissa Amdur, *Linda Ronstadt* (New York: Chelsea House, 1993); *Newsweek*, April 23, 1979, 26; *People*, April 30, 1979; Mark Bego, *Linda Ronstadt, It's So Easy* (Austin: Eakin Press, 1990), 101–2.

24. *Los Angeles Times*, May 4, 1979, 1.

25. *Los Angeles Times*, May 24, 1979, Part II, 6; *Esquire*, June 19, 1979, 6; *PP*, 809.

26. *Los Angeles Times*, May 6, 1979, 1, 3; *Esquire*, June 19, 1979, 6; *Washington Post*, May 6, 1979, 12.

27. *Time*, May 21, 1979, 20; *New York Times*, May 12, 1979, 19.

28. *Variety*, May 16, 1979, 9.

29. *New York Times Magazine*, April 22, 1979, 30, 32; *New Republic*, May 19, 1979, 22; *Village Voice*, April 30, 1979, 51.

30. *New York Times Magazine*, April 22, 1979, 32; *Time*, April 30, 1979, 69.

31. *Los Angeles Times*, May 9, 1979, 1; *Washington Post*, May 12, 1979, 12; *Time*, May 7, 1979, 77; *Washington Post*, May 11, 1979, 1.

32. *PP*, 840.

33. *National Journal*, March 17, 1979, 425, 426.

34. Eizenstat Exit Interview, Jimmy Carter Library; Peter Bourne, *Jimmy Carter* (New York: Scribner's, 1997), 187.

35. *National Journal*, June 9, 1770, 946.

36. Reagan quoted in Adam Clymer, *Drawing the Line at the Big Ditch: The Panama Canal Treaties and the Rise of the Right* (Lawrence: University Press of Kansas, 2008), 34; William Link, *Righteous Warrior: Jesse Helms and the Rise of Modern Conservatism* (New York: St. Martin's Press, 2008), 190–94.

37. *New York*, May 28, 1979, 104; letter in Francis Ford Coppola Name File, Jimmy Carter Library.

38. Anna Kashfi Brando, *Brando for Breakfast* (New York: Crown, 1979), 259; *People*, June 4, 1979, 28; *Washington Post*, May 25, 1979, E8.

39. *New York Times*, May 21, 1979, C15.

40. *Newsweek*, May 21, 1979, 97; *Washington Post*, May 21, 1979, B9.

41. *Washington Post*, May 13, 1979, 1, May 1, 1979, 1.

42. Adam Clymer, *Edward M. Kennedy: A Biography* (New York: William Morrow, 1999), 279; *Washington Post*, June 4, 1979, A3; *Village Voice*, June 18, 1979, 14.

43. *Cleveland Plain Dealer*, May 28, 1979, 20, May 4, 1979, 1, May 5, 1979, 1, May 16, 1979, 1, June 13, 1979, 10, May 27, 1979, 1 (and committee person quoted on page 9).

44. Garry Wills, *The Kennedy Imprisonment* (New York: Simon & Schuster, 1982); *Washington Post*, April 18, 1979, B3; see in general Clymer, *Edward Kennedy*.

45. *New York*, June 25, 1979, 13.

46. Caddell Memo to DNC from Cambridge Survey Research, May 25, 1979, Chief of Staff Jordan Series, Administration Coordination, 4/78, Box 33, File Caddell (3); "Of Crisis and Opportunity," April 23, 1979, Staff Offices Press Powell: Memoranda: President Carter Box 40, Folder: Memoranda: President Carter, 1/10/79-4/23/79, page 16, both in Jimmy Carter Library.

47. Rafshoon to President, "Style," n.d., Jimmy Carter Library: Rafshoon Collection, Box 28: Memoranda from Jerry Rafshoon, June, July, and August 1979. He opens by saying that he's been at the White House for a year, and since he came in May 1978, I date the memo around May 1979.

48. *Time*, July 3, 1978, online archive, n.p.; Tim Kraft to Jimmy Carter, May 21, 1979, Jimmy Carter Library, Tim Kraft Collection, Box 1: Folder "Memos 1978 to 1979."

49. *Los Angeles Times*, May 25, 1979, 2; Bourne, *Jimmy Carter*, 441; *Washington Post*, May 21, 1979, 1.

50. *Time*, June 4, 1979.

51. *Los Angeles Times*, May 23, 1979, 1 (Late Final); *Cleveland Plain Dealer*, May 24, 1979, 1.

52. Michael Schudson, *Watergate in American Memory* (New York: Basic Books, 1992), 77–78.

53. Caddell to DNC, May 25, 1979, Jimmy Carter Library, Chief of Staff Jordan Collection, Administration Coordination, 4/78, Box 33: File, Pat Caddell (3), pp. 70, 92.

54. *PP*, 948–54.

55. *Washington Post*, May 26, 1979, 2.

56. Bourne, *Jimmy Carter*, 332; Steven Gillon, *The Democrats' Dilemma: Walter Mondale and the Liberal Legacy* (New York: Columbia University Press, 1992), 256.

57. Speech transcript, Minnesota Historical Society.

58. Bourne, *Jimmy Carter*, 443.

59. Ronald Reagan, *In His Own Hand*, ed. Kiron Skinner, Annelise Anderson, and Martin Anderson (New York: Free Press, 2001), 322–23.

60. *Washington Post*, June 1, 1979, C8.

61. *Wall Street Journal*, June 5, 1979, 22.

62. *PP*, 972–75.

63. *New York Times*, June 14, 1979, A29.

64. *New Republic*, June 30, 1979, 6.

65. *New York Times*, April 22, 1979, D35, January 16, 1979, C14.

66. Joan Baez, *And a Voice to Sing With: A Memoir* (New York: Plume, 1987), 276–77.

67. *Washington Post*, June 1, 1979, A12; *Time*, June 11, 1979, 21; *Los Angeles Times*, July 1, 1979, 20; *Washington Post*, June 29, 1979, C1.

68. *New York Times*, June 8, 1979, A30; *National Review*, June 8, 1979, 720; Ronald Reagan in *Reagan's Path to Victory*, ed. Kiron Skinner, Annelise Anderson, and Martin Anderson (New York: Free Press, 2004), 457, 458.

69. *Los Angeles Times*, Calendar Section, May 13, 1979, 83; Lee Marshall, *Bob Dylan: The Never Ending Star* (Cambridge, Mass.: Polity, 2007), 149.

70. Quotes are from the DVD *The Late Great Planet Earth*; Hal Lindsey, *The 1980s: Countdown to Armageddon* (King of Prussia, Penn.: Westgate, 1980), 28, 46; Paul Boyer, *When Time Shall Be No More* (Cambridge, Mass.: Harvard University Press, 1992).

71. Howard Sounes, *Down the Highway: The Life of Bob Dylan* (New York: Grove, 2001), 324; *New York*, September 24, 1979, 76–80.

72. Caddell memo, Jimmy Carter Library, Box CF/O/A: #743, Box 1 of 3, Folder: Caddell, Pat, 1/77-3/80: Caddell to President, "State of America," January 17, 1979, p. 19.

73. Peter Steinfels, *The Neoconservatives* (New York: Simon & Schuster, 1979), 165 (Steinfels discusses Bell's comment about being a socialist, liberal, and conservative simultaneously); Daniel Bell, *The Cultural Contradictions of Capitalism* (New York: Basic Books, 1976), 54.

74. *Washington Monthly*, October 1978, 37; *Washington Monthly*, February 1979, 10, 12.

75. Andrew McFarland, *Common Cause* (Chatham, N.J.: Chatham House, 1984), 8; John Gardner, *Morale* (New York: Norton, 1978), 14, 15, 23, 52, 82, 83.

76. *Los Angeles Times*, Calendar Section, May 27, 1979, 4, 5. See also Marshall Frady, *Jesse: The Life and Pilgrimage of Jesse Jackson* (New York: Random House, 1996) and Ernest House, *Jesse Jackson and the Politics of Charisma* (Boulder: Westview, 1988).

77. See Richard Wightman Fox, "An Interview with Christopher Lasch," *Intellectual History Newsletter* 16 (1994): 12–13. This account of the dinner is from a memoir that Daniel Bell wrote, Christopher Lasch Papers, University of Rochester, Rush Rhees Library.

78. Quoted in Peter Carroll, *It Seemed Like Nothing Happened* (New York: Holt, Rinehart, & Winston, 1982), 189.

79. Caddell to President Carter memo, Jimmy Carter Library: May 30,

1979, Powell Collection: Box 55, Folder: Dinner with Bill Moyers, et al., 5/30/79.

80.   See Stan Jones to Mrs. Carter, April 3, 1979, Jimmy Carter Library, John W. Gardner Name File. See also Richard Wightman Fox, "An Interview with Christopher Lasch."

81.   Christopher Lasch to Mr. Nahmias, February 2, 1985, letter, Christopher Lasch Papers, University of Rochester, Rush Rhees Library.

82.   Charles Peters interview with author, January 30, 2007.

83.   John Gardner to Mrs. Carter, June 6, 1979, letter, John W. Gardner Name File, Jimmy Carter Library; Christopher Lasch to Nahmias, February 2, 1985, Christopher Lasch Papers.

84.   *Los Angeles Times*, May 31, 1979, Part II, 6.

85.   DVD version of *Convoy*; on the revival of the movie, see *New Yorker*, May 28, 1979, 21–22.

3. "THE WORST OF TIMES"

1.   John Gardner, *Morale* (New York: Norton, 1978), 23.

2.   Memos in Jimmy Carter Library, Chief of Staff Jordan, Administration Coordination, 4/78, Box 33: File Caddell (3), memo from Caddell to President, June 11, 1979; Chief of Staff Jordan, Administration Coordination, 4/78, Box 33: File Caddell (3), John Gorman memo to Hamilton Jordan, June 15, 1979.

3.   *Los Angeles Times*, June 7, 1979, 18; *New Yorker*, June 11, 1979, 29; *New York Times*, June 5, 1979, A1 and June 7, 1979, A7.

4.   Carter in the *Public Papers of the Presidents of the United States, Jimmy Carter, 1979 (in two books), Book I—January 1 to June 22, 1979* (Washington, D.C.: United States Government Printing Office, 1980), 992, 993, 995, 996, 1009–1010 (hereafter cited as *PP*). See also *Cleveland Plain Dealer*, June 3, 1979, 8.

5.   Quoted in William Goodman and James Price, *Jerry Falwell: An Unauthorized Profile* (no place of publication listed: Paris and Associates, 1981), 25.

6.   Dinesh D'Souza, *Falwell: Before the Millennium* (Chicago: Regnery, 1984), 109; Sara Diamond, *Not By Politics Alone: The Enduring Influence of the Christian Right* (New York: Guilford, 1998), 66–67.

7.   *Harper's*, October 1980, 22; *New Republic*, July 7 and 14, 1979, 19–21; Larry Sabato, *The Rise of Political Consultants* (New York: Basic Books, 1981),

224; Richard Viguerie, *The New Right* (Falls Church, Va.: Viguerie Books, 1980), 123; see also Carol Flake, *Redemptorama* (Garden City: Anchor, 1984), 229.

8. Viguerie, *The New Right*, 219.

9. Lee Edwards, *The Conservative Revolution* (New York: Free Press, 1999), 197; Frances Fitzgerald, *Cities on a Hill* (New York: Simon & Schuster, 1986), 129–30; Dinesh D'Souza, *Falwell*, 109–11.

10. *Harper's*, October 1980, 24–25; David Snowball, *Continuity and Change in the Rhetoric of the Moral Majority* (New York: Praeger, 1991), 43; *Harper's*, October 1980, 25; *U.S. News & World Report*, September 24, 1979, 38.

11. William Link, *Righteous Warrior: Jesse Helms and the Rise of Modern Conservatism* (New York: St. Martin's Press, 2008), 178. One of the best books on this matter is still William Martin, *With God on Our Side: The Rise of the Religious Right in America* (New York: Broadway, 1996).

12. *Washington Post*, June 11, 1979, A2.

13. *New York*, April 23, 1979, 11; *Washington Post*, June 13, 1979, 3; *Newsweek*, June 25, 1979, 40; *Washington Post*, June 14, 1979, 7; *Los Angeles Times*, June 13, 1979, 1; *Time*, June 4, 1979, 20.

14. Adam Clymer, *Edward M. Kennedy: A Biography* (New York: William Morrow, 1999), 86.

15. *New York Times*, June 22, 1979, 17; for more on ADA, see Steven Gillon, *Politics and Vision: The ADA and American Liberalism, 1947–1985* (New York: Oxford University Press, 1987).

16. *Washington Post*, June 25, 1979, B1, B2, and June 24, 1979, 3.

17. *New Republic*, July 7 & 14, 1979, 16; *Washington Star*, June 28, 1979, A-2.

18. Mark Feeney, *Nixon at the Movies* (Chicago: University of Chicago Press, 2004), 85–86; *Washington Post*, June 13, 1979, A32. See also Randy Roberts and James Olson, *John Wayne: American* (New York: Free Press, 1995).

19. *Washington Post*, June 13, 1979, E9; *Wall Street Journal*, June 13, 1979, 26.

20. Ronald Reagan, *In His Own Hand*, ed. Kiron Skinner, Annelise Anderson, and Martin Anderson (New York: Free Press, 2001), 412, 413.

21. James Patterson, *Restless Giant* (New York: Oxford University Press, 2005), 122; *Time*, June 25, 1979, 10–15.

22. *Los Angeles Times*, June 16, 1979, 1; *New York Times*, June 19, 1979, A13.

23. See Leo Ribuffo, "Jimmy Carter and the Selling of the President, 1976–1980," in *The Presidency and Domestic Policies of Jimmy Carter*, ed. Herbert

Rosenbaum and Alexej Urginsky (Westport, Conn.: Greenwood, 1994), 150; *New York Times*, September 20, 1979, 13.

24. *New York Times*, June 19, 1979, 20.

25. *Washington Post*, June 9, 1979, A1.

26. *Washington Post*, June 16, 1979, C1; Daniel Yergin, *The Prize: The Epic Quest for Oil, Money, and Power* (New York: Free Press, 1992), 692; *Washington Post*, June 16, 1979, C1; *New York Times*, June 25, 1979, 1.

27. *Washington Post*, June 17, 1979, A1, and June 16, 1979, C1.

28. *Los Angeles Times*, June 1, 1979, 1; *New York Times*, June 26, 1979, 1; *New York Times*, June 28, 1979, B11.

29. *New York Times*, June 26, 1979, B6; *Washington Post*, June 17, 1979, A1.

30. *Washington Post*, June 10, 1979, B1; *New York Times*, July 2, 1979, B6.

31. *Washington Post*, June 17, 1979, A5, and June 25, 1979, A18.

32. *Village Voice*, July 2, 1979, 17; *New York Times*, June 22, 1979, B6; *Time*, July 9, 1979, 18; *Newsweek*, July 16, 1979, 78, and July 9, 1979, 26.

33. *People*, May 28, 1979, 26; *New York Post*, July 2, 1979, 6.

34. *Washington Post*, June 23, 1979, A20, June 25, 1979, A18, and July 7, 1979, A12; *Los Angeles Times*, June 27, 1979, 1; *Harper's*, May 1978, 38.

35. *Washington Post*, May 21, 1979, A22.

36. *New York Times*, July 4, 1979, B4.

37. *Cleveland Plain Dealer*, June 23, 1979, 16A; "pioneers" quote from Robert Keefer, "Mike Parkhurst: Leading the Last Cowboys," *Harvard Crimson*, July 16, 1974, online; *New York Times*, June 15, 1979, 1.

38. *Wall Street Journal*, July 2, 1979, 1; *Newsweek*, February 12, 1979, 34; John Heidenry, *What Wild Ecstasy: The Rise and Fall of the Sexual Revolution* (New York: Simon & Schuster, 1997), 229.

39. *Cleveland Plain Dealer*, June 3, 1979, sec. 2, 8; *Los Angeles Times*, June 7, 1979, 15; *Cleveland Plain Dealer*, June 13, 1979, 13, and June 15, 1979, 1.

40. *New York Times*, June 17, 1979, 22.

41. Eizenstat to President, June 16, 1979, Eizenstat Box 294: Folder: "Trucking Strike"; Eizenstat to President, June 21, 1979, Eizenstat Box 294: Folder "Trucking Strike"; both, Jimmy Carter Library.

42. *Cleveland Plain Dealer*, June 1979, 4 ; *New York Times*, June 21, 1979, 1; White House News Summary, June 20, 1979, Jimmy Carter Library; *Cleveland Plain Dealer*, June 27, 1979, 14, and June 13, 1979, 13; *Time*, July 9, 1979, 18.

43. *Cleveland Plain Dealer*, June 11, 1979, 11; *Newsweek*, July 2, 1979, 22; *Time*, July 9, 1979, 18.

44.   Eizenstat to Tony Coelho, July 19, 1979, Jimmy Carter Library, Eizenstat Collection, Box 100, Folder: 7/18–7/20/79; *Cleveland Plain Dealer*, June 23, 1979, 1; *New York Times*, June 23, 1979, 1; Staff Offices: Office of Staff Secretary, Handwriting File, Box 137: File: Trip to Japan and Korea, 6/22/79–7/1/79, Memo from Jack Watson, June 26, 1979; Jack Watson to President, July 1, 1979, Staff Secretary, Handwriting—Box 137, Folder 7/2/79; all, Jimmy Carter Library; *Cleveland Plain Dealer*, June 23, 1979, 16A.

45.   *New York Times*, June 24, 1979, 16.

46.   *Bucks County Courier Times*, June 20, 1979, 1.

47.   *Bucks County Courier Times*, June 22, 1979, 3; *Cleveland Plain Dealer*, June 26, 1979, 14.

48.   Song at http://blogfiles.wfmu.org/KF/2006/05/oil/Bobby_Butler _-_Cheaper_Crude_Or_No_More_Food.mp3. See also *Newsweek*, May 21, 1979, 28.

49.   *Bucks County Courier Times*, June 24, 1979, 1, 3.

50.   *Bucks County Courier Times*, June 25, 1979, 1, 5, July 6, 1979, 1, and June 25, 1979, 1, 5.

51.   *Bucks County Courier Times*, June 25, 1979, 3, and June 25, 1979, 6.

52.   *Bucks County Courier Times*, June 26, 1979, 1.

53.   *Wall Street Journal*, June 26, 1979, 20; *Bucks County Courier Times*, June 27, 1979, 1.

54.   Jimmy Carter Library, Staff Offices: Office of Staff Secretary, Handwriting File, Box 137: File: Trip to Japan and Korea, 6/22/79–7/1/79, Trip to Japan and Korea File (2): "Departure for Tokyo" (Presidential Statement), June 23, 1979.

55.   Jimmy Carter, *Keeping Faith: Memoirs of a President* (Fayetteville: University of Arkansas Press, 1995), 117, 118; *Time*, June 25, 1979, 16–17; *Los Angeles Times*, June 27, 1979, 2; Dankwart Rustow, *Oil and Turmoil: America Faces OPEC and the Middle East* (New York: Norton, 1982), 217, 228; *Los Angeles Times*, June 10, 1979, V, 1; *Time*, July 9, 1979, 14; *Time*, July 30, 1979, 23.

56.   David Frum, *How We Got Here: The 70's* (New York: Basic, 2000), 25; *Wall Street Journal*, June 18, 1979, 10; *PP*, 1171 and 1166.

57.   *New York Times*, June 29, 1979, 1; *Los Angeles Times*, June 29, 1979, 2; *New York Times*, June 29, 1979, 1.

58.   *Washington Post*, June 29, 1979, 31; *Los Angeles Times*, June 28, 1979, 1.

59.   Jimmy Carter Library: Staff Offices: Press, Powell, Box 40: Folder: Memoranda: President Carter, 5/1/79–9/24/79.

60.   *Washington Post*, June 29, 1979, 25; *New York Times*, June 30, 1979, 29.

61. White House News Summary, June 27, 1979, Jimmy Carter Library.

62. *Bucks County Courier Times*, June 28, 1979, B12; *New York Times*, July 1, 1979, 4F.

63. *New York Times*, June 27, 1979, 14.

64. James Reston Jr., *The Lone Star: The Life of John Connally* (New York: Harper & Row, 1989); *Human Events*, May 12, 1979, 391.

65. *Conservative Digest*, July 1979, 4; *Human Events*, February 17, 1979, 141, May 5, 1979, 4, and May 12, 1979, 5–6; *National Journal*, May 12, 1979, 802; *Human Events*, May 19, 1979, 409.

66. *Human Events*, March 17, 1979, 215; Lee Annis, *Howard Baker* (Knoxville: University of Tennessee Press, 2007), 163; *Los Angeles Times*, June 15, 1979, 30; *Washington Post*, April 9, 1979, 3; Caddell on Reagan in Jonathan Moore, ed., *The Campaign for the President: 1980 in Retrospect* (Cambridge, Mass.: Ballinger, 1981), 15.

67. *Human Events*, February 17, 1979, 1.

68. *New York Times*, July 2, 1979, A14.

69. Memos Jordan sent to Carter (especially in early July), Jimmy Carter Library: Chief of Staff Jordan: Press—President Through WH Staff Coordination, Box 37, File: Speech, President's 7/10/79.

70. Hertzberg quoted in Robert Schlesinger, *White House Ghosts: Presidents and Their Speechwriters* (New York: Simon & Schuster, 2008), 299; Powell to Ms. Rosalyn Swetlow, July 10, 1979, Jimmy Carter Library, Staff Offices: Powell, Box 27, File: Correspondence (Chron), 7/2/79–7/30/79.

71. *National Review*, July 27, 1979, B105.

72. Memo reprinted in Daniel Horowitz, ed., *Jimmy Carter and the Energy Crisis of the 1970s: The "Crisis of Confidence" Speech of July 15, 1979* (Boston: Bedford, 2005), 81–86.

73. Horowitz, ed., *Jimmy Carter and the Energy Crisis of the 1970s*, 88–90.

4. "ONE OF MY BEST"

1. From the speech, as reprinted in Daniel Horowitz, ed., *Jimmy Carter and the Energy Crisis of the 1970s: The "Crisis of Confidence" Speech of July 15, 1979* (Boston: Bedford, 2005), 113. When the speech is quoted, I have used this version. This chapter's title, "One of My Best," comes from Carter's own remark about the speech, as quoted in Peter Bourne, *Jimmy Carter* (New York: Scribner's, 1997), 445.

2. *New York Times*, July 1, 1979, sec. 4, 20E.

3. Jimmy Carter Library: Jack Watson to President, July 1, 1979, Staff Secretary Handwriting File, Box 137, File on 7/2/79.

4. *Cleveland Plain Dealer*, July 3, 1979, 1; *New York Post*, July 7, 1979, "Week in Review," 11.

5. Jimmy Carter Library: Eizenstat and Kitty Schirmer to Carter, "Meeting with Energy Advisors," July 3, 1979, Speechwriter Subject File, Box 8, File: Energy Address, 7/5/79—6/1/79–7/31/79; Office of Staff Secretary Handwriting File, Box 137, File on 7/2/79. Quote from Eizenstat and Kitty Schirmer to President, July 3, 1979 in File 7/3/79.

6. Quoted in Robert Schlesinger, *White House Ghosts: Presidents and Their Speechwriters* (New York: Simon & Schuster, 2008), 300.

7. Jimmy Carter Library: writing staff to Rafshoon, 6/29/79, and Greg Schneiders to Rick, July 3, 1979, both, Staff Offices: Speechwriters Chron File, Box 50, File: Proposed Remarks on Energy (2); Hertzberg, Miller Center Interview, Miller Center Interviews, Box 1, 61–62. Also, author interview with Gordon Stewart and Hendrik Hertzberg, March 1, 2008.

8. *Wall Street Journal*, July 6, 1979, 3.

9. Jimmy Carter Library: Eizenstat, Miller Center Interview, 79, Miller Center Interviews, Box 1, and Eizenstat to President, July 4, 1979, Wexler Collection, Box 17, Folder: Energy [4].

10. Patrick Caddell in "Playboy Interview: Pat Caddell," *Playboy*, February 1980, 79.

11. Powell quoted in *Wall Street Journal*, July 6, 1979, 3.

12. Jimmy Carter Library, Eizenstat Miller Center Interview, 80.

13. Jimmy Carter Library: Caddell Breakthrough memo, Utilities Confidential, UT through Exec. folder, Box UT-1, File: 5/19/79–1/20/81; Kitty to Stu, Caddell Memo, July 5, 1979 (handwritten), White House Central File, UT through Exec. folder, Box UT-1, File: 5/19/79–1/20/81 (Kitty is Kitty Schirmer, an assistant to Eizenstat).

14. Author interview with Jody Powell, April 25, 2008.

15. *New York Times*, July 7, 1979, 22.

16. *Washington Star*, July 13, 1979, 10; governor quoted in Jack Germond and Jules Witcover, *Blue Smoke and Mirrors* (New York: Viking, 1981), 33.

17. Douglas Frantz and David McKeen, *Friends in High Places: The Rise and Fall of Clark Clifford* (Boston: Little, Brown, 1995); *Washington Star*, July 13, 1979, A10.

18. Jimmy Carter Library: "Remarks of the President at Lunch with

Camp David Meeting Participants," July 30, 1979, Box 5 of Staff Offices Speechwriters-Subject File; Jimmy Carter, *Keeping Faith: Memoirs of a President* (Fayetteville: University of Arkansas Press, 1995), 122–23.

19.   Jimmy Carter Library: Jackson to Carter, July 10, 1979, follow-up on meeting, Office of Staff Secretary Handwriting File, Box 137, 7/5–7/12 File; *Chicago Tribune*, July 15, 1979, 12.

20.   *Time*, July 23, 1979, 27.

21.   *New York Times*, July 9, 1979, 1.

22.   Haynes Johnson, *In the Absence of Power* (New York: Viking, 1980), 174. See also Judy Kessler, *Inside People* (New York: Villard, 1994).

23.   *People*, July 2, 1979, 18–21.

24.   *Washington Post*, July 7, 1979, B1, B3.

25.   *U.S. News & World Report*, July 16, 1979, 20; *Washington Post*, July 13, 1979, 1; Joseph Goulden, *Jerry Wurf: Labor's Last Angry Man* (New York: Atheneum, 1982).

26.   The Jimmy Carter Library has an excellent set of photographs taken by White House photographers, which gives a nice history of the summit that doesn't exist yet on paper entirely. I have used these photographs for this paragraph and often to get a sense of the mood of participants during the summit.

27.   White House News Summary, July 10, 1979.

28.   *New York Times*, July 11, 1979, B5; Frank Moore to President, July 9, 1979, Jimmy Carter Library, Eizenstat Collection, Box 162, Folder: Camp David Summit [1].

29.   Alfred Kahn to Carter, July 11, 1979, in File 7/5/79–7/12/79 (2) and Galbraith to President, July 9, 1979, same dates, File 7, both in Office of Staff Secretary Handwriting File, Box 138, Jimmy Carter Library; White House News Summary, July 11, 1979; Galbraith to Eizenstat, July 3, 1979, Galbraith to President, July 9, 1979, found in John K. Galbraith Name File, Jimmy Carter Library; Carter, *Keeping Faith*, 123.

30.   *Chicago Tribune*, July 15, 1979, 12; *New York Post*, July 16, 1979, 4; Marc Tanenbaum, "The Malaise of America—Piety or Reality?" and Dick Ryan, "Rabbi Tanenbaum: A Forceful Voice," both in Tanenbaum Name File, Jimmy Carter Library; see also the biography in Judith Banki and Eugene Fisher, eds., *A Prophet for Our Time: An Anthology of the Writings of Rabbi Marc Tanenbaum* (New York: Fordham University Press, 2002).

31.   Daniel Horowitz, *The Anxieties of Affluence* (Amherst: University of Massachusetts Press, 2004), 218–19; Robert Bellah, *Beyond Belief* (New York: Harper & Row, 1970), xi–xxi; Robert Bellah, *The Broken Covenant*

(New York: Seabury Press, 1975), 3; Robert Bellah, "Human Conditions for a Good Society," *St. Louis Dispatch*, March 25, 1979, 8–12.

32. Robert Bellah, *The Broken Covenant*, 63; John Raeside, "A Night at Camp David," *Express (East Bay)*, July 27, 1979, 3.

33. Walter Mondale to the president, July 4, 1979, reprinted in Horowitz, ed., *Jimmy Carter and the Energy Crisis of the 1970s*, 95; Raeside, "A Night at Camp David," 3.

34. *New York Times*, July 10, 1979, C2; *Washington Post Magazine*, April 8, 1979, 11; *New York Post*, July 6, 1979, 3; *New York Times*, July 2, 1979, 16.

35. *Washington Post*, July 1, 1979, B1; *Washington Star*, June 28, 1979, 2; *Seven Days*, April 27, 1979, 26.

36. *New York Times*, July 12, 1979, A1.

37. *The Progressive*, June 1979, 29; Christopher Booker, "Reaching for the Moon," in *The Seventies* (New York: Stein & Day, 1980), 307; *Cleveland Plain Dealer*, June 12, 1979, 1B. For more on Chrysler, see Peter Carroll, *It Seemed Like Nothing Happened: America in the Seventies* (New Brunswick: Rutgers University Press, 1990), 222–23 and David Frum, *How We Got Here: The 70's* (New York: Basic Books, 2000), 25. See also James Hansen, *First Man: The Life of Neil A. Armstrong* (New York: Simon & Schuster, 2005).

38. *U.S. News & World Report*, July 16, 1979, 20.

39. Jimmy Carter Library: Staff Secretary, Handwriting File, Box 141, File, 8/7/79, from a speech Clinton gave soon after the summit, given to Carter by Anne Wexler; *Los Angeles Times*, July 10, 1979, 1, 14; *Washington Star*, July 9, 1979, A-15.

40. *New York Times*, July 12, 1979, D15.

41. *Los Angeles Times*, July 13, 1979, 10; *New York Times*, July 13, 1979, 10; *Washington Star*, July 13, 1979, A-10.

42. *Village Voice*, November 12, 1979, 36, 37; Albert Goldman, *Disco* (New York: Hawthorn, 1978), 118; for more on this theme, see Peter Braunstein, "The Last Days of Gay Disco," *Village Voice*, June 30, 1998, 58.

43. *Chicago Tribune*, July 13, 1979, sec. 5, 1, 3.

44. *New York Times*, July 13, 1979, A16.

45. Marc Eliot, *Rockonomics: The Money Behind the Music* (New York: Franklin Watts, 1989), 186–89.

46. *Chicago Tribune*, July 12, 1979, 4.

47. Hugh Sidey, "A Man Searching for Consensus," *Time*, July 23, 1979, 22; *Washington Star*, July 15, 1979, D-3; White House News Summary, July 14, 1979.

48.   *Washington Post*, July 14, 1979, 1, 8; Ayers to Rosalynn Carter, October 12, 1979, and accompanying draft of article, Jimmy Carter Library, H. Brandt Ayers, Name File.

49.   Germond and Witcover, *Blue Smoke and Mirrors*, 34–35; *Washington Star*, July 13, 1979, 1; "From Jim King—re Friday Morning," Jimmy Carter Library, Office of Staff Secretary Handwriting File, Box 138, File 7/5–7/12/79 (5).

50.   Rafshoon to President, 7/10/79, Jimmy Carter Library, Speechwriters Chronological File, Box 50, Folder: Address to the Nation, Energy, Crisis of Confidence (I); draft of speech found in Speechwriter Chron File—Box 50, Folder titled "Address to the Nation, Energy, Crisis of Confidence" (1). Draft entitled "DRAFT 7/2/79, but I believe that's a typo and should read 7/12/79; drafts of the speech also found in these files in the Jimmy Carter Library.

51.   Rafshoon to President, 7/10/79, Jimmy Carter Library, Speechwriters Chronological File, Box 50, Folder: Address to the Nation, Energy, Crisis of Confidence (1); author interview with Gordon Stewart and Hendrik Hertzberg, March 1, 2008.

52.   Ruth Carter Stapleton, *In His Footsteps: The Healing Ministry of Jesus* (San Francisco: Harper & Row, 1979), 2. For more on Peale, see Donald Meyer, *The Positive Thinkers* (New York: Pantheon, 1980).

53.   Various drafts of speech with note to "Rick" from "Susan," dated 8/2/79: Staff Secretary: Handwriting File—Camp David, Box 138, and File: President's Address to the Nation, all, Jimmy Carter Library.

54.   Schneiders to Rafshoon, July 10, 1979, Jimmy Carter Library, Speechwriters Chron File—Box 50, Folder: "Address to Nation, Energy, Crisis of Confidence" (1).

55.   Rafshoon Exit Interview, posted at the Jimmy Carter Library Web site, 9.

56.   Schlesinger, *White House Ghosts*, 303–4. Gordon Stewart recounted this story to me as well when I interviewed him and Hertzberg.

57.   *New York Times*, July 11, 1979, B5; *Wall Street Journal*, July 5, 1979, 2; *Los Angeles Times*, July 10, 1979, 1.

58.   *TV Guide*, July 14–20, 1979, A30–A32; *Time*, July 23, 1979, 20.

59.   Caddell, "Playboy Interview," 80; see also memo reprinted in Horowitz, ed., *Jimmy Carter and the Energy Crisis of the 1970s*, 150–51.

60.   *New York Review of Books*, July 19, 1979, 32.

61.   All letters, Jimmy Carter Library: Staff Offices: Office of Staff Secretary Handwriting File, Box 139, File: President's Remarks to the Nation July 15, 1979: File: President's Address (3).

62. *Newsweek*, July 30, 1979, 22, 23.

63. Jimmy Carter in the *Public Papers of the Presidents of the United States: Jimmy Carter, 1979 (in two books), Book II—June 23 to December 31, 1979* (Washington, D.C.: U.S. Government Printing Office, 1980), 1248, 1242 (hereafter cited as *PP*).

64. Jimmy Carter Library: Box 5 from Staff Offices Speechwriters-Subject File, Folder on Crisis of Confidence Speech, Anne Wexler to the President, August 4, 1979, JCL Library: Office of Staff Secretary, Handwriting File: Box 141, File 8/4/79.

65. Hertzberg Miller Center Interview, 67.

66. *New York Post*, July 2, 1979, 1; *New York Times*, July 11, 1979, 20.

67. Caddell, "Of Crisis and Opportunity," April 23, 1979, Jimmy Carter Library, Staff Offices Press Powell: Memoranda: President Carter Box 40, Folder: Memoranda: President Carter, 1/10/79–4/23/79, 54, 55.

68. Hugh Sidey, "Trying to Show His Toughness," *Time*, July 30, 1979, 20; *Washington Star*, July 15, 1979, A-1; *New Republic*, July 21 and 28, 1979, 7, and August 4 and 11, 1979, 5.

69. *Washington Post*, July 15, 1979, E6; Martin Schram, "Carter: Back on the Track and Eager to Retake the Lead," *Washington Post*, July 17, 1979, A14; *Washington Star*, July 14, 1979, 7; David Broder, "Camp David Denouement," *Washington Post*, July 15, 1979, A10.

70. *Los Angeles Times*, July 16, 1979, 15; *Washington Star*, July 16, 1979, 10; *Washington Post*, July 16, 1979, 19.

71. See op-ed that Ayers included in his communication with Carter, July 31, 1979, in Ayers Name File, Jimmy Carter Library.

72. Daniel Bell to Pat Caddell, August 28, 1979, letter in possession of Daniel Bell and shared with the author.

5. THE SPEECH BECOMES A "TURNING POINT"

1. Dick Wirthlin, *The Greatest Communicator* (Hoboken: Wiley, 2004), 35.

2. *Time*, July 30, 1979, 10–16; Leo Ribuffo, "'Malaise' Revisited: Jimmy Carter and the Crisis of Confidence," in John Patrick Diggins, ed., *The Liberal Persuasion* (Princeton, N.J.: Princeton University Press, 1997), 175; see also *Newsweek*, July 30, 1979, 22–28.

3. *New York Times*, July 22, 1979, 1; *Time*, July 30, 1979, 13.

4. Jimmy Carter, *Keeping Faith: Memoirs of a President* (Fayetteville:

University of Arkansas Press, 1995), 127; Bruce Mazlish and Edwin Diamond, *Jimmy Carter* (New York: Simon & Schuster, 1979), 209.

5.   Jordan memo discussing staff changes, Jordan to President, July 3, 1979, Jimmy Carter Library, Chief of Staff Jordan: President Through White House Staff Coordination, Box 37: File: Speech, president's 7/10/79.

6.   Rafshoon to President on "Style," Rafshoon: Box 28, Folder: Memoranda from JR: June, July, and August 1979; Rafshoon and Hertzberg to the President, July 23, 1979, Staff Offices: Office of Staff Secretary Handwriting File, Box 140, File: 7/23/79, both, Jimmy Carter Library.

7.   Jody Powell, Miller Center Interview, 121, Jimmy Carter Library.

8.   Eizenstat, Miller Center Interview, 82, Jimmy Carter Library.

9.   Gordon Stewart Exit Interview (audio), Jimmy Carter Library; this observation also draws from the interview I conducted with Hertzberg and Stewart on March 1, 2008.

10.   Pat Caddell to President, July 19, 1979, Jimmy Carter Library, Staff Offices: Powell, Box 27, File: Memoranda, Jody Powell, 7/2/79–7/31/79.

11.   *Time*, August 6, 1979, 11.

12.   *Los Angeles Times*, July 16, 1979, 15; *New Republic*, August 4 and 11, 1979, 15; the "cross of malaise" comment is quoted in Adam Clymer, *Edward M. Kennedy: A Biography* (New York: William Morrow, 1999), 283; see also *New York Times*, August 2, 1979, B4.

13.   Schneiders to Rafshoon, July 10, 1979, Jimmy Carter Library, Speechwriters Chron File—Box 50, Folder: "Address to the Nation, Energy, Crisis of Confidence" (1).

14.   Greg Schneiders, "Goodbye to All That," *Newsweek*, September 14, 1979, 23.

15.   *Cleveland Plain Dealer*, July 15, 1979, 4.

16.   Clymer, *Edward M. Kennedy: A Biography*, 283.

17.   *New Times*, January 8, 1979, 75; James MacGregor Burns, *Edward Kennedy and the Camelot Legacy* (New York: Norton, 1976), 335.

18.   Kennedy's speech is reprinted in Daniel Horowitz, ed., *Jimmy Carter and the Energy Crisis of the 1970s: The "Crisis of Confidence" Speech of July 15, 1979* (Boston: Bedford, 2005), 165, 166; on Kennedy's announcement and Joan's appearance, see Clymer, *Edward Kennedy*, 293.

19.   Richard Reeves, "The Inevitability of Teddy," *Esquire*, February 13, 1979, 6.

20.   *Human Events*, July 28, 1979, 1; *Wall Street Journal*, July 17, 1979, 18.

21.   Howard Jarvis, *I'm Mad as Hell: The Exclusive Story of the Tax Revolt*

and Its Leader (New York: Times Books, 1979); *National Review*, July 6, 1979, 838.

22.   Patrick Caddell, "Of Crisis and Opportunity," 53; April 23, 1979, Jimmy Carter Library, Staff Offices Press Powell: Memoranda: President Carter Box 40, Folder: Memoranda: President Carter, 1/10/79–4/23/79.

23.   James C. Roberts, *The Conservative Decade* (Westport: Arlington, 1980), 308, 329.

24.   *American Spectator*, March 1979, 13.

25.   Charles Horner, "From Nixon to Pol Pot," *Commentary*, August 1979, 66.

26.   See, for instance, Guenter Lewy, "Vietnam: New Light on the Question of American Guilt," *Commentary*, February 1978, 29–49, also his book, *America in Vietnam* (New York: Oxford University Press, 1978), especially 429; Carl Gersham, "After the Dominoes Fell," *Commentary*, May 1978, 47–54; and the intelligent review essay written by Theodore Draper, "Ghosts of Vietnam," *Dissent*, Winter 1979, 34.

27.   James Neuchterlein, "Watergate: Toward a Revisionist View," *Commentary*, August 1979, 38–45.

28.   Jerry Falwell, *America Can Be Saved!* (Murfreesboro, Tenn.: Sword of the Lord Publishers, 1979), 21, 7, 34, 97, 115, 64.

29.   Jerry Falwell, *Listen America!* (Garden City, N.Y.: Doubleday, 1980), 117; *U.S. News & World Report*, September 24, 1979, 38.

30.   *Washington Post*, July 8, 1979, K1; *Kansas City Times*, July 16, 1979, 2; James Reston, Jr., *The Lone Star: The Life of John Connally* (New York: Harper & Row, 1989), 565; *U.S. News & World Report*, September 24, 1979, 40.

31.   *Los Angeles Times*, May 11, 1979, 3; *Washington Post*, July 9, 1979, 23.

32.   Ronald Reagan, *An American Life* (New York: Simon & Schuster, 1990), 205; Garry Wills, *Lead Time* (Garden City, N.Y.: Doubleday, 1983), 261. On Reagan and the issue of sin, see John Patrick Diggins, *Ronald Reagan* (New York: Norton, 2007).

33.   This speech is reprinted in Horowitz, ed., *Jimmy Carter and the Energy Crisis of the 1970s*, 167–71.

34.   Dick Wirthlin, *The Greatest Communicator*, 39–40; I also draw from communication via e-mail with Wirthlin's assistant, Wynton Hall, as well as Hall's own article, "The Invention of 'Quantifiably Safe Rhetoric': Richard Wirthlin and Ronald Reagan's Instrumental Use of Public Opinion Research in Presidential Discourse," *Western Journal of Communication* 66 (2002): 319–46.

35.   Wirthlin in *The Campaign for President: 1980 in Retrospect*, ed. Jonathan

Moore (Cambridge, Mass.: Ballinger, 1981), 39; Wynton Hall Interview, via e-mail, December 10, 2007. He quoted from the "black book" in this interview.

36.　*Cleveland Plain Dealer*, June 25, 1979, 9; *Washington Post*, July 8, 1979, 4.

37.　*Time*, August 13, 1979, 17.

38.　I rely here on the following: synopsis of the NBC Evening News for Saturday, August 25, 1979, Vanderbilt Television News Archive (online); *New York Times*, June 29, 1979, B1; *New York*, November 12, 1979, 46–50; *Esquire*, April 24, 1979, 57; *Village Voice*, January 15, 1979, 1, 17.

39.　*Time*, September 10, 1979, at Time.com archives.

40.　Powell screaming at Maxa, *New Times*, January 8, 1979, 76; *Time*, September 24, 1979, 18.

41.　*Washington Post*, August 30, 1979, 1.

42.　*New York Times*, August 3, 1979, 10; *Time*, August 6, 1979, 13.

43.　That graffiti comes from Thomas Frank, *What's the Matter with Kansas?* (New York: Holt, 2004), ch. 7. On neoconservatives and Carter in 1979, see Jacob Heilbrunn, *They Knew They Were Right* (New York: Doubleday, 2008), 154.

44.　Garland Haas, *Jimmy Carter and the Politics of Frustration* (Jefferson, N.C.: McFarland, 1992), 86–87.

45.　Maddox to Powell, July 20, 1979, Jimmy Carter Library, Powell Box 37, Folder: Memoranda: Jody Powell, 7/2–7/31/79; see also Perry Deane Young, *God's Bullies* (New York: Holt, Rinehart, & Winston, 1982), 198.

46.　Reston, *The Lone Star*, 570–75.

47.　The Treptow story comes from Lou Cannon, *President Reagan: The Role of a Lifetime* (New York: Public Affairs, 1991), 76–77. I viewed the speech online at the YouTube Web site.

48.　Joan Didion, *We Tell Ourselves Stories in Order to Live* (New York: Everyman's Library, 2006), xv.

EPILOGUE: IN DREAMS THERE BEGIN
NO RESPONSIBILITIES

1.　John Updike, *Problems and Other Stories* (New York: Knopf, 1979), 44.

2.　Jimmy Carter, *Why Not the Best* (New York: Bantam, 1976), 65.

3.　Jimmy Carter, *A Government as Good as Its People* (New York: Simon &

Schuster, 1977), 63; Carter quoted in Douglas Brinkley, *The Unfinished Presidency: Jimmy Carter's Journey Beyond the White House* (New York: Viking, 1998), xi.

4.   Bruce Schulman, *The Seventies* (New York: DaCapo Press, 2001), 143; *New West*, January 29, 1979, 29.

5.   *Washington Star*, July 6, 1979, A-3; *Washington Post*, July 6, 1979, E3 and July 10, 1979, B3; *Cleveland Plain Dealer*, May 24, 1979, 12; and Margaret Trudeau, *Consequences* (Toronto: McClelland & Stewart, 1982).

6.   "Time of Pause," see *Time*, December 25, 1978, 84; David Frum, *How We Got Here: The 70's* (New York: Basic Books, 2000), 289.

7.   Sean Wilentz, *The Age of Reagan* (New York: HarperCollins, 2008), 98. It's interesting to note in this context that Wilentz gets details about the speech wrong: He says Christopher Lasch was at Camp David when he wasn't, and that Chris Matthews—the now-famous MSNBC pundit—helped with the speech, but Matthews first came to the White House in October. For another example of Wilentz's interpretation, see James Patterson, *Restless Giant: The United States from Watergate to Bush v. Gore* (New York: Oxford University Press, 2005), 128, and Nicholas Lemann, "How the Seventies Changed America," in *A History of Our Time: Readings on Postwar America*, ed. William Chafe, Harvard Sitkoff, and Beth Bailey (New York: Oxford University Press, 2003).

8.   Garry Wills, "That National Malaise Is Galloping Caddell," *Washington Star*, August 29, 1979; article in the Jimmy Carter Library, Office of the First Lady, Gretchen Poston's Social Office Administrative Office Files: Box 53, File: Press Clips—Caddell, Pat.

BIBLIOGRAPHIC NOTE

In researching this book, I used the usual assortment of historical tools: interviews (listed in my acknowledgments), archival collections, and published sources, including newspapers, magazines, and books.

MANUSCRIPT COLLECTIONS

The most important collection of public papers for this book resides at the Jimmy Carter Library in Atlanta, Georgia. I have cited a variety of memos and used photographic histories in the collection to piece together some of the history I tell here. There are various drafts of the July 15, 1979, speech available there as well. In addition, the library has copies of exit interviews done by the Miller Center of the University of Virginia that are extraordinarily helpful. Some have been transcribed, some remain on audio tape.

I have also consulted papers in the Christopher Lasch Collection at the Rush Rhees Library at the University of Rochester as well as a few Mondale sources at the Minnesota Historical Society.

NEWSPAPERS

With all newspapers, I have quoted from the front sections (versus local or arts and entertainment sections) unless otherwise noted. So if a page number is listed without a letter in front of it (i.e., "1" instead of "A1"), the story is in the front section. I have not quoted story titles or authors in my notes, unless the source was an in-depth treatment or the author's listing seemed crucial to understanding the source or the context. The following newspapers were used for the period of April to August, 1979:

Bucks County Courier Times
Chicago Tribune
Cleveland Plain Dealer
Los Angeles Times
New York Post
New York Times
Wall Street Journal
Washington Post
Washington Star

MAGAZINES

I have cited these in the same way as newspapers. I have usually gone through all articles during the year of 1979 in each magazine, listing the publication date and page number of what's being quoted or cited. Only in rare cases when the author and title of the story matter to the context do I list those. The best source that I have found for reporting events in the Carter administration is the *National Journal*, a magazine that did consistently good and deep reporting about Carter and many members of his administration. Besides the *National Journal*, I have consulted the following magazines for 1979:

American Spectator
Atlantic Monthly
Businessweek
Christianity Today
Conservative Digest
Dissent
Esquire
Harper's
Human Events
Interview
Life
Maclean's (Canada)
Mother Jones
Ms.
Nation

National Review
New Age
New Republic
New West
New York
New York Review of Books
New Yorker
Newsweek
People
Politics Today
Progressive
Rolling Stone
Seven Days
Time
TV Guide
U.S. News & World Report
Variety
Village Voice
Vogue
Washington Monthly

OTHER SOURCES

There are, as expected, numerous books on the Carter presidency. It's a hard presidency to define as it was rather diffuse in the issues the administration confronted. So most books cover a large ground. The best, for my purposes, were Jimmy Carter's own memoir, *Keeping Faith* (1982; reprint, Fayetteville: University of Arkansas Press, 1995); Haynes Johnson, *In the Absence of Power* (New York: Viking, 1980); Peter Bourne, *Jimmy Carter* (New York: Scribner's, 1997); John Dumbrell, *The Carter Presidency: A Re-Evaluation* (Manchester, U.K.: Manchester University Press, 1995); and Kenneth Morris, *Jimmy Carter: American Moralist* (Athens: University of Georgia Press, 1996).

On the speech itself, I rely upon the extraordinarily helpful collection of sources found in Daniel Horowitz, ed., *Jimmy Carter and the Energy Crisis of the 1970s: The "Crisis of Confidence" Speech of July 15, 1979* (Boston: Bedford, 2005) as well as the final chapters from his *The Anxieties of Affluence* (Amherst: University of Massachusetts Press, 2004). The best account written close to the time of the speech (and still very helpful today) is Elizabeth Drew, "A Reporter at Large: Phase: In Search of a Definition," *New Yorker*, August 27, 1979. Two excellent scholarly treatments are Leo Ribuffo, " 'Malaise' Revisited: Jimmy Carter and the Crisis of Confidence," in *The Liberal Persuasion*, ed. John Patrick Diggins (Princeton, N.J.: Princeton University Press, 1997) and J. William Holland, "The Great Gamble: Jimmy Carter and the 1979 Energy Crisis," *Prologue*, Spring 1990. Ribuffo has written other important pieces on Carter. Also important here is Robert Schlesinger, *White House Ghosts* (New York: Simon & Schuster, 2008). On the jeremiad tradition that Carter drew from, the best source is still a book that was, ironically, published around the time of Carter's speech: Sacvan Bercovitch, *The American Jeremiad* (Madison: University of Wisconsin Press, 1978).

Historians now see the importance of the 1970s as a decade in defining what America is today. Much of their work is important in the context of this book. On the 1970s as a whole, see Bruce Schulman, *The Seventies* (New York: Da Capo Press, 2001); David Frum, *How We Got Here: The 70's* (New York: Basic, 2000); Peter Carroll, *It Seemed Like Nothing Happened* (New York: Holt, Rinehart, & Winston, 1982); Edward Berkowitz, *Something Happened: A Political and Cultural Overview of the Seventies* (New York: Columbia University Press, 2006).

On the culture, popular and otherwise, of the seventies, I have relied upon Anthony Haden Guest, *The Last Party: Studio 54, Disco, and the Culture of the Night* (New York: Morrow, 1997); Howard Sounes, *Seventies: The Sights, Sounds, and Ideas of a Brilliant Decade* (New York: Simon & Schuster, 2006); some parts of Bob Colacello, *Holy Terror: Andy Warhol Close Up* (New York: Cooper Square Press, 2000); and Pagan Kennedy, *Platforms: A Microwaved Cultural Chronicle of the 1970s* (New York: St. Martin's Press, 1994). See also the very interesting essay by Victor Bockris, "Visions of the Seventies: The Rise and Fall of a Cultural Challenge," *Gadfly*, January/February 2001 (found online).

One of the best observers on the 1970s is a British essayist, Christopher Booker. See his collection *The Seventies* (New York: Stein & Day, 1980) which is too often overlooked. Another good observer is the left-wing journalist Andrew Kopkind, *The Thirty Years' War* (New York: Verso, 1995).

On the energy crisis, there is the encyclopedic book by Daniel Yergin, *The Prize* (New York: Simon & Schuster, 1991).

There are of course also numerous sources on Carter's critics. For more on the religious right, see William Martin, *With God on Our Side: The Rise of the Religious Right in America* (New York: Broadway, 1996). An older book that discusses the surge of evangelicalism that posed difficulties for Carter is still well worth reading: Carol Flake, *Redemptorama: Culture, Politics, and the New Evangelicalism* (Garden City, N.Y.: Doubleday, 1984).

On Ted Kennedy, there's an excellent biography that documents the senator's growing alienation from Carter: Adam Clymer, *Edward M. Kennedy: A Biography* (New York: Morrow, 1999).

On neoconservatives, see Jacob Heilbrunn, *They Knew They Were Right: The Rise of the Neocons* (New York: Doubleday, 2008), and Garry Dorrien, *The Neoconservative Mind: Politics, Culture, and the War of Ideology* (Philadelphia: Temple University Press, 1993).

Of course, a central figure here is Ronald Reagan. Lou Cannon's books are very helpful, including *President Reagan: The Role of a Lifetime* (New York: Simon & Schuster, 1991). But for the worldview of Reagan, especially his lack of attention paid to sinfulness and his idea of national redemption, I relied upon John Patrick Diggins, *Ronald Reagan* (New York: Norton, 2007).

I have used many other sources than those listed here, of course. They are cited throughout in the endnotes.

INDEX

A NOTE ON THE AUTHOR

Kevin Mattson is the Connor Study Professor of Contemporary History at Ohio University. He is the author of *Rebels All!*, *When America Was Great*, *Upton Sinclair and the Other American Century*, and *Intellectuals in Action*. He has written for the *American Prospect*, *Dissent*, the *Nation*, the *New York Times Book Review*, and many other publications.